In the Shadow of the Great War

In the Shadow of the Great War
Physical Violence in East-Central Europe, 1917–1923

Edited by
Jochen Böhler, Ota Konrád, and Rudolf Kučera

berghahn
NEW YORK • OXFORD
www.berghahnbooks.com

First published in 2021 by
Berghahn Books
www.berghahnbooks.com

© 2021, 2024 Jochen Böhler, Ota Konrád, and Rudolf Kučera
First paperback edition published in 2024

IMRE KERTÉSZ KOLLEG JENA
Europas Osten im 20. Jahrhundert. Historische Erfahrungen im Vergleich

 MASARYK INSTITUTE AND ARCHIVES OF THE CAS, v.v.i

 FACULTY OF SOCIAL SCIENCES
Charles University

All rights reserved. Except for the quotation of short passages
for the purposes of criticism and review, no part of this book
may be reproduced in any form or by any means, electronic or
mechanical, including photocopying, recording, or any information
storage and retrieval system now known or to be invented,
without written permission of the publisher.

Library of Congress Cataloging-in-Publication Data
Names: Böhler, Jochen, 1969– editor. | Konrád, Ota, 1973– editor. | Kučera, Rudolf, 1980– editor.
Title: In the shadow of the Great War : physical violence in East-Central Europe, 1917–1923 / edited by Jochen Böhler, Ota Konrád and Rudolf Kučera.
Description: New York : Berghahn Books, 2021. | Includes bibliographical references and index.
Identifiers: LCCN 2020033026 (print) | LCCN 2020033027 (ebook) | ISBN 9781789209396 (hardback) | ISBN 9781789209402 (ebook)
Subjects: LCSH: Violence—Europe, Central—History—20th century. | Peace-building—Europe, Central—History—20th century. | Nation-building—Europe, Central—History—20th century. | World War, 1914–1918—Social aspects—Europe, Central.
Classification: LCC HN380.7.Z9 V548 2021 (print) | LCC HN380.7.Z9 (ebook) | DDC 303.60943—dc23
LC record available at https://lccn.loc.gov/2020033026
LC ebook record available at https://lccn.loc.gov/2020033027

British Library Cataloguing in Publication Data
A catalogue record for this book is available from the British Library

ISBN 978-1-78920-939-6 hardback
ISBN 978-1-80539-128-9 paperback
ISBN 978-1-80539-388-7 epub
ISBN 978-1-78920-940-2 web pdf

https://doi.org/10.3167/9781789209396

Contents

Introduction   1
     Jochen Böhler, Ota Konrád, and Rudolf Kučera

Chapter 1. The *Baltikumer*: Collective Violence and German Paramilitaries after 1918   10
     Mathias Voigtmann

Chapter 2. Pogroms and Imposture: The Violent Self-Formation of Ukrainian Warlords   28
     Christopher Gilley

Chapter 3. Toward an Interactional Theory of Sexual Violence: The White Terror in Hungary, 1919–1921   45
     Béla Bodó

Chapter 4. The Many Lives of Mrs. Hamburger: Gender, Violence, and Counterrevolution, 1919–1930   65
     Emily R. Gioielli

Chapter 5. "A Little Murderous Party": Poland after World War I in the Works of Joseph Roth   89
     Winson Chu

Chapter 6. Suicide Discourses: The Austrian Example in an International Context from World War I to the 1930s   107
     Hannes Leidinger

Chapter 7. The "Healthy Nerves" of the Nation: War Neuroses in Austria-Hungary and its Successor States   123
     Maciej Górny

Chapter 8. Forging a "Winning Spirit": The North American YMCA and the Czechoslovak Army, 1918–1921   142
     Ondřej Matějka

Chapter 9. When the Defeated Become Victorious: Averting
Violence with Football in Post-1918 Romania 163
Cătălin Parfene

Afterword: The End of the Great War and Postwar Problems 183
Boris Barth

Introduction

Jochen Böhler, Ota Konrád, and Rudolf Kučera

For a very long time, World War I in Central and Eastern Europe had been widely ignored in historiography. Although the Eastern Front witnessed the same period of heavy fighting as did the Western, and although significant parts of land there were under foreign occupation for years, knowledge of these events and their impact on the troops engaged there and on the local population was sparse. During the 1920s and 1930s, enthusiasm over the newly won national independence had dominated the discourse in the states between Russia and Germany. After World War II, when these very countries ended up in the sphere of influence of the Soviet Union, the Cold War created an atmosphere where what had happened in the years before 1918 seemed of only minor importance.[1] With the turn of the millennium, things began to change (Baczkowski and Ruszala 2016; Borodziej and Górny 2014; Gumz 2009; Kučera 2016b; Liulevicius 2000; Mędrzecki 2000; Watson 2014), but there was still little notion of what happened immediately after the Great War, when imperial rule had ended but the region had not yet come to a rest. On the contrary, it witnessed armed conflicts and ethnic violence for years, with anti-Jewish excesses and the emergence of proto-fascist paramilitary groups being only the most visible transnational phenomenon (Hagen 2018; Hanebrink 2018; Gerwarth 2008).

Within the past decade or so, many seminal works have started to fill this void successfully. The notion that the armistices of 1918 did not constitute a watershed between armed conflict and peace has since been well established, and this not only goes for Central and Eastern Europe but also includes the experiences of countries such as Great Britain, Italy, France, or even beyond (Barth 2003; Prusin 2005; Wilson 2010; Klabjan 2011; Gerwarth and Horne 2012; Gerwarth and Manela 2014; Newman 2015; Jones 2016; Borodziej and Górny 2018; Millington 2018).[2] Nevertheless, where Central, Eastern, and Southeastern Europe is concerned, physical violence has been treated so far rather as an isolated phenomenon, widely detached from the unfinished demobilization and the ongoing conflicts connected with the building of new states.

The victorious narratives of many newly created states tended to downplay violence as one of the shaping factors of their emergence and concentrated instead on forging legitimizing narratives based on the notions of civility, peace, and a much more successful postwar reconstruction overall than those states that were deemed to have lost the war. This notion has also partly been adopted by the relevant historiography, which sometimes tends to draw a dividing line between the states that were defeated in the war and those that were treated as war winners. While the defeated states are seen as those suffering from a war that "failed to end" (Gerwarth 2016) long into the interwar period, many of the winning states have been described as enjoying a faster recovery and postwar stabilization, paving the way for subsequent economic prosperity and social stability. However, most recent works suggest that postwar reconstruction could have also been problematic in some of the victorious states that were forced to cope with similar problems stemming from the war, which challenged the unproblematic victorious narratives (Newman 2010; Frank and Szabó 2015; Kučera 2016b; Beneš 2017; Egry 2017; Böhler 2018; Konrád 2018). That is why treating defeated states such as Germany, Austria, or Hungary separately from the war winners of the region such as Romania, Czechoslovakia, Poland, or Yugoslavia might obscure fundamental issues that can become apparent in a mutual comparison. Therefore, this volume has brought together historians of Hungary, Austria, and Germany together with those dealing with Czechoslovakia, Romania, and Poland to ask a common set of questions and ponder the similarities and differences regarding not only the break-up of European empires around 1918 but also the tools to master it and build the pillars of the new order.

It is a commonplace in contemporary historiography that to cross the boundaries of a nation-centered historiography and venture onto transnational and comparative ground has proved fruitful for generating fresh perspectives on European as well as non-European history. That is also true for the particular field of World War I and postwar violence. Among the first comparative works, Sven Reichardt's book on the practices of Italian Fascist paramilitary commandos *Squadre d'Azione* and German *Sturmabteilung* was probably the most prominent contribution that showed how the concept of violence as a legitimate tool of political communication of both organizations was closely associated with the prevailing idea of masculinity (2009).[3] The scope was further widened by studies of paramilitary violence treated as a transnational phenomenon that appeared in practically all the defeated states of Central and East-Central Europe and emerged from the specific "culture of defeat" in the aftermath of World War I. Paramilitary violence here was interpreted as a phenomenon brought about by the collective shock over the military defeat, weak statehood, and threat of communist revolutions (Schumann 2003; Kershaw 2005; Horne 2005; Gerwarth 2008; Gerwarth and Horne 2011).

However, as already mentioned, the categories of "culture of defeat" and "culture of victory" have analytical limits. The various and complex postwar period cannot be described as having such clear path-dependencies between war defeat and violence. The contributions of this book address forms of demobilization in victorious and defeated states of East-Central Europe, examine public violence and its state and nonstate actors, and investigate the role this violence played in the public discourse about the postwar reconstruction. From a cultural history angle, the volume addresses the aftermath of the Great War, that is, the various ways that individual East-Central European societies set off from the war into the postwar period. In this context, violence played an important role. What appeared crucial were specific and various frameworks in which individual postwar societies developed their specific "settings of mind" and learned to handle and understand violent experiences.

The first two chapters discusses state collapse and violent collectives, situational aspects of violence as well as a longer predisposition for the emergence and formation of postwar paramilitary violence from the perspective of the perpetrators. Mathias Voigtman deals with a classic case of "culture of defeat," i.e. Germany after the war. He focuses on the so-called *Baltikumer*, members of the German paramilitary groups that got involved in the fighting in the Baltics in 1919. Under the circumstances of the new type of warfare, characterized by small, mostly independent combat groups, many of the members of these groups made an experience with a brutal culture of violence, where the collective performance of violence became a crucial socialization factor. The violent experiences complicated the demobilization, and the reintegration of these men and their postwar social networks and memory threatened the postwar democratic political order in Germany.

While in Germany the concept of the culture of defeat appears to be an appropriate analytical framework for understanding paramilitary violence and its impact on the postwar society, in the case of Ukraine, as described by Christopher Gilley, it does not explain much. While Ukraine underwent a stormy political development during the war and in its immediate aftermath, defeat could turn into victory and vice versa depending on specific regional conditions and actors. The power vacuum shaped the specific spaces of violence, in which the individual actors of paramilitary violence, the Ukrainian warlords, became prominent. Gilley analyzes their changing self-representations and identities in the revolution and in the postrevolutionary phase, which were closely connected to the rhetoric and use of violence.

Béla Bodó's study of anti-Semitic and sexual violence, deals with another "space of violence," i.e. postwar Hungary, particularly during the period of the White Terror after the defeat of the short-lived communist regime of Béla Kun. Bodó stresses the importance of the specific situation of violence, which can escalate even in brutal, performative violence in which the perpetrators, victims, and bystanding public are mutually connected. According to Bodó, "violent artists" were central in escalating and shaping particular violent situations. However, at the same time, he stresses the role of the long-term ideological paradigms and cultural settings, like anti-Semitism, conservative notions about women, and how men from the middle classes used to be educated and socialized.

All these chapters stress the importance of the space and situation in which violence occurred. The dissolution of an old order, the specific power vacuum, and a subsequent unstable political situation leading into a civil war made it possible to create specific spaces and situations of violence in which otherwise unthinkable fantasies could emerge. These fantasies than shaped the performance of violence that drew upon long traditions of nationalism, anti-Semitism, and antifeminism, but at the same time also created something new: new collectives as well as individual identities. These experiences, further disseminated by social networks of the perpetrators and their memory, gave birth to new narratives that were threatening the postwar order.

The following chapters of the book are dedicated to violence as a part of transnational discourses and its use in transnational political and literary disputes. Emily Gioielli deals with the same case as Béla Bodó does—with the humiliation and torture of Mrs. Hamburger. However, Gioielli is interested in the "second life" of this case of brutal sexual violence. She analyzes the ways how the case of Mrs. Hamburger became one of the most known cases of postwar violence in interwar Europe. She is especially interested in partly different accents and meanings that were ascribed to this case by various actors who made public the case of Mrs. Hamburger (British Labour Party, Jewish organizations, and Mrs. Hamburger herself). After World War I, when women called for emancipation and equal participation in public life, violence against them became a sensitive issue and also played a symbolic function. Analyzing the medialization of this specific case of sexual violence, Gioielli stresses the importance of violence for the emerging postwar transnational public and the active role of women and women's organizations in this process.

Winson Chu also concentrates on the process of medialization of postwar violence. He deals with the journalism of Joseph Roth who informed the (defeated) German readership about violence in postwar Poland, i.e. one of the countries that, contrary to Germany, benefited from the results of the war. This situation, and specifically Roth's nostalgia for the former Austro-Hungarian Empire, framed his interpretation of postwar violence in "Eastern Europe." Once again, physical violence played a crucial role in casting Roth's plots and embedded his narratives with clear notions of culture and barbarism, thus translating the intricate situation in the East into a coherent narrative that was understandable for his German readers. Similarly to the case of Mrs. Hamburger's incident, here violence also proved to be a central means in transnational media discourse about the immediate aftermath of the Great War.

The chapters by Leidinger and Górny also deal with the representations and reflections of violence, this time, however, in the framework of scholarly communities and discourses. Hannes Leidinger and Maciej Górny analyze the expert discourses that strived to understand the violence that emerged or intensified during the war and in some cases shaped local societies well into the 1920s and 1930s. Leidinger analyzes the statistics of suicide and the respective sociological scholarship that tried to understand it. While Leidinger insists that the war did not mean any significant rupture in the understanding of this kind of violence, Górny, on the other hand, underlines the importance of the changing of war and postwar contexts for the psychiatric knowledge and its treatment of the "war psychosis." During the war, the German-speaking psychiatry ethnicized the "war psychosis" as an example of the "weak nerves." After the war, psychiatrists in Czechoslovakia and Poland developed a concept of the "strong nerves" of men who—thanks to their victory— knew what they fought for and will fight for again in the future. The changing cultural framework, stresses Górny, became decisive for the reflection of violence and construction of the respective expert discourses.

To sum up, these chapters are interested in the medialization of violence in postwar Europe and its reflections in expert knowledge. Violence is not only about immediate practice aiming at harming or killing enemy bodies but is also used at the same time as a symbol to mobilize postwar societies or to make sense of the problematic postwar reconstruction. Although emerging in specific local contexts and frameworks, some of the chapters show how it became a transnational phenomenon shaping far more than just the agency and experience of the immediate perpetrators and victims.

The last chapters by Matějka and Parfene continue in the analysis of the states, which mainly benefited from the new postwar order and looks on different strategies of taming the violent potential stemming from the war and postwar demobilization. The case of the activities of the YMCA in postwar Czechoslovakia shows the precondition of a successful de-escalation of (ethnic as well as social) tensions in the postwar Czechoslovak society. The geostrategic importance of the new Czechoslovakia for Western European countries and the United States combined with a widespread feeling of war victory and valuable war sacrifice made it possible for the YMCA to successfully support the emerging democratic regime by de-escalating the postwar violence.

The last chapter illustrates, however, the limits of such an integrative culture of victory. In the case study of the national football team in postwar Romania, Cătălin Parfene analyzes an attempt to integrate even the "defeated" ethnic groups of the postwar Romania in a new, victorious Romanian state. However, as the author underlines, this attempt was eventually not successful. The narrative of victory, one can conclude, was tied to a specific nation, which made it challenging to represent the whole multiethnic society of the (re)newed states in central and eastern Europe after the war. As the Romanian case study shows, there were cultures of victory and defeat in one state simultaneously, with far-reaching consequences for the escalation of the potential of violent rhetoric and even practice in the future.

Altogether, the chapters of this book show that postwar violence was a complex phenomenon with various forms, meanings, understandings, and impacts on postwar societies. Looking on the societies in the aftermath of the Great War can unravel lots of differences, but also some surprising similarities. War victory indeed provided a better starting point for taming the violent potential but was by no means a guarantee of a peaceful exit from the imperial frame. By appropriating the victorious narratives, the new "state nations" of what Pieter Judson (2016: 442–52) calls "little Empires" of interwar Central and East-Central Europe tried to monopolize the interpretation of the past. This automatically generated new or deepened already existing conflicts between the ethnic majority and ethnic minorities within these new states.

This book also shows that violence was not important only for local contexts and actors but that it could easily become a transnational tool of communication and representation. As the cases of the YMCA in Czechoslovakia and the Romanian national football team show, this transnational aspect can be used to highlight both the chances and limits of transnationalism for postwar reconstruction.

For a long time overlooked by scholarship, the transition from war to peace in the wake of the Great War was a crucial phase in European history that significantly shaped the interwar years. Paramilitary milieus with antistate agendas continued to exist and destabilize the postwar order, while initially democratic governments that had emerged out of a turmoil of war, civil war, and revolution soon tended to lean toward authoritarianism (Barth 2016; Leonhard 2018, Tooze 2014). The processes at work were multilayered and entangled at the same time, and thus defy a monocausal explanation. The feeling of defeat and victory changed depending on time, space, and actors.

In some cases, both could coexist even at the same time and place. The analysis of various and changeable postwar frameworks and "setting of minds" brought by this book helps to understand the individual perspective of historical actors, specific forms of violence, its emergence, and its de-escalation in specific situations and regions in the shadows of the Great War.

Jochen Böhler is director of the Vienna Wiesenthal Institute for Holocaust Studies. His publications include *Civil War in Central Europe: The Reconstruction of Poland, 1918-1921* (Oxford University Press, 2018).

Ota Konrád is a full professor of modern history at Charles University in Prague. His publications include *Paths out of the Apocalypse Physical Violence in the Fall and Renewal of Central Europe, 1914-1922* (Oxford University Press, 2022. Together with Rudolf Kučera) and *Geisteswissenschaften im Umbruch. Die Fächer Geschichte, Germanistik und Slawistik an der Deutschen Universität in Prag 1918-1945* (Berlin 2020).

Rudolf Kučera is director of the Masaryk Institute and Archives of the Czech Academy of Sciences and associate professor of history at the Charles University in Prague. His publications include *Paths out of the Apocalypse Physical Violence in the Fall and Renewal of Central Europe, 1914-1922* (Oxford University Press, 2022. Together with Ota Konrád) and *Rationed Life: Science, Everyday Life, and Working Class Politics in the Bohemian Lands, 1914-1918* (Berghahn Books, 2016).

Notes

1. Nevertheless, the following were published in this period: Holzer and Molenda (1967); Pichlík, Křížek, and Vávra, (1967); Křížek (1968); Stone (1975); Jindra (1984).
2. See also Eichenberg and Newman (2010) and the following contributions in this special issue.
3. See also Goodfellow (2013) or Bauerkämper and Rossolinski-Liebe (2017).

References

Barth, Boris. 2003. *Dolchstoßlegenden und politische Desintegration: Das Trauma der deutschen Niederlage im Ersten Weltkrieg 1914-1933*. Düsseldorf.
———. 2016. *Europa nach dem Großen Krieg: Die Krise der Demokratie in der Zwischenkriegszeit 1918-1938*. Frankfurt.
Baczkowski, Michal, and Kamil Ruszala, eds. 2016. *Doświadczenia żołnierskie Wielkiej Wojny: Studia i szkice z dziejów frontu wschodniego I wojny światowej*. Kraków.
Bauerkämper, Arnd, and Grzegorz Rossoliński-Lieb, eds. 2017. *Fascism without Borders: Transnational Connections and Cooperation between Movements and Regimes in Europe from 1918 to 1945*. New York.
Beneš, Jakub. 2017. "The Green Cadres and the Collapse of Austria-Hungary in 1918." *Past & Present* 236(1): 207-41.
Böhler, Jochen. 2018. *Civil War in Central Europe, 1918-1921: The Reconstruction of Poland*. Oxford.

Borodziej, Włodzimierz, and Maciej Górny. 2014. *Nasza Wojna*. Vol. 1: *Imperia, 1912–1916*. Warszawa.

———. 2018. *Nasza Wojna*. Vol. 2: *Narody, 1917–1923*. Warszawa.

Eichenberg, Julia, and John Paul Newman. 2010. "Aftershocks: Violence in Dissolving Empires after the First World War." *Contemporary European History* 19(3): 183–94.

Egry, Gábor. 2017. "The World between Us: State Security and the Negotiation of Social Categories in Interwar Romania." *East Central Europe* 44(2): 17–46.

Frankl, Michal, and Miloslav Szabó. 2015. *Budování státu bez antisemitismu: Násilí, diskurz, loajality a vznik Československa*. Praha.

Gerwarth, Robert. 2008. "The Central European Counter-Revolution: Paramilitary Violence in Germany, Austria and Hungary after the Great War." *Past & Present* 200(1): 175–209.

———. 2016. *The Vanquished: Why the First World War Failed to End, 1917–1923*. London.

Gerwarth, Robert, and John Horne, eds. 2012. *War in Peace: Paramilitary Violence in Europe after the Great War*. Oxford.

Gerwarth, Robert, and Erez Manela, eds. 2014. *Empires at War, 1911–1923*. Oxford.

Gumz, Jonathan E. 2009. *The Resurrection and Collapse of Empire in Habsburg Serbia, 1914–1918*. Cambridge.

Hagen, William W. 2018. *Anti-Jewish Violence in Poland, 1914–1920*. Cambridge.

Hanebrink, Paul. 2018. *A Specter Haunting Europe: The Myth of Judeo-Bolshevism*. Cambridge.

Holzer, Jerzy, and Jan Molenda. 1967. *Polska w pierwszej wojnie światowej*. Warszawa.

Horne, John. 2005. "Kulturelle Demobilmachung 1919–1939: Ein sinnvoller historischer Begriff?" In *Politische Kulturgeschichte der Zwischenkriegszeit 1919–1939*, edited by Wolfgang Hardtwig, 129–50. Göttingen.

Jindra, Zdeněk. 1984. *První světová válka*. Praha.

Jones, Mark. 2016. *Founding Weimar: Violence and the German Revolution of 1918–1919*. Cambridge.

Judson, Pieter M. 2016. *The Habsburg Empire: A New History*. Harvard.

Kershaw, Ian. 2005. "War and Political Violence in Twentieth-Century Europe." *Contemporary European History* 14(1): 107–23.

Klabjan, Borut. 2011. "Scramble for Adria: Discourses of Appropriation of the Adriatic Space before and after World War I." *Austrian History Yearbook* 40: 16–32.

Konrád, Ota. 2018. "Two Post-war Paths: Popular Violence in the Bohemian Lands and in Austria in the Aftermath of World War I." *Nationalities Papers* 46(5): 759–75.

Kučera, Rudolf. 2016a. "Exploiting Victory, Bewailing Defeat: Uniformed Violence in the Creation of the New Order in Czechoslovakia and Austria 1918–1922." *Journal of Modern History* 88(4): 827–55.

———. 2016b. *Rationed Life: Science, Everyday Life and Working-Class Politics in the Bohemian Lands, 1914–1918*. New York.

Křížek, Jaroslav. 1968. *První světová válka*. Praha.

Leonhard, Jörn. 2018. *Der überforderte Frieden: Versailles und die Welt; 1918–1923*. München.

Liulevicius, Vejas G. 2000. *War Land on the Eastern Front: Culture, National Identity and German Occupation in World War I*. Cambridge.

Mędrzecki, Włodzimierz. 2000. *Niemiecka interwencja militarna na Ukrainie w 1918 roku*. Warszawa.

Millington, Chris. 2018. "Getting Away with Murder: Political Violence on Trial in Interwar France." *European History Quarterly* 48(2): 256–82.

Newman, John Paul. 2010. "Post-imperial and Post-war Violence in the South Slav Lands, 1917–1923." *Contemporary European History* 19(3): 249–65.
———. 2015. *Yugoslavia in the Shadow of War: Veterans and the Limits of State Building, 1903–1945.* Cambridge.
Pichlík, Karel, Jaroslav Křížek, and Vlastimil Vávra. 1967. *Červenobílá a rudá: Vojáci ve válce a revoluci 1914–1918.* Praha.
Prusin, Alexander Victor. 2005. *Nationalizing a Borderland: War, Ethnicity, and Anti-Jewish Violence in East Galicia, 1914–1920.* Alabama.
Reichardt, Sven. 2009. *Faschistische Kampfbünde: Gewalt und Gemeinschaft im italienischen Squadrismus und in der deutschen SA.* Cologne.
Schumann, Dirk. 2003. "Europa, der Erste Weltkrieg und die Nachkriegszeit: Eine Kontinuität der Gewalt?" *Journal of Modern European History* 1(1): 24–43.
Stone, Norman. 1975. *The Eastern Front, 1914–1917.* New York.
Tooze, Adam. 2014. *The Deluge: The Great War and the Remaking of Global Order, 1916–1931.* London.
Watson, Alexander. 2014. *Ring of Steel: Germany and Austria-Hungary at War, 1914–1918.* London.
Wilson, Tim. 2010. *Frontiers of Violence: Conflict and Identity in Ulster and Upper Silesia, 1918–1922.* Oxford.

CHAPTER 1

The *Baltikumer*
Collective Violence and German Paramilitaries after 1918

Mathias Voigtmann

Introduction

> We march to the sound of a muffled drum,
> How dark the visage, how gloomy the song.
> O Germany, our hearts are so heavy,
> For we are the last of the old army.
>
> We have stood our ground through every disaster,
> The enemy has never made us waver.
> We have held fast in an age without faith,
> To our flag, our leaders, our true German oath.
>
> Now home calls us to foreign command.
> We must go back, though danger's at hand,
> We conquered our fear, and will not fall,
> Yet this is the hardest duty of all.[1]

This "Kampflied der Baltikumer" (Battle song of the Baltic troops) is good indicator of the stylized self-image of the German Army units that fought in the Baltic countries after World War I. It also refers to the immediate aftereffects of that war on Eastern Europe; that is, its effects on relationships and events in the immediate postwar years. For many people, especially in Eastern Europe, the war did not end in 1918. In many places, a return to peace and normality was impossible. Death, murder, expulsion, and deportation continued to be part of everyday life. The period between 1917 and 1923 was marked by a variety of conflicts and wars that overlapped and merged into one another. Not infrequently, the tactics of the Great War were reintroduced, and many people felt that they were living through a single vast experience of violence. This entire period was shaped by revolutionary wars, ethnic cleansing and pogroms, wars of independence, civil wars, state and state-building wars, and guerrilla warfare. One characteristic of the age, cutting across geography and society, was extreme, violent paramilitary activity in the *shatterzones of empires* (Liulevicius 2002; Wróbel 2003; Eichenberg and Newman 2010; Gatrell 2010; Prusin 2010; Bódo 2011; Gerwarth and Horne 2013: 7; Böhler 2014; Gerwarth and Mandela 2014; Sapper and Weichsel 2014; Bartov and Weitz 2016).

One extremely radical example of a paramilitary (Dupuy 1993: 2104–7; Moran and Moran 2002; Gerwarth and Horne 2013: 8) was the German "Free Corps" units, known as the *Baltikumer*, which were primarily deployed in Latvia in 1919. This chapter seeks to shed light upon the actors and combatants in the conflict in the Baltics. It explains the motivations expressed by those fighting there and how they correlated with the self-image of the various German units.[2] These *Gewaltgemeinschaften* (communities of violence) can be understood as social groups or networks that were characterized by physical violence that was applied or threatened in a particular *Gewaltraum* (area of violence). Besides the motivations and self-perceptions of the combatants, this chapter analyzes the importance of joint acts of violence, that is, how joint military actions reinforced group identity and cohesion. Furthermore, this chapter considers the extent to which it was possible for German paramilitaries to reenter normal civilian life in the Weimar Republic after returning home to Germany. Did a specific culture of remembrance or a particular narrative develop from the historical depiction of their period of active combat? Another question pursued here is the nature of the long-term consequences of the fighting for both the individuals involved and the political system they found themselves in after the war.

Recruitment and Motivation of the *Baltikumer*

The *Baltikumer*, a word that very quickly entered the literary canon of the Weimar Republic, are Germans who fought under various banners and in various constellations against their enemies in 1918, but mainly in 1919. They primarily engaged in action in Latvia against the Bolsheviks of Russia, but later also against Latvians and Estonians in the context of civil war.[3] Originally intended as security units for retreating German troops in World War I, the German volunteer units, and the units of the Baltic armies that fought alongside them, soon reinterpreted their role (Koch 2002: 123). They took the offensive, with Riga as their main objective (Volkmann 1970; Hehn 1977; Purkl 1997; Stopinski 1997; Knigge 2003; Bleiere 2008). At the beginning of the "Baltic

Project," the Allies were keen that German troops should be deployed against the Bolsheviks. As justification, they relied on Article XII of the Armistice agreement, which, roughly summarized, envisaged a German obligation to occupy and defend the Baltics for as long as the Allies deemed necessary.[4]

One important incentive for the *Baltikumer*, especially for volunteer units from Germany, was an alleged promise by the Latvian government to provide them with land for settlement purposes. This "settlement promise" was never expressed in an official document or contractually agreed upon, but the German government referred to it continually, creating one of the most important incentives for recruiting volunteers. It had its origin in an agreement between the Latvian government and the German state signed on 29 December 1918. To simplify matters, that agreement set forth terms for the support of German troops against further advance of the Bolsheviks and granted German soldiers Latvian citizenship after four weeks of service.

Ultimately, this evoked a "Baltic fever," to quote a later German defense minister, Gustav Noske (1920: 177). Recruited by the Anwerbestelle Baltenland (Baltic Recruitment Office),[5] which was specially created for the purpose, and influenced by posters on advertising kiosks and in shop windows and by large numbers of newspaper advertisements, thousands of volunteers set off for Latvia and the Baltic in the spring of 1919, some with completely unrealistic expectations (Zobel 1934: 74; Sammartino 2010: 49–52).[6] For the most part, the recruits were demobilized World War I officers, Imperial Army cadets who had enjoyed a military education but had not been able to participate actively in the hostilities of the Great War, and nationalist university and high school students (Schulze 1969: 47–54).

Aside from the purported incentive of land for settlement, the recruits' motives and reasons for joining the paramilitary structures were not the same for all those involved. To the contrary: insofar as one can rely on the personal documents and somewhat untrustworthy reports retrospectively composed after the conflict, their individual motives were extremely diverse.[7] Even where ideological convictions can be detected as an initial motivation, other reasons were always a factor as well, and the recruits' willingness to be deployed cannot be explained without them. A desire for adventure played a role. So did many recruits' feeling that they had been born too late to serve in World War I and that this new combat mission could overcome the ignominy of defeat in World War I. Thus, defeat had a certain mobilizing force for some combatants (Schivelbusch 2003). For example, Erich Balla, who was a battalion commander in the Iron Division, the most famous military formation of the German Free Corps in the Baltics, wrote,

> What a relief from dull hopelessness and the hand of fate it was to him, when one day he read in the newspaper that German troops in the Baltic were still fighting

Bolshevism and that volunteers with front-line experience were being sought. Once again, there was a task; there was a goal worth living for! (Balla 1932: 16)

For men like Balla, deployment in the Baltic was a kind of salvation, enabling them to do their patriotic duty as soldiers. For many, the East was a sort of stylized, mythical place of fulfilment. A volunteer soldier, Franz Nord, wrote,

> Everywhere in Germany where men refused to give in to defeat, an indefinite hope of the East began to grow. The first who dared to think of the coming kingdom knew with a lively instinct that the outcome of the war had utterly destroyed all Germany's ties to the West, and that a courageous fellow dared to ride into the broad swathe between us and Asia, which for us Germans seems covered in a mystical glow, and that at every crossroads, this ride offered unimagined prospects and exhilarating opportunities. . . . And it was this feeling and insight which made the Baltic seem like a magical eye in the midst of the storm of the first post-war years, a new German field of influence, which could replace that lost home . . . (Nord 1929: 63)

Financial incentives and the prospect of new career options should not be neglected as motivations. All the volunteers in the Baltic Corps received an extra allowance in addition to their normal pay. Last but not least, they had an opportunity to live out romanticized fantasies of military life and to actively prove themselves in battle. Ernst von Salomon, the unofficial chronicler of this younger generation of paramilitaries, seemed somewhat fatalistic when he wrote,

> But there still probably had to be something, something that couldn't be calculated or weighed up—in the end, an idea? O God, these big words! I didn't have any ideas, unless you count the cheap slogans of our warfare in the Baltic as something like that. No, we marched without an idea, without a purpose, without a goal. And that was good, that was three times as good. Hell, finally here was something that didn't offer easy answers, which couldn't be estimated or weighed. (Salomon 1929: 106)

Evidence that the Baltic Project also appealed to people who acted out of base motives is found in the records of Walter von Rohrscheidt, a subaltern in Latvia: "These old soldiers encountered throngs of rootless folk of all kinds, adventurers, work-shy, highly morally questionable elements, whom they primarily wanted to restore to health out there" (Rohrscheidt 1938: 29; Voigtmann 2015: 122–40).

These short extracts illustrate reasons why so many volunteers could be found for the Baltic Project. In retrospect, their perceptions of their own motivations were often polarized between extremes. Edgar von Schmidt-Pauli, one of the chroniclers of the volunteer corps and later a convinced National Socialist, fell in line with the times when he referred to the volunteer combatants as the "best Germans" (Schmidt-Pauli 1936: 30). In sharp contrast, the historian Boris Barth saw them as "the criminal residue of the Imperial Army" (Barth 2003: 261).

The *Baltikumer* as a Special Paramilitary *Gewaltgemeinschaft*

As a result of aggressive recruitment and the high expectations of the volunteers, Rüdiger Graf von der Goltz, the commander of all units in the Baltics, had about fourteen thousand men at his disposal by March 1919 (Schulze 1969: 134). As an offensive against the Bolsheviks began in March, it rapidly became clear what type of war was being waged in the Baltics, although its nature was subject to transformation and change. On balance, the conflict was a running battle of a "wild and permissive nature," as former soldier Franz Nord wrote in retrospect (Nord 1929: 63). It had guerrilla-war-like features, to which the small, independently operating units of the volunteer corps seemed particularly suited. The German units initially saw the Bolsheviks as their main opponents.[8]

It is important to state at this point that events in the Baltics cannot be viewed in isolation from the civil war and revolution in Russia. Fear of Bolshevism was a mobilizing factor, and there were direct contacts with the enemy Red Army and links to the White units (Gerwarth and Horne 2013). For the German volunteers, the Red Army was not the only enemy, however. The local rural and urban communities also posed a potential threat.[9] Although only a certain proportion of the local population sympathized with the Bolsheviks, the German troops in the Baltics encountered latent opposition everywhere. This led to a very particular dynamic of violence.[10] Looting, violent appropriation, and confiscations frequently occurred in engagements in various localities, at the initiative of individual subgroups. They often forced entry into homes and "lived a few hours *on the house*," or "off the land,"[11] to use the common terminology of the time. "The soldiers descend on the houses like a pack of wolves, often forcing their way in. It cannot be pleasant to experience such stormy quartering,"[12] as the personal notes of one soldier put it.

The members of the *Gewaltgemeinschaft* generally cultivated an elitist and interventionist understanding of violence, seeing themselves as the violent vanguard of the anti-Bolshevist effort. This inevitably led them to seek to transform the society they had infiltrated and terrorized. However, they lapsed into violent crime, opportunistic vandalism, and other acts of violence, which became characteristic of the *Gewaltgemeinschaft*.

In his essay "The Nature of Violence as a Problem of Sociology," Jan Philipp Reemtsma identified the following types of violence, which can also be identified in the Baltic conflict:

1. "Localized violence": In this case, the opponent, i.e. the other body, is simply an obstacle to be overcome.
2. "Raptive violence": This is understood as the physical penetration of a body, for example in sexual violence, particularly rape.
3. "Autotelic violence": This refers to the absolute, deliberately planned destruction of a body. (Reemtsma 2008: 52–54; Voigtmann 2015: 127)

These three types of violence occurred and continually recurred in various proportions in Latvia. Apart from its decidedly physical component, violence always has a symbolic message as well (Popitz 1986: 73; Lindenberger 1995: 7; Trotha 1997). When the bodies of murdered Bolsheviks were put on public display, the act of violence was a message addressed to a third party, the survivors.[13]

Combat was experienced as a period of biographical compression, in which one's virility could be experienced most intensively. This is seen in the memoirs written for the Baltische Landeswehr (Baltic Territorial Army) in 1968 by Nikolaus von Grote, a former adjutant of a battalion fighting in the Baltics:

"I have never lived so intensely as I did in the *Landeswehr*," wrote a former member of the shock troops from a distant continent. We agree with this statement, not because we were young in 1918–1920, but because later on, we were rarely as engaged as we were in those years. This impacted on the spirit of the troops, creating a strong community. They benefited from the fact that concepts like patriotism, fidelity, obedience, and comradeship were not questioned. This only happened later, because these virtues were abused. Our camaraderie was spontaneous. . . .[14]

The following must be stated regarding the experience of community and group cohesion described by von Grote. For the *Baltikumer*, involvement in a *Gewaltgemeinschaft* was often loaded with intense emotion. In this situation, many of them found themselves in an "emotional tunnel of violence" (Collins 2011: 544–57). It is possible to trace a particular dynamic of brutalization, which was very much shaped by external conditions. A defining feature of the *Baltikumers'* particular group identity is undoubtedly found in collective violence, whether in dealing with the enemy or internally in the group's self-discipline. In some subunits, violence had a dual function: it was both a social element and the defining guiding principle (Voigtmann 2015: 130).

The experience of joint struggle and the real danger of death were intensely unifying factors, but they also presupposed that the group members could rely on each other unconditionally. If one member of the group did not act as was deemed necessary for survival in the extreme conditions of running battle, the majority of the group unleashed a rapid and self-adjusting cleansing process: "It was certainly possible that one of the crowd opposed the iron laws of the clan. In this case the company convened into a brief field court, and after the mutineer was crushed, the Hamburg group moved on, singing their pirate song with angry scorn for technicalities" (Salomon 1930: 81). Besides its internal disciplinary function, collective violence always had an external confirmatory effect, excluding others. One former member of the volunteer corps remembers it like this: "It was dangerous to even step on one of their toes; anyone careless immediately had the whole pack of them at his throat" (Salomon 1930: 80). Or, according to Felix Schnell, "Collective violence is a very effective means of saying 'we'" (Salomon 1930: 80).

The collective violence and the spatial experience associated with it gradually changed the self-image of a large proportion of the fighting units. In Latvia in 1919, "different roles in German history" were not simply "tested and exchanged for others," as Vejas Liulevicius puts it, but indeed the whole "stage [seemed] like a huge, violent costume party" (Liulevicius 2002: 289).

In hindsight, the majority of the former combatants saw themselves as mercenaries rather than regular soldiers (Salomon 1929: 113; Balla 1932; Theweleit 2009). This self-image can be repeatedly deduced from the memoirs of various combatants. As the aforementioned Ernst von Salomon wrote,

> The stragglers invested the spent, derogatory word with new content, and proudly called themselves mercenaries and their wars mercenary. . . . This was most visible in the gradual change in their cohesion. The formations of the Great War, defined by the experience and tradition of Old Prussian rule, increasingly lost their character as ordered members of a large, purposeful military organization. They became smaller and smaller groupings, under a lesser flag, in their own jealously guarded sections, which did not observe the general law of the whole army, but the will of a revered leader, whose name they all wore on their sleeves. And since these small . . . squads, with their swashbuckling actions, were constantly facing a majority which dominated in terms of both numbers and equipment, they were soon shaped by the need to defeat the greater mass with greater force. These military personnel became war technicians who learned to master any weapon, any terrain and any conditions. Attack became the most effective weapon of a minority, and gained newly pointed significance. (Salomon 1929: 113)

The Baltic Project came to an unofficial end when the last German units crossed the border back into Germany in December 1919. An order from Berlin to leave the Baltics immediately had previously been ignored by some of the troops, which equated to open mutiny and defection from the German state. This did not, however, alter the fact that German volunteer units were increasingly at a military disadvantage. Their rearguard actions were characterized by extremely brutal acts, applying the scorched earth principle, using petrol to raze whole parks and orchards to the ground for pure pleasure. When they withdrew from certain villages, strategically important buildings such as provisions offices and barracks were set on fire.[15]

According to Jörg Baberowski and Felix Schnell, it is also possible to discuss Latvia and the people fighting there in terms of a particular *Gewaltraum* (i.e. a space where violence is practiced). In this context, the *Gewaltraum* in the Baltics can be identified on both the real geographical level and the social level. It was defined by the idea that the use of physical force is the form of social action that ensures the best chance of success in fulfilling the group's objectives and interests. The violence the group commits thus keeps it together, creating a spiral of violence.

Another characteristic of the *Gewaltraum* was the existence of networks in which locals and nonlocals shared a very specific distribution of tasks. In the case of the combat units in Latvia, nonlocals—primarily the German volunteer formations—had the external contacts necessary to access the logistical and financial resources essential for the use of violence. Nonlocal Baltic troops also fulfilled a leadership function. Around these violent groups there were other groups of actors who were not actual members of the *Gewaltgemeinschaft* but who contributed the detailed knowledge of local conditions that was required.

Transformation Processes in the *Gewaltgemeinschaften* and the Formation of a Particular Culture of Remembrance

In *Krieg im Frieden* (War in peace) Robert Gerwarth compares the lines of communication in the violent counterrevolutionary subculture of postwar Europe to a spider's web.[16] Such networks and mutual influences continued to exist in the Weimar Republic, based on parallels in the personal life stories of their members (Voitgmann 2013: 135).

Historical research has focused on the violent careers and generation-specific experience of violence in the post–World War I period for some time now. Bruno Thoß notes that, for the generations born before 1900, "the context of the two world wars characterized the age and was the real sign of the times experienced" (Thoß 2002: 7). According to Joachim Tauber, the experience of violence in World War I meant that many men "were no longer able or willing to return to civilian society" (Tauber 2008: 7; Haslinger and Petronis 2013: 346). It is possible in that context to identify forms of processing, traditions, the perpetuation of violence, and the consequences of each on remembrance practices and group cohesion after the demobilization of *Gewaltgemeinschaften* in the Baltic. The transitions in this typology may of course be fluid and not at all static.[17]

Some returnees made a clear and complete break with this episode in their biographies and with their experience of violence. They abandoned their temporary communities forever and cut themselves off from all contact with their former comrades. This meant a full withdrawal into normal private life. Naturally, their stories were lost and it soon became difficult to uncover them.

Some other former combatants also made a decision to distance themselves from acts of violence. However, this group suffered from an inability to completely detach themselves from war, violence, the volunteer corps, and paramilitarism. Through a wide variety of artistic expression, these chroniclers of violence sought to process their experiences and convey them to those who had stayed at home and to successive generations. They could glorify and affirm them, but they could also criticize and condemn them.[18] One example is the biographical and literary career of the German poet and writer Karl Christian Müller, also known as Teut or Teut Ansolt.

Müller, like so many of the *Baltikumer* born at the turn of the century, served primarily in the volunteer corps in Western Latvia, "in Liebermann's volunteer battalion." In his early poems, he showed disappointment over the opportunity he had missed to fight in the Great War and the burden of being born too late. His personal memoirs of his time in the volunteer corps, however, show that his romantic expectations of heroic combat soon proved illusory. His diary entries are characterized by deprivation, hardship, the troops' poor supplies of materiel, and the negative experiences of fighting.[19]

There was yet another, entirely different type of life after the return from the Baltics. Some soldiers returned to Germany shaped by uncompromising offensive warfare, conducted on their own terms, which reflected virtually unconditional and absolute activism and an extreme readiness to take the initiative. They did not appear willing to adapt to the structures and relationships of normal civilian life. A variety of memoirs, diary entries and personal correspondence make it clear that the specific experience of the culture of violence in Latvia had a lasting effect on these men.[20] Some of them brought what they had lived, learned, and internalized in the Baltics back to Germany, a process that can be regarded as the migration or transfer of violence. In the early 1920s, this type of man had hardly any opportunities to join the political leadership. He could join in on violent actions, such as the various attempted coups d'état, but he could not organize or lead them himself. Ernst von Salomon was one of these veterans of violence. In Salomon's case, his socialization to violence in the Baltic was reflected in arms smuggling, acts of sabotage, and political assassinations in the early 1920s. For example, Salomon was indirectly involved in the assassination of Walther Rathenau by closely observing him to find out details of his daily routine.[21]

The various actions by former volunteer combatants and their associations were organized and led by men who can best be described as "networkers of violence." When the *Baltikumer* returned to Germany, the government was keen to completely disband the existing formations.[22] In order to resist the effects of demobilization and to keep in touch, many former soldiers got involved in the *Arbeits- und Siedlungsdienst* (Employment and Settlement Service) and other organizations.²³ These men were exemplified by Gerhard Roßbach and the organizations he led. With his volunteer corps, Roßbach, who was born in 1893 and had served as an infantry lieutenant in World War I, made a significant contribution to the reasonably orderly and successful withdrawal of the *Baltikumer* from Latvia in late 1919.

Back in Germany, Roßbach's storm-trooper formations were officially disbanded on 28 January 1920, but they continued to exist as described above. Roßbach publicly praised the service of his now camouflaged corps in newspaper advertisements. He and his men offered their services to big landowners in Mecklenburg, Pomerania, and Silesia, where they acted as a type of territorial protection force, marked by a readiness to use expert violence.²⁴ The following eyewitness account describes the group's actions:

> The *Roßbacher* (Roßbach's men) exerted terrible pressure on the farm workers. When there are strikes the *Roßbacher* come (with weapons of course) immediately to help the landowner beat up the workers and work as scabs, receiving cigarettes, wine, ham sandwiches and monetary compensation for their labor. In the East Wismar area alone, approximately 500 *Roßbacher* work on the estates. Each Roßbach man has weapons—some have firearms, others daggers or a truncheon—which he has to keep hidden in his house. Each property has a squad, depending on the size, and each squad has a leader provided by the local leadership. The internal operations are entirely military. When an officer appears, the cry *attention!* rings out through the barracks and the whole company clicks their heels together, until the order *at ease* is given. (Gumbel 1979: 89–90)

Besides these extremely violent, radical acts that maintained the group identity of the Baltic troops after active hostilities were over, there were also more moderate, civilian attempts to maintain some kind of organization. Many former combatants organized themselves into various fellowships. One of the largest of these was the Kameradschaft ehemaliger Baltikumer- und Freikorpskämpfer (Fellowship of Former Baltic Troops and Volunteer Combatants). These fellowships spread all over Germany, especially in Berlin and the surrounding region, where a disproportionate number of former Baltic troops were organized. Regular fellowship evenings usually took place once a month, at which the veterans gave talks that were based on their common experiences. These talks often glorified exceptional episodes and the "heroic deeds" of the Baltic veterans (*Der Reiter gen Osten* 7, 1936: 15).

It is striking that certain events took on prominence. A culture of remembrance developed in which select battles were emphasized and placed at the heart of common memory. One such central event was the conquest, or "liberation," of Riga on 22 May 1919. Riga is a constantly recurring theme in various memoirs. As Hamilkar von Foelkersahm wrote in a letter to a comrade in 1972, "Old army comrades refer to those days as the time of their lives, and this is especially true of the 22nd of May; for me, too, this day will always be a highlight of my life."[25]

Numerous volunteer corps magazines were also devoted to the common memory, glorification, and justification of the volunteer corps' actions both in service and in postwar Germany. The bestselling, highest-circulation of these was published monthly from 1930 until December 1943, *Der Reiter gen Osten* (The Eastward Rider) or *RgO*. Recurrent themes in the publication were the Feme murders committed by far-rightists against their political opponents, German paramilitaries' engagement in Upper Silesia, the Baltic Project, and disparaging criticism of the Weimar Republic. Edited by the Bund der Freunde Schlageters (League of Friends of Schlageter) or Bund Schlageter e.V., the *RgO* maintained traditions and commemorated past events in order to preserve them for posterity.[26]

Yet the magazine also served different purposes. It was a means of communication, a newsletter, and an organizational aid to help the numerous former Baltic troops stay in touch and maintain their community structures. The magazine published information about the current addresses of former members of the volunteer corps in the Baltic. The *RgO* also announced their marriages and deaths and fielded enquiries as to their current whereabouts and spheres of activity. Thus, the *RgO* fulfilled a dual function: on the one hand it acted as a repository of memory, significantly contributing to the creation of the myth surrounding the volunteer corps, and on the other, it was instrumental in maintaining and consolidating group structures.

Conclusion

The creation of large, well-developed paramilitary organizations with expansive social networks and radical subversive ideas was particularly exemplified by the *Baltikumer*. This was a trend that spanned entire societies and areas of Europe after World War I. Paramilitary *Gewaltgemeinschaften* occupied a special position in the postimperial fault zone of Latvia in 1919, where the *Baltikumer* sought to fill a power vacuum and achieve a new balance of power. The temporary weakening of the state monopoly on violence also created particular conditions and markets for violence. It enabled the formation of structures that, on the one hand, combined nonlocals with local actors who had knowledge of the area, with a very specific allocation of tasks. On the other hand, there were characteristics of an outsourcing strategy based on a division of labor, which resembled other forms of state violence.

The individual combatants' motives for engagement in the Baltic were extremely complex and by no means equally important to all involved. In addition to the prospect of settlement land promoted by the German government, they were driven by ideological convictions and a thirst for adventure, enhanced by the feeling that they had been born too late for combat in World War I. Last but not least, the opportunity to live out a fantasy of a romanticized military life and to prove themselves in battle was decisive to their enlistment.

Since the majority of the Baltic troops had an elitist and interventionist understanding of violence, there was a certain tendency to autonomy, accompanied by an intent to transform the society that they had infiltrated and terrorized. This tendency led to violent crimes, opportunistic vandalism, and other violent acts, which were a particular pattern of behavior of the *Gewaltgemeinschaften*. Collective violence was one of the defining characteristics of some units. Violence fulfilled a dual function, both as a social element and as a guiding principle. The majority of the former combatants viewed themselves in hindsight as having been mercenaries with violent tendencies rather than regular soldiers. Their group understanding and the gradual removal of common social norms under the extreme conditions of guerilla warfare had a direct impact on their psyches. Interpersonal dynamics and interdependencies made it almost impossible for men to leave their formations and also made it easier for radicalized individuals to quickly gain influence over the groups.

After the paramilitary forces returned from the Baltic, some contributed to the destabilization of the Weimar Republic and played a role in the radicalization of public life. The paramilitary *Gewaltgemeinschaften* that had operated in the Baltics were maintained in a new form by some ex-combatants. While some Baltic troopers were ready to return to normal civilian life, others felt they were neither able nor willing to do so. The networks formed in the Baltic continued to function in peacetime, and their activities were a case of transfer of violence.

The former combatants retained a special sense of community even after the period of active violence in the Baltics was over. Former combatants met in their own specially established fellowships and remembered the past, focusing on certain select events that dominated and shaped their discourse of remembrance, such as the "liberation" of Riga. Autobiographical sketches and the collection of various experiences and life stories also served to put their authors in control of the uncertainty in their own biographies, allowing them to distance themselves from their former selves and relocate themselves in history.

Gunther Mai was one of the first to assert that the interwar period in Europe was marked "by a bewildering *accumulation of configurations that favored violence*" (Mai 2001: 13). The *Baltikumers*' involvement in the *Gewaltgemeinschaften* and paramilitary networks created structures and opportunities to realize their new vision of order and community, drawing on a continuation of violence after World War I. Consequently, paramilitary associations in East-Central Europe between the two world wars were not just a transitional phenomenon but also a particularly violent vanguard, which had significant impact on both existing and newly forming political and social orders. It is no coincidence that in the German case, they provided a fertile recruiting ground for the personnel of the Gestapo, SA, and SS.

Mathias Voigtmann studied European history and European cultural history at the Technical University Chemnitz and at the European University Viadrina Frankfurt (Oder). In 2011 he finished his master's thesis "Literature as Historical Source—New Insights to Soviet Camps after Reading Varlam Šalamov." He is currently a doctoral student at the Herder Institute for Historical Research on East Central Europe in Marburg (working title of his thesis: "Paramilitärische Verbände im Ostmitteleuropa der Zwischenkriegszeit—Gewalt als Gemeinschaftserlebnis am Beispiel der baltischen Freikorps"). His research topics include history of Eastern Europe, social history of the GDR, history of the Soviet Union, and paramilitarism.

Notes

1. "Es geht bei gedämpftem Trommelklang / Wie finster das Antlitz, wie trüb der Gesang / O Deutschland, wie ist uns das Herz so schwer / Wir sind ja die letzten vom alten Heer. / Wir haben gestanden auf eiserner Wacht, / Der Feind hat uns nimmer zum Wanken gebracht. / Wir haben gehalten in treuloser Zeit /Der Fahne, den Führern den treudeutschen Eid. / Nun ruft uns die Heimat auf fremdes Gebot./ Wir müssen zurück, ob Gefahr uns auch droht, Wir haben gestanden, wir fürchten uns nicht, / Doch das aber ist unsere härteste Pflicht." "Kampflied der Baltikumer" (*Der Reiter gen Osten* 5, 1938: 29).
2. Different aspects of this text are part of the doctoral thesis by the author, which is being developed within the DFG research project, Gewaltgemeinschaften, at the Herder Institute for Historical Research on East Central Europe, Marburg.
3. See, regarding the pejorative usage of the term, Noske (1920: 183–84).
4. See Schluze (1969: 131–32). In this context, Schulze deviates strongly in his interpretation of the ceasefire agreement from its interpretation by the Germans. See Bernhard (1995: 2–4; Sauer 1995: 36).
5. Forschungsanstalt für Kriegs- und Heeresgeschichte, ed., 1937. Darstellungen aus den Nachkriegskämpfen deutscher Truppen und Freikorps, Zweiter Band, Der Feldzug im Baltikum bis zur zweiten Einnahme von Riga, Januar bis Mai 1919 (Berlin), 140-42. The headquarters of the Anwerbestelle Baltenland was in Berlin, but several local branches spread over all of Germany. Although its work was officially authorized by the war ministry, situations arose that evoked memories of the "time of Wallenstein." See concerning this, Noske (1920: 116); Maercker (1921: 226).
6. For the significance of the so-called "settlement promise," see also Blücher (1951: 70). To Blücher, the settlement promise was "the starting point of the so-called Baltic project." See also Stavenhagen (1919); cf. also, regarding the idea of settlement, Goltz (1936: 136–37).

7. One of the biggest problems in analyzing primary sources—that is, diaries, memoirs, and letters—is the prejudiced character of the sources. Despite their indispensability, they need to be critically evaluated, not least because they are commonly self-serving and exaggerate events. Quotations from novels and personal reminiscence writings will be particularly used in this study if their statements can reflect an atmosphere or mood that gives an insight to inner motives. These sources are considered as complementary information to historiography that needs to be critically observed within its context.
8. Altogether, we can talk of three different military campaigns: the *Bolschewistenzug* of December 1918–May 1919, the *Estenkrieg* of May 1919–September 1919, and the *Lettenkrieg* of September 1919–December 1919. In all three military campaigns, the political situation around the *Freikorps* exposed it to change. See Klein (2002: 53).
9. Regarding a paramilitary unit of the Latvians, the Aizsargi, see Balkelis (2013: 202). For an English version, see Balkelis (2012: 44). Unfortunately, I do not have access to the English edition and therefore do not have the correct page reference for that edition. See also Butulis (1995: 113–24).
10. Regarding the effect of World War I on the Baltic region and on the development of new, violent group conflicts, see Liulevicius (2002; 2006a: 46–65); for the eastern front and for *Ober Ost* see Liulevicius (2006b: 295–310); as source, Oberbefehlshaber Ober Ost 1917. Still crucial is Stone (1976), and Diehl (2003: 97–112).
11. Herder Institute for Historical Research on East Central Europe Marburg, Dokumentensammlung (DSHI) 190 BR/BLW 2.
12. DSHI 120 BR/BLW 52.
13. DSHI 120 BR/BLW 9.
14. DSHI 120 BR/BLW 2; see also DSHI 120 BR/BLW 161.
15. Cf. the literature of the last months of the war in footnote 7 and the "scorched earth principle": DSHI 190 BR/BLW 19. Cf. Schnell (2012); Baberowski (2012: 7–28).
16. Gerwarth (2013: 108–33) [in this exceptional case, we can use the German translation because the image of the spider web is not prominent in the English original: JB]; on the connections between paramilitaries and nationalistic groups, cf. Bergien (2012); Sauer (2004); on the metaphor of the web, cf. Salomon (1936: 99–100); Roth (1970).
17. The typology presented here was referenced by the author in another article. That article was published at the end of 2016 in the concluding volume of the research group Gewaltgemeinschaften. See Haslinger (2017).
18. On the complexity and inner inconsistency of the literature by *Freikorps* veterans, see Schellhase (2016).
19. For the biography of Müller, see Mergen (2010: 329–49; 2012) and Schleiden (1992: 25–36). On the artistic processing of the experiences in *Freikorps* by Müller, see Ansolt (1929: 56–57; 1934); Müller (1974).
20. Regarding the emotions and fears as well as the values and the self-imagination of the volunteer corps, see Theweleit (2009).
21. On the life of Ernst v. Salomons after his return, see Klein (2002: 67–124).
22. Many former *Freikorps* members operated informally and secretly, often in different cover organizations, such as detective agencies, traveling circuses and cartage companies. See also Salomon (1936: 98).
23. On the development and structure of the employment and settlement services, see *Der Reiter gen Osten* 7 (1934: 12) and *Der Reiter gen Osten* 4 (1935): 13.
24. Sauer (2002: 7). On the actions of the *Roßbacher*, see Gumbel (1979: 89–90). On the *Freikorps* magazines as information source: *Der Reiter gen Osten* 5 (1934: 12) and *Der*

Reiter gen Osten 6 (1935: 13); see also Voigtmann (2013: 137–38). For a partial description of what Georg Elwert called *Gewaltmärkte*, see Elwert (1997: 86–101).
25. DSHI 120 BR/BLW 57. Regarding the special group understanding and the growing solidarity of some subunits, see DSHI 120 BR/BLW 53, 85.
26. On the special position of the Baltic project, see *Der Reiter gen Osten*, "*Baltikum Sondernummer*" 2 (1935), and *Der Reiter gen Osten* 5 (1934: 3). Albert Leo Schlageter was a soldier in World War I. After 1918 he was part of different Free Corps in the Weimar Republic. After sabotaging French occupying troops, he was arrested and executed. His militant career and his execution fostered a martyrdom around his person, which was cultivated by German nationalist groups, in particular the Nazi Party during the Third Reich.

References

Baberowski, Jörg. 2012. "Einleitung: Ermöglichungsräume exzessiver Gewalt." In *Gewalträume: Soziale Ordnungen im Ausnahmezustand*, edited by Jörg Baberowski, 7–27. Frankfurt am Main.
Balla, Erich. 1932. *Landsknechte wurden wir . . . Abenteuer aus dem Baltikum*. Berlin.
Balkelis, Tomas. 2012. "Turning Citizens into Soldiers: Baltic Paramilitary Movements after the Great War." In *War in Peace: Paramilitary Violence in Europe after the Great War*, edited by Robert Gerwarth and John Horne, 126–45. Oxford.
———. 2013. "Von Bürgern zu Soldaten: Baltische Paramilitärische Bewegungen nach dem Ersten Weltkrieg." In *Krieg im Frieden: Paramilitärische Gewalt in Europa nach dem Ersten Weltkrieg*, edited by Robert Gerwarth, 201–25. Göttingen.
Barth, Boris. 2003. *Dolchstoßlegenden und politische Desintegration: Das Trauma der deutschen Niederlage im Ersten Weltkrieg 1914–1933*. Düsseldorf.
Bartov, Omer, and Eric D. Weitz, eds. 2013. *Shatterzone of Empires: Coexistence and Violence in the German, Habsburg, Russian, and Ottoman Borderlands*. Bloomington.
Bergien, Rüdiger. 2012. *Die bellizistische Republik: Wehrkonsens und "Wehrhaftmachung" in Deutschland 1918–1933*. München.
Bódo, Béla. 2011. *Pál Prónay: Paramilitary Violence and Anti-Semitism in Hungary, 1919–1921*. Pittsburgh.
Bleiere, Daina, ed. 2008. *Geschichte Lettlands. 20. Jahrhundert*. Riga.
Blücher, Wipert von. 1951. *Deutschlands Weg nach Rapallo: Erinnerungen eines Mannes aus dem zweiten Gliede*. Wiesbaden.
Böhler, Jochen, et al., eds. 2014. *Legacies of Violence: Eastern Europe's First World War*. München.
Butulis, Ilgvars. 1995. "Die Schutzkorpsorganisation in Lettland (1919–1940)." In *Autoritäre Regime in Ostmitteleuropa 1919–1944*, edited by Erwin Oberländer, 113–24. Mainz.
Collins, Randall. 2011. *Dynamik der Gewalt: Eine mikrosoziologische Theorie*. Hamburg.
Diehl, James M. 2003. "No More Peace: The Militarization of Politics." In *The Shadows of Total War: Europe, East Asia, and the United States 1919–1939*, edited by Roger Chickering, 97–112. Cambridge.
Dupuy, Trevor N., ed. 1993. *International Military Defense Encyclopedia*. Washington.
Eichenberg, Julia, and John Paul Newman. 2010. "Aftershocks: Violence in Dissolving Empires after the First World War." *Contemporary European History* 3: 183–94.
Elwert, Georg. 1997. "Gewaltmärkte: Beobachtungen zur Zweckrationalität der Gewalt." In *Soziologie der Gewalt, Sonderheft 37*, edited by Trutz von Trotha, 86–101. Opladen/Wiesbaden.

Gatrell, Peter. 2010. "War after the War: Conflicts, 1918-1922." In *A Companion to World War I*, edited by John Horne, 558-75. Chichester.

Gerwarth, Robert. 2013. "Im 'Spinnennetz': Gegenrevolutionäre Gewalt in den besiegten Staaten Mitteleuropas." In *Krieg im Frieden: Paramilitärische Gewalt in Europa nach dem Ersten Weltkrieg*, ed. Robert Gerwarth, 108-33. Göttingen.

———. 2017. *The Vanquished: Why the First World War Failed to End, 1917-1923*. London.

Gerwarth, Robert, and John Horne. 2013. "Paramilitarismus in Europa nach dem Ersten Weltkrieg: Eine Einleitung." In *Krieg im Frieden: Paramilitärische Gewalt in Europa nach dem Ersten Weltkrieg*, edited by Robert Gerwarth, 7-27. Göttingen.

Gerwarth, Robert, and Erez Manela. 2014. *Empires at War 1911-1923*. Oxford.

Goltz, Rüdiger v. d. 1936. *Als politischer General im Osten (Finnland und Baltikum) 1918 und 1919*. Leipzig.

Gumbel, Emil Julius. 1979. *Verschwörer: Zur Geschichte und Soziologie der deutschen nationalistischen Geheimbünde 1918-1924*. Heidelberg.

Haslinger, Peter. 2017. "Frontiers of violence: Paramilitärs als Gewaltgemeinschaften im Ostmitteleuropa der 1920er Jahre." In *Gewaltgemeinschaften in der Geschichte: Entstehung, Kohäsionskraft und Zerfall*, edited by Winfried Speitkamp, 233-54. Göttingen.

Haslinger, Peter, and Vytautas Petronis. 2013. "Erster Weltkrieg, Systemkonsolidierung und kollektive Gewalt in Ostmitteleuropa: Litauen und der 'Eiserne Wolf.'" In *Gewaltgemeinschaften: Von der Spätantike bis ins 20. Jahrhundert*, edited by Winfried Speitkamp, 343-69. Göttingen.

Hehn, Jürgen von, ed. 1977. *Von den baltischen Provinzen zu den baltischen Staaten: Beiträge zur Entstehungsgeschichte der Republiken Estland und Lettland 1918-1920*. Marburg/Lahn.

Klein, Markus Josef. 2002. *Ernst von Salomon: Revolutionär ohne Utopie*. Aschau i. Ch.

Knigge, Jobst. 2003. *Kontinuität deutscher Kriegsziele im Baltikum: Deutsche Baltikum-Politik 1918/19 und das Kontinuitätsproblem*. Hamburg.

Koch, Hannsjoachim W. 2002. *Der deutsche Bürgerkrieg—Eine Geschichte der deutschen und österreichischen Freikorps 1918-1923*. Dresden.

Liulevicius Vejas, Gabriel. 2002. *Kriegsland im Osten: Eroberung, Kolonisierung und Militärherrschaft im Ersten Weltkrieg*. Hamburg.

———. 2006a. "Der Osten als apokalyptischer Raum: Deutsche Frontwahrnehmungen im und nach dem Ersten Weltkrieg." In *Traumland Osten: Deutsche Bilder vom östlichen Europa im 20. Jahrhundert*, edited by Gregor Thum, 47-65. Göttingen.

———. 2006b. "Von 'Ober Ost' nach 'Ostland'?" In *Die Vergessene Front: Der Osten 1914/15; Ereignis, Wirkung, Nachwirkung*, edited by Gerhard P. Groß, 295-310. Paderborn.

Lindenberger, Thomas, ed. 1995. *Physische Gewalt: Studien zur Geschichte der Neuzeit*. Frankfurt am Main.

Maercker, Georg. 1921. *Vom Kaiserheer zur Reichswehr: Geschichte des freiwilligen Landesjägerkorps; Ein Beitrag zur Geschichte der deutschen Revolution*. Leipzig.

Mai, Gunther. 2001. *Europa 1918-1939: Mentalitäten, Lebensweisen, Politik zwischen den Weltkriegen*. Stuttgart.

Mergen, Torsten. 2010. "Erlebte und gedeutete Geschichte: Der Erste Weltkrieg im Werk von Karl Christian Müller." In *Im Banne von Verdun: Literatur und Publizistik im deutschen Südwesten zum Ersten Weltkrieg von Alfred Döblin und seinen Zeitgenossen / Internationales Alfred-Döblin-Kolloquium*, edited by Ralf Georg Bogner, 329-49. Bern.

———. 2012. *Ein Kampf für das Recht der Musen: Leben und Werk von Karl Christian Müller alias Teut Ansolt (1900-1975)*. Göttingen.

Moran, Daniel, and Arthur Moran, ed. 2002. *People in Arms: Military Myth and National Mobilization since the French Revolution*. Cambridge.

Müller, Karl Christian. 1974. *Der Meerhornruf: Reigen.* Heidenheim.
Nord, Franz. 1929. "Der Krieg im Baltikum." In *Der Kampf um das Reich*, edited by Ernst Jünger. Essen.
Noske, Gustav. 1920. *Von Kiel bis Kapp: Zur Geschichte der deutschen Revolution.* Berlin.
Oberbefehlshaber Ober Ost, ed. 1917. *Das Land Ober Ost: Deutsche Arbeit in den Verwaltungsgebieten Kurland, Litauen und Bialystok-Grodno.* Stuttgart.
Philipp, Jan. 2006. "Die Natur der Gewalt als Problem der Soziologie." In *Die Natur der Gesellschaft: Verhandlungen des 33. Kongresses der Deutschen Gesellschaft für Soziologie in Kassel 2006*, edited by Karl-Siegbert Riekenberg, 42–64. Frankfurt am Main.
Popitz, Heinrich. 1986. *Phänomene der Macht: Autorität—Herrschaft—Gewalt—Technik.* Tübingen.
Prusin, Alexander Victor. 2010. *The Lands Between: Conflict in the East European Borderlands, 1870–1992.* New York.
Purkl, Andreas. 1997. *Die Lettlandpolitik der Weimarer Republik: Studien zu den deutsch-lettischen Beziehungen der Zwischenkriegszeit.* Münster.
Reichardt, Sven. 2013. "Vergemeinschaftung durch Gewalt: Der SA-'Mördersturm 33' in Berlin-Charlottenburg." In *SA-Terror als Herrschaftssicherung: "Köpenicker Blutwoche" und öffentliche Gewalt im Nationalsozialismus*, edited by Stefan Hördler, 110–29. Berlin.
Rohrscheidt, Walter von. 1938. *Unsere Baltikumkämpfer: Die Ereignisse im Baltikum 1918 und 1919.* Braunschweig.
Roth, Joseph. *Das Spinnennetz.* Frankfurt am Main.
Sapper, Manfred, and Volker Weichsel. 2014. "Editorial." In *Totentanz: Der Erste Weltkrieg im Osten Europas*, edited by Manfred Sapper et al., 5–6. Berlin.
Salomon, Ernst von. 1929. "Sturm auf Riga." In *Der Kampf um das Reich*, edited by Ernst Jünger. Essen.
———. 1929. "Die Versprengten." In *Der Kampf um das Reich*, edited by Ernst Jünger. Essen.
———. 1936. *Nahe Geschichte: Ein Überblick.* Berlin.
Sammartino, Annemarie H. 2010. *The Impossible Border: Germany and the East 1914–1922.* Ithaca, NY.
Sauer, Bernhard. 1995. *Die Baltikumer.* Berlin.
———. 2002. "Gerhard Roßbach—Hitlers Vertreter für Berlin: Zur Frühgeschichte des Rechtsradikalismus in der Weimarer Republik." In *Zeitschrift für Geschichtswissenschaft* 50(1): 5–21.
———. 2004. *Schwarze Reichswehr und Fememorde: Eine Milieustudie zum Rechtsradikalismus in der Weimarer Republik.* Berlin.
Schellhase, Robert. 2016. "Vergessenes Genre. Freikorpsliteratur 1918–1945." *Freunde und Alumni der Bergischen Universität.*
Schivelbusch, Wolfgang. 2003. *The Culture of Defeat: On National Trauma, Mourning, and Recovery.* New York.
Schleiden, Karl August. 1992. "Literatur an der Saar im Spannungsfeld von Politik und Geschichte." In *Literatur an der Grenze: Der Raum Saarland—Lothringen—Luxemburg—Elsass als Problem der Literaturgeschichtsschreibung; Festgabe für Gerhard Schmidt-Henkel*, edited by Uwe Grund, 25–36. Saarbrücken.
Schmidt-Pauli, Edgar v. 1936. *Geschichte der Freikorps 1918–1924: Nach amtlichen Quellen, Zeitberichten, Tage-büchern und persönlichen Mitteilungen hervorragender Freikorpsführer.* Stuttgart.
Schnell, Felix. 2012. *Räume des Schreckens. Gewalträume und Gruppenmilitanz in der Ukraine, 1905–1933.* Hamburg.
Schulze, Hagen. 1969. *Freikorps und Republik 1918–1920.* Boppard am Rhein.

Stavenhagen, Kurt. 1919. *Die eigene Scholle in der Baltenmark*. Stuttgart.
Stone, Norman. 1976. *The Eastern Front 1914–1917*. London.
Stopinski, Sigmar. 1997. *Das Baltikum im Patt der Mächte: Zur Entstehung Estlands, Lettlands und Litauens im Gefolge des Ersten Weltkrieges*. Berlin.
Tauber, Joachim. 2008. "Editorial." In *Über den Weltkrieg hinaus: Kriegserfahrungen in Ostmitteleuropa 1914–1921*, Neue Folge 17: 7–12.
Theweleit, Klaus. 2009. *Männerphantasie 1 + 2*. München.
Thoß, Bruno. 2002. "Die Zeit der Weltkriege—Epochen als Erfahrungseinheit?" In *Erster Weltkrieg—Zweiter Weltkrieg. Ein Vergleich. Krieg, Kriegserlebnis, Kriegserfahrung in Deutschland*, edited by Bruno Thoß, 7–42. Paderborn.
Voigtmann, Mathias. 2015. "Die 'Baltikumer'—Deutsche Freikorps im Lettland des Jahres 1919 als Schule der Gewalt." In *Nach dem Zerfall der Imperien: Historische Zäsur und biografische Erfahrung im östlichen Europa / After the Fall of Empires: Historical Turning Points and Biographical Experience in Eastern Europe*, edited by Katrin Steffen, 122–40. Lüneburg.
Volkmann, Hans-Erich. 1970. *Die deutsche Baltikumpolitik zwischen Brest-Litowsk und Compiègne: Ein Beitrag zur "Kriegszieldiskussion."* Cologne.
Wróbel, Piotr. 2003. "The Seeds of Violence: The Brutalization of an Eastern European Region, 1917–1921." *Journal of Modern European History* 1: 125–49.
Zobel, Johannes. 1934. *Zwischen Krieg und Frieden: Schüler als Freiwillige in Grenzschutz und Freikorps*. Berlin.

CHAPTER 2

Pogroms and Imposture
The Violent Self-Formation of Ukrainian Warlords

Christopher Gilley

Warlordism in Ukraine, 1917–1922

The fall of empires creates opportunities for national minorities to realize hitherto impossible or even unimagined projects. This was certainly true of those territories of today's Ukraine that before 1917 were part of the Russian Empire. Here, a Ukrainian national movement had existed before 1914, but it was largely confined to intellectuals, many of whom were socialists who advocated the transformation of the Romanov Empire into a democratic federation in which both Russia and Ukraine would be equal partners. Few self-identified Ukrainians sought Ukrainian independence before the Great War. After the fall of the Romanov dynasty, the Central Rada—the assembly that claimed to speak on behalf of the "Ukrainians" in the former Russian Empire—continued to seek a federal solution to the Ukrainian question through negotiations with the Russian Provisional Government. However, the Bolsheviks' overthrow of the Provisional Government, the Red Army's invasion of Ukraine, and the need for international support forced the Central Rada to declare independence so that it could ally with the Central Powers.[1]

There followed a series of multisided wars that saw invasions and interventions in Ukraine from the Bolsheviks, Whites, Poles, the Central Powers, and the Entente. Peasant rebels opposed requisitioning and conscription by all the warring parties, yet they also fought one another to gain control of the property of dispossessed landowners. Nationally conscious Ukrainians sought to orient themselves within this chaos. Many moved increasingly toward a nationalist stance, some oscillated between nationalist and socialist goals, and others saw independence as a temporary measure until a federation with Russia could again become a possibility. The Ukrainian People's Republic (UNR) headed by Symon Petliura became the main representative of Ukrainian national aspirations and the new cause of Ukrainian independence. However, as a result of a lack of consensus about the desirability of independence and differing stances on social liberation, the UNR did not command the loyalties of all nationally conscious Ukrainians. For example, the Independentists, a leftist splinter group from Petliura's own Ukrainian Social Democratic Workers' Party, tried in the spring and summer of 1919 to create a Ukrainian soviet[2] state subservient to neither the Bolsheviks nor the UNR.[3]

In November 1920, the UNR forces ended their open struggle against the Bolsheviks, crossed into Poland, and were interned; they had failed to create an independent, non-Soviet state. This was not only due to lack of foreign aid or the absence of a Ukrainian national consciousness—the two most common explanations[4]—but also to the fact that many nationally conscious Ukrainians did not support the UNR. However, given the fact that most Ukrainian intellectuals had not even advocated the creation of an independent state before 1917, preferring a socialist federation with Russia, one can question whether the "Ukrainian revolution" was a failure. Certainly part of the Ukrainian intelligentsia was willing to see the creation of the Ukrainian Socialist Soviet Republic as the realization of their traditional goals, albeit an imperfect one (Gilley 2009). At the same time, a large number who had fought the Bolsheviks emigrated. Many émigrés increasingly became attracted by doctrines of ultranationalism that called for an unrelenting struggle against the occupiers of Ukrainian land. They advocated authoritarianism, anti-Semitism, and charismatic leadership. They saw other fascist movements as their ideological kin and created the Organization of Ukrainian Nationalists (OUN), which collaborated with the Nazis during World War II.[5]

The chaos of the revolution and civil war in Ukraine created ideal conditions for military commanders who operated autonomously from the major warring parties. They led groups of peasant partisans that often consisted of a small, hardened core of permanent insurgents organized around a prominent leader. During the various uprisings, they called upon local peasants to support them. The peasants found these commanders to be useful allies against the powers trying to requisition their produce and conscript their sons. When the rebellions met serious opposition, the peasants returned to their fields. The partisans then went underground or moved to a less dangerous place, only to rise again when the time was right. Many warlords preferred to operate near their home villages, often creating self-proclaimed "republics." However, in order to remain active, they often found themselves fighting in different parts of the country.[6]

The most famous commander was Nestor Makhno, a putative anarchist who led thousands of peasant insurgents in the region surrounding Hulai-Pole (today in southeastern Ukraine). Between 1917 and 1920, Makhno fought against Ukrainian nationalists, Austro-German occupiers, White Russians, and—when his on-again, off-again alliance with the Bolsheviks failed—the Red Army.[7] Other leaders styled themselves as *otamany* (singular: *otaman*) after the leaders of the early modern Zaporozhian Cossacks, whom Ukrainian nationalist historians had long celebrated as the forebears of Ukrainian statehood in the sixteenth and seventeenth centuries. Makhno, who rejected nationalism, never used this title. *Otaman* is often loosely translated as "warlord"; in this text, the two words shall be used interchangeably. The *otamany* committed some of the bloodiest pogroms of the civil wars in Ukraine. The most notorious *otaman* pogromist was Nykyfor Hryhor'iev, a former captain in the Imperial Russian Army, who commanded a band active primarily in southern Ukraine that captured Odesa for the Bolsheviks and then rebelled against them (Adams 1963; Horak 1998). In Kyiv province, two of the most active *otamany*, who were also responsible for a wave of anti-Semitic violence, were Danylo Terpylo (aka *Otaman* Zelenyi) and Il'ko Struk. Both were former village teachers who had served in the Great War; they commanded insurgent bands in their home regions to the south and north of the city of Kyiv, respectively (Gilley 2014).

The collapse of the state's monopoly on force enabled the *otamany* to remain active, but their violence made it harder for any one single force to reestablish that monopoly. At the end of 1918, many warlords allied with the UNR to overthrow Pavlo Skoropads'kyi, the ruler put in place by the Germans. However, during the war between the UNR and the Bolsheviks for control of Ukraine that erupted soon afterward, a large number abandoned Petliura or switched their allegiances to the Red Army. That new loyalty did not last long; in the spring and summer of 1919, the warlords were prominent in the uprisings against the new Bolshevik government in Ukraine. These uprisings forced the Red Army to retreat before the counterrevolutionary Whites under the command of Anton Denikin. Although a few *otamany* allied with Denikin, the majority were involved in an insurgency against his rule. This ensured that the Whites did not control great swaths of the Ukrainian hinterland. Some *otamany* fought in the name of the UNR and others in that of the Bolsheviks. Denikin's rule collapsed in winter 1919 following a Bolshevik counterattack. Thus, between the end of 1918 and the end of 1919, the warlords had helped bring down four governments in Ukraine.

Thereafter, the warlords played a less central role. Those who allied with the Bolsheviks were incorporated into the Red Army or sidelined, as the new rulers of the country built up their regular military forces. The many *otamany* who continued to fight for the UNR no longer threatened to topple the Bolshevik government. However, into the early 1920s, they were still able to disrupt the construction of the Soviet state and economy by attacking the country's economic infrastructure and state representatives. Only by strengthening their punitive forces, developing a more systematic approach to counterinsurgency, and offering amnesties to the insurgents were the Bolsheviks able to end the threat.

With the rise in nationalist interpretations of Ukrainian history since 1991, it has become popular to present the *otamany* as Ukrainian national heroes who consistently fought against the Bolsheviks for Ukrainian independence. One prominent popularizer of this view is Roman Koval',[8] although many professional Ukrainian historians view his work critically (Koval'chuk 2012: 249–50). The apotheosis of this trend is the legal recognition of the *otamany*, alongside other insurgents and partisans of the civil wars, as "fighters for the independence of Ukraine in the twentieth century" in Ukraine's 2014 legislation regulating historical memory. As such, they receive the law's protection against "disrespect."[9]

By contrast, historians based in the West who have studied the warlords dispute claims that these groups fought for independence. Serhy Yekelchyk argues that the *otamany* expressed the "dreams and phobias of mostly illiterate peasant rebels through the vocabulary of modern socialism or nationalism." The main factor in Ukraine was the question of land redistribution (Yekelchyk 2013: 124). Another scholar, Felix Schnell, argues that the fall of the Romanovs created a "space of violence," a social space where violence was the form of interaction that offered actors the best chance of successfully pursuing their interests. It was a paradise for those predisposed to violence, who could live out fantasies that in a peaceful society were impossible. This violence was "contagious." The threat of violence from others encouraged individuals to use violence themselves, and those less inclined toward violence became more susceptible to using it (Schnell 2008: 195–221; Schnell 2012: 19–25, 256–62, 363–65). Nestor Makhno and the *otamany* headed militant communities that offered their members strength and protection. Violence held them together. It underpinned their leaders' authority, determined their status within the bands' hierarchy, and united their members in a shared experience of combat and complicity in terrorizing the weak. As was the case for other actors in the space of violence, ideology played no role in the activity of the *otamany*. Violence was not a means to their ideological ends. Ideology was more a rationalization of violence after the fact, while violence was a method of communicating belonging and identity that possessed its own self-perpetuating dynamics (Schnell 2012: 19–25, 256–62, 363–65).

Certainly, Schnell and Yekelchyk have done a great service in highlighting the complexities of the situation in Ukraine. Peasants rarely took up arms to fight for an ideological cause, seeking instead to pursue their own more limited desires and goals within the dangerous conditions of a chaotic civil war. Moreover, Schnell identifies a dynamic that undoubtedly existed: violence and the threat of violence drove individuals to become more violent. However, the "space of violence" approach has a drawback, in that it rules out the use of a set of sources—the leaflets and newspapers published by the *otamany*—before the historian has even looked at them to assess their value.

How then is it possible to use the leaflets of the *otamany* as a source while still accepting that their loyalties and alliances were often a response to situational factors rather than deep ideological convictions? This chapter will proceed using an approach inspired by Sheila Fitzpatrick. She argues that

> successful revolutions tear off masks: that is, they invalidate the conventions of self-presentation and social interaction that obtained in pre-revolutionary society. This happened in Russia after the October 1917 revolution. . . . In such upheavals, people have to reinvent themselves, to create or find within themselves personae that fit the new postrevolutionary society. The process of reinvention is at once a process of reconfiguration (a new arrangement of data about oneself) and one of discovery (a new interpretation of their significance). It always involves strategic decisions (how should I present myself in this new world?) and may also prompt ontological reflection (who am I really?). (Fitzpatrick 2005: 3)

In addition, she writes, "All identity projects require impersonation. . . . But, at a certain point, or in certain circumstances, impersonation becomes imposture" (Fitzpatrick 2005: 18).

From this perspective, statements by the *otamany* regarding their political goals were a means of expressing a new identity that fit the postrevolutionary situation, a method of self-formation. Some of the personae they created were most likely impostures. However, whether or not an identity was "genuine" is less important than the fact that the warlords sought to project that identity. It is more important to ask what personae the *otamany* sought to construct, in what circumstances, and with what purpose.

Some of these personae were created during the civil wars, at the time of the violence itself. Others developed afterward in order to explain the warlords' civil war careers and meet the needs of the postwar circumstances. For example, Il'ko Struk presented himself as a constant supporter of Ukrainian independence in the form of a presidential republic. After the civil wars, he claimed,

> I am entirely devoted to the will and desires expressed by the Ukrainian people, and particularly by my glorious knights, who are from the people, from the peasants, and they wanted and want only that Ukraine will be an independent, people's republic, at the head of which would stand a president, who would take part in governing the country.[10]

However, Struk had fought for numerous masters—the UNR, the Whites, and the Independentists—but had maintained strong autonomy from his nominal superiors. He thereby repeatedly undermined the attempts to create a non-Bolshevik state, on the one hand by turning against the UNR, on the other by tainting the UNR's image with his lawlessness and violence while he was allied with it. His statement quoted above was therefore a retrospective attempt to impose order on his checkered career in the civil wars. As such, it was yet another case of impersonation and imposture.

The Civil War Personae of the Warlords

One also finds numerous examples of impersonation and imposture that occurred during the civil wars themselves. Many warlords operated under pseudonyms. Nykyfor Hryhor'iev was most likely born as Oleksandr Servetnyk and took his surname from the village in which he grew up (Horak 1998: 8). *Noms de guerre* were extremely popular and seem to have identified characteristics with which a particular *otaman* wanted to be associated. Some took appellations to evoke a fearsome countenance, such as *Otaman* Bida ("Misery"), while other names evoked the natural world, for instance *Otaman* Zelenyi ("Green"). However, some of the most common handles were those adopted from the Zaporozhian Cossacks. Examples include *Otaman* Mamai (after the folk hero Kozak Mamai) and *Otaman* Bohun (after Ivan Bohun, an advisor to Bohdan Khmel'nyts'kyi, the leader of the 1648 Cossack uprising against Polish-Lithuanian rule) (Savchenko 2011: 8).

This indicates how important Ukrainian warlords found it to construct for themselves a persona as a Zaporozhian Cossack. Iukhym Bozhko provides one example. He was the organizer and commander of several units that fought for the UNR against the Bolsheviks, but he was also difficult to control and discipline. He finally died while taking part in a mutiny against Petliura. In November 1918, he created a unit called the "Zaporozhian Sich" that acknowledged the authority of the UNR Directory. He declared himself *otaman* of the New Zaporozhian Sich, a re-creation of the camp of the seventeenth-century Cossacks. He made his base on the island of Khortytsia in the Dnipro River on the site of the earlier camp. With this re-creation in mind, he was reported (perhaps apocryphally) to have demanded that the director of the historical museum of Katerynoslav send him the museum's Cossack artifacts and an old Cossack Bible. Bozhko and some of his supporters cultivated a neo-Cossack appearance, shaving their heads and sporting topknots, long mustaches and uniforms modeled on the garb of the Zaporozhians (fur hats with a cloth tail, high-collared jerkins with large buttons, baggy trousers, and broad belts) (Sereda 1930: 10–12; Savchenko 2011: 115–21).

Moreover, imposture was an essential tactic of partisan warfare. False flag operations were common. One White intelligence report describes the activities of *Otaman* Zelenyi, a former peasant, teacher, and political activist who had allied, in turn, with the UNR, the Bolsheviks, and the Independentists before joining the UNR again (Tynchenko 2007: 174). The report claimed that, after failing to incite a peasant settlement to rise up against the White Russian Volunteer Army, Zelenyi's men dressed up as White soldiers to attack and pillage the village. Once the "Whites" had left, Zelenyi appeared again to decry the evils that the "Volunteer Army" had committed and call upon the peasants to join his ranks.[11]

Imposture was also a useful means of infiltrating an enemy-held village. Numerous partisan memoirs recall such events. One finds several examples in the account of A. Taranenko, an anti-Bolshevik insurgent in the Kyiv province. He describes how his partisan detachment arrived at a settlement where a Cheka unit was garrisoned. The leader of the insurgents, one Cornet Morozov, told the locals that he headed a Bolshevik punitive detachment and demanded to see the chairman of the local executive committee. Morozov ordered it to feed and equip his troops, which indeed happened. Morozov then called an assembly. This too took place. The partisans used the meeting to determine who was a communist. They then arrested the communists and commissars, beat them up, and moved on.[12]

One finds further examples of how living in a "space of violence" forced repeated impostures upon the partisans in other memoirs. One good example is the account by Andrei Vladimirov, a Russian-speaking landowner from Kyiv province who served as an officer in the Russian Army during World War I. After the revolution, he adopted—or was forced to adopt—several personae, many of which involved an element of imposture. In 1917, he pretended to be a private soldier in order to return home from the front unmolested. During the first Bolshevik occupation of his native region in early 1918, he became an actor in a pro-Soviet theatrical group and wrote poems "in a revolutionary spirit" to avoid persecution by the authorities. During the German occupation later that year, he was forced, against his will, to join a group of peasant partisans. Then, during the second Bolshevik occupation of the area in 1919, he had a new persona thrust upon him, that of partisan leader, when the local peasants asked him to lead their uprising against the Bolsheviks. He felt he had little choice but to join the insurgents, as he feared reprisals if he refused. During the uprising, he issued a statement calling other peasants to his "cause." He claimed, "We are fighting not against soviet power, but against the Communists, Bolsheviks, and Jewish commissars and Chekists. Our slogan is, 'Long live the soviets, but without Communists and Bolsheviks.'" In his memoir, Vladimirov felt that he had to explain such a strange stance to his readers, who might find it "funny or even absurd." He wrote that many, if not all, peasants in the area understood the power of the soviets to be the power of the peasants. They were very disappointed that instead of peasant soviets, they found themselves under the control of soviets dominated by Communists and (supposedly) Jews. "My order," he explained, "aimed to influence the peasant masses, who had to play in this struggle the main, decisive role."[13]

In this way, the Russian landowner and monarchist presented himself as a supporter of the soviet system of government in order to mobilize support. From the perspective of the creation of postrevolutionary personae, it is unimportant whether his declarations described his "real" goals. More significant is that he projected a persona in order to swell his ranks and gain legitimacy for his violence. Adopting slogans and promulgating them in leaflets was one way of doing this. Indeed, the personae adopted were a survival strategy. In the conflict it was necessary to tell others (truthfully or not) whose side one was on, whether one was an officer disguising himself as a private or one was a partisan publishing leaflets stating one's goals.

Vladimirov himself claimed to have no interest in Ukrainian nationalism.[14] However, one can look at the statements by the nationally conscious Ukrainian *otamany* in the same way. For example, one Ukrainian commander, Iurii "Iurko" Tiutiunnyk, had an extremely checkered career during the Russian civil wars, fighting numerous enemies and serving several masters. He participated in the anti-German risings of summer 1918. In early 1919, he became chief of staff to *Otaman* Hryhor'iev, meaning he fought first as part of the Red Army and then rose against the Bolsheviks along with Hryhor'iev. Following the dispersal of Hryhor'iev's forces, he briefly allied with the Independentists in their uprising against the Bolsheviks. The failure of their revolt led Tiutiunnyk to join the UNR army that fought the Bolsheviks until it had to abandon the country for Poland in autumn 1920. After emigrating, he supported the insurgents remaining in Ukraine and led the so-called Second Winter Campaign, a disastrous raid into Soviet territory at the end of 1921. He continued to try organizing opposition to the Bolsheviks from abroad, until the GPU tricked him into returning to Soviet Ukraine in 1923. He was captured, after which he defected and made pro-Soviet statements. Tiutiunnyk lived in Soviet Ukraine unmolested until 1929, when he became one of the first victims of the purges of the Ukrainian intelligentsia at the end of the decade (Gilley 2015: 328–52).

During the civil wars, Tiutiunnyk issued numerous leaflets and appeals in which he set out his political goals and adopted political slogans. Order No. 1, which Tiutiunnyk published during Hryhor'iev's uprising, took a stance that was anti-imperialist, antibourgeois, pro-soviet, and pro-labor, presenting his partisans as a leftist Ukrainian alternative to the pseudo-communist Bolshevik speculators.[15] This was largely in accordance with the line taken by Hryhor'iev at the time. His Order No. 2, proclaimed later during his short-lived alliance with the Independentists, was more obviously nationalist. While he continued to pay lip service to the concept of a non-Bolshevik, soviet state as proclaimed by the Independentists, his declaration was stridently anti-Russian and anti-Semitic, calling for Ukraine to be ruled by Ukrainians rather than "our eternal enemy, the Great Russians, and their assistants the Jews."[16] Leaflets published while he was serving the UNR stressed more the need for a single, centralized Ukrainian leadership to strengthen Ukrainian statehood and fight for social and economic independence.[17] He used images of Ukrainian national heroes, such as the mid-seventeenth-century Cossack leader Bohdan Khmel'nyts'kyi, to mobilize the Ukrainian population.[18]

After the defeat of the UNR army, Tiutiunnyk continued to oppose the Bolsheviks. He sought to establish contacts with other émigré military groups and right-wing thinkers. He met leaders of the Ukrainian Military Organization that conducted a terrorist campaign against the Poles in Eastern Galicia to discuss spreading their activity to Soviet Ukraine (Shatailo 2000: 84–85). He worked with the rabidly anti-Russian Dmytro Dontsov, an émigré from the former Russian empire who became the prophet of the far-right brand of nationalism that gained many adherents among the soldiers of the defeated Ukrainian army (Golczewski 2010: 512–20). Tiutiunnyk's letters from the time reveal that he advocated many of the central tenets of Dontsov's nationalism.[19]

After the Bolsheviks tricked him into returning to Ukraine (Fauzlin 2011: 383–404), he faced the choice of execution or recognizing the regime against which he had fought. He asked to be rehabilitated. This involved issuing statements in favor of Soviet Ukraine that praised its promotion of Ukrainian culture and statehood after the introduction of the 1923 policy of Ukrainization; he depicted Soviet Ukraine as the best supporter of the Ukrainians living in Poland, Romania, and Czechoslovakia. In this way, Tiutiunnyk presented himself as penitent leftist nationalist who had come to see the error of his opposition to the Bolsheviks. His private letters reveal that this was an imposture and that he continued to see the Bolsheviks as alien occupiers of Ukraine (Fauzlin 2013: 297–98). Nevertheless, it was clearly important to construct a persona as a penitent warlord to explain the reconciliation. For the Bolsheviks, at least, that was central to the propaganda value they hoped to gain from pardoning Tiutiunnyk.

One should not simply dismiss Tiutiunnyk's numerous shifts in loyalty and the changing tone of his leaflets as conclusive evidence of the ideological inconstancy of the warlords and the unimportance of their ideas. Viewed from the perspective of construction of postrevolutionary identities as described by Fitzpatrick, those statements were a means of expressing the persona that Tiutiunnyk thought necessary to project at the particular time. They explained his current loyalties to himself and others and sought to mobilize support. Some were undoubtedly impostures (for example, the persona of the contrite *otaman*), yet there is no real way of sifting all the "fake" personae out from the "genuine." Tiutiunnyk may indeed have moved from a more leftist to a more nationalist position during the civil wars; many other nationally conscious Ukrainians seem to have made the same journey. However, ultimately the genuineness of the persona is less important than the fact that Tiutiunnyk believed that it was worth projecting.

The Warlords' Personae and Their Violence

Erik Landis, the historian of the Tambov revolt in Russia, has stressed the importance of such attempts to create and project identities to irregular forces during the civil wars in the former Russian Empire. He argues that there were numerous groups with ready access to arms that were dissatisfied with both the White and Red governments and that were willing to offer armed resistance. However, the great majority of these failed to develop into mass movements. This indicates that such movements required not only opportunity and material resources but also a politicized collective identity. He stresses that

> collective … identity claims must be asserted, contextualized, and continually rearticulated. An important component to the collective-identity claims made in this regard involves the narrative connections that link underlying issues such as grievances, worthiness, solidarity, and objectives." (Landis 2010: 33, 46)

The Tambov rebels' stated desire to restore the Constituent Assembly was therefore not an expression of support for constitutional democracy but part of the narrative explaining their activity. They sought to identify themselves as supporters of the 1917 revolution and challenge the Bolsheviks' claim to be its sole custodians. This met the need of both leaders and participants "to frame their activities in terms of worthiness and possibility" and thus maintain a prolonged mass movement (Landis 2004: 217–19, 236).

The personae constructed and projected by the warlords provided the central element of the narrative developed by the Ukrainian insurgents. The *otamany* created numerous narratives based on their identity and adapted them through the war. Their personae were also connected to the violence. As mentioned above, the *otamany* were among the worst perpetrators of the pogroms that swept Ukraine during the civil wars. *Otaman* Hryhor'iev was responsible for the bloodiest—each of the pogroms committed by his troops claimed, on average, sixty-seven victims, more than double the number for those perpetrated by White forces. More generally, the pogroms were most virulent during spring and summer of 1919, the high point of the uprisings led by the *otamany* against the Bolsheviks (Abramson 1999: 114, 116).

This violence was closely related to the personae and narratives constructed by the different bands who allied in the attempt to overthrow the Bolshevik government. Like Tiutiunnyk, they described themselves as supporters of the soviet system of government who were seeking to wrest the soviets from the clutches of the Russo-Jewish pseudo-socialists. One can piece together the elements of this self-image from the leaflets issued by the warlords. For example, *Otaman* Zelenyi, who was also responsible for many brutal pogroms, ended his leaflets with slogans such as "Long live the Independent Ukrainian Socialist Republic!" and "Long live the peasant, workers' and soldiers' power of soviets!"[20] At the same time, he emphasized how the Bolsheviks had abused the soviet system of government: they had come as brothers to help the laboring people of Ukraine but instead requisitioned their produce and conscripted their sons, inflicting violence upon those in the village who resisted. Zelenyi portrayed himself as the defender of the Ukrainian laboring people, in particular the peasants, against this outrage.[21]

While many of his leaflets portrayed the Bolsheviks as Russians, we can also see that Zelenyi found the Jews to be particularly complicit in the communists' crimes. He emphasized that "the Rumanian Jew Rakovskii"[22] headed the Bolshevik Soviet government of Ukraine.[23] A song celebrating the feats of Zelenyi's troops, titled "Otaman Zelenyi's Army Is So Strong," described the Bolshevik Ukrainian government as "Little Jews" who "dictated the law to our glorious Ukraine."[24] Zelenyi extended this belief in the Jewishness of the Bolshevik government to suspicion of the Jewish population in general. In his orders issued after taking Rzhyshchev in June 1919, Zelenyi told the city's inhabitants that all the city's Jewish population had run away. He described their flight (which, if his claim was true, was most likely an attempt to escape a feared pogrom) as a provocation by the Jews. He ordered Jews not to flee. All the members of the Jewish population who supported Rakovskii's government were to give up their weapons by 4:30 P.M. Those who failed to do so would be shot.[25]

The persona constructed by Hryhor'iev is remarkably similar. Like Zelenyi, he portrayed himself as a representative of the Ukrainian laboring people against the elites who had betrayed them and a supporter of an independent soviet Ukraine. At the start of his uprising, Hryhor'iev issued a *universal* describing his aims. The word *universal* was the term used by early modern Cossacks to describe their proclamations. In it, Hryhor'iev explicitly condemned pogroms and called for the punishment of those responsible for them. Yet, in the very same text, one finds anti-Semitic canards: Hryhor'iev described Bolshevik Chekists and commissars as coming from Moscow and "the land where Christ was crucified." Here, he combined the traditional anti-Semitic canard of Jewish deicide with the modern one of Judeo-Bolshevism.[26]

Like Zelenyi, Hryhor'iev emphasized Rakovskii's supposed Jewishness and claimed that Jews dominated the Bolshevik leadership in general. This, he stated, was the cause of the pogroms, meaning that the Jews were themselves responsible for the violence against them. In one leaflet written at the end of his uprising, Hryhor'iev denied that his troops had committed pogroms, but then wrote,

> I turn to the Jews and loudly declare to the entire world that the pogroms and slaughter of Jews are the fault of the Jews themselves who have crawled by any means into the [Bolshevik] leadership and Cheka.
>
> Comrade Jews. You know very well that in Ukraine you only make up five or six percent, but the Cheka and commissars are 99 percent Jewish. And, here it is, your 99 percent of the Cheka Jews have led you to pogroms. This is how the people deal with the Jewish commissar; for this reason it beats up Jews.[27]

Indeed, this leaflet threatened further anti-Jewish violence: if the Jews fighting against him did not lay down their arms within the week, they would be beaten and their property and homes would be destroyed. Throughout his uprising, Hryhor'iev abjured responsibility for the pogroms in one breath[28] but justified them in the next, in part by portraying the agents of anti-Semitic violence as the people themselves.

As the warlords' claims to represent the Ukrainian *laboring* people remind us, there was a social component to their personae, not just an ethnic one. Other independent commanders placed greater emphasis on class solidarity, particularly those connected to Nestor Makhno. One finds some broad similarities between Makhno's program and those put forward by the *otamany*: Makhno and his followers presented themselves as representatives of the laboring classes—peasants and workers—against their exploiters. They called for the creation of free soviets not dominated by the Bolsheviks.[29] However, Makhno rejected the Ukrainian warlords' use of nationalist slogans, arguing that they aided bourgeois counterrevolution by stirring up ethnic hatreds, particularly against Jews, and harmed socialist unity with Russia.[30] These aspects of Makhno's identity were closely bound up with his self-depiction as an anarchist. Whether Makhno "really" was an anarchist is therefore less important than the fact that he considered it important to describe himself as such.

As in the case of the *otamany*, the personae developed by Makhno and his supporters included the construction of an image of the enemy against which they contrasted themselves. They generally sought to insert their violence into a narrative of defending the exploited against the exploiters. For example, the Makhnovite commander Aleksei Chubenko was once sent to the town of Pologi because local peasants were complaining that the commander of a detachment was terrorizing them. On his arrival, Chubenko found the charges to be true and had the miscreants executed.[31] Later he was sent to another settlement, where, in a similar way, the local population was complaining about partisan commanders treating them poorly. On investigation, Chubenko decided that the accusations had been concocted by forces loyal to Petliura, who wanted to compromise the partisans in revenge for their merciless treatment of the bourgeoisie. Instead of arresting the partisans, he convinced them to join Makhno.[32] For Chubenko, the first case of partisan violence was unjustified because it targeted the exploited; the second case, directed at the exploiters, was justified.

Certainly, there could be disagreement about appropriate targets of violence. Makhno fell out with his deputy Fedor Shchus' for a time when the latter attacked a German settlement, despite the fact that Shchus' justified his violence by claiming that he was punishing the bourgeoisie.[33] As Schnell (2008: 217) argues, this incident may indeed indicate that Makhno understood the importance of maintaining control over acts of violence as a means of underpinning his personal authority. Nevertheless, it also demonstrates that Shchus' thought in categories of justifiable and unjustifiable violence and that he assumed (albeit, in this case, wrongly) that Makhno would accept them as he shared the same narrative of defending the exploited. During the altercation between Makhno and Shchus,' the latter pointed out that Makhno had brutally murdered a priest. When he used violence to bolster his authority, Makhno certainly seemed to prefer victims who could be depicted as exploiters, be they representatives of the old order such as the priest or even one of his own troops who was proven guilty of robbing local peasants.[34] Even if these categories for choosing victims might sometimes be applied arbitrarily or ignored completely, the perpetrators did think about them. These categories connected the violence to the personae the insurgents sought to project.

Conclusion

The violence in the former Romanov Empire was a response to state collapse: the state's loss of its authority and monopoly on force created a spiral of violence that encouraged men to use violence to survive and prosper. This does not mean that the ideas expressed by the violent men involved in the war are unimportant, even in the case of the *otamany*, whose loyalties repeatedly changed. Those living in the "space of violence" could create, or had to create, new identities for themselves in order to respond to the conditions in which they found themselves. The Ukrainian warlords cultivated, among others, the personae of leftist opponents of the (supposedly) pseudo-socialist Russo-Jewish Bolsheviks, proponents of a Ukrainian national state, and descendants of the Cossacks. Sometimes they employed these personae at the same time. This was not necessarily contradictory.

Part of the process of constructing identity was voluntary, but the threat of violence and the need to mobilize support meant that this self-formation often involved impersonation and imposture as a survival strategy. Within that process, it is not always possible to separate "fake" from "genuine" identities—nor is that always the most important question. Finding themselves on a battleground in which actors espoused various ideologies, the *otamany* seem to have felt the need to construct identities that referenced and incorporated disparate elements of those ideologies. Their personae entailed narratives about the warlords' activity that gave meaning to their actions in their own eyes and in others'. They thus represented a tool for mobilizing support (albeit one that was often unsuccessful) and a means of holding the bands of insurgents together, if only for a short time. Identifying the enemy was an important part of the narratives. Consequently, the personae of the *otamany* were closely linked to their violence.

There was nothing uniquely Ukrainian about these processes of constructing identity. As mentioned above, Erik Landis has described the personae created by insurgents in other parts of the former Russian Empire (2010, 2014). One can also view the political statements and violent acts of combatants elsewhere as a means of forming new identities. Thus, future paramilitary leaders such as Ernst von Salomon, who abetted the assassination of German foreign minister Walther Rathenau, constructed for themselves a romanticized warrior self-image in response to the shock of military defeat, the collapse of the old order, and the lost opportunity to prove themselves on the battlefields of World War I. Viewed in this way, the "subcultures of ultra-militant masculinity" that sprang up throughout Central Europe after the war were examples of the self-formation of new personae to fit the new postrevolutionary situation, no less so than the identities constructed by the Ukrainian warlords.[35]

The particularity of the Ukrainian context is perhaps the sheer number of warring parties in the country, each with its own ideological precepts and state-building projects. Among them were the Whites, Bolsheviks, Poles, the Ukrainian People's Republic, and Ukrainian leftists who favored a soviet but non-Bolshevik Ukraine. On the one hand, the many contenders for power, and the willingness of ad hoc military formations to switch allegiances from one to another, made it very difficult for any one faction to establish a monopoly of force in the country. On the other, it meant that all those involved in the fighting had to construct personae and narratives to position themselves in relation to their allies and opponents. The result was the confusion of political statements and programs that was so characteristic of the civil wars in Ukraine.

Christopher Gilley wrote his doctorate at the University of Hamburg on Sovietophilism in the interwar Ukrainian emigration. His postdoctoral research, funded by the German Research Foundation, examined warlordism in Ukraine during the civil war, 1917–1921. He is currently working at Durham University Library Archives and Special Collections while also undertaking a Diploma in Archive Administration at Aberystwyth University. Gilley's most recent publication is "Beat the Jews, Save . . . Ukraine: Antisemitic Violence and Ukrainian State-Building Projects, 1918–1922," *Quest: Issues in Contemporary Jewish History; Journal of Fondazione CDEC* 15.

Notes

1. On the Ukrainian intelligentsia's stance on independence, see Rudnytsky (1987: 389–416).
2. In this text, I use the noncapitalized "soviet" to refer to the principle of government centered on class-based councils and the capitalized "Soviet" for the state set up by the Bolsheviks.
3. The best overview of the civil wars in Ukraine is Kasianov (2015: 76–131).
4. For a discussion, see Hrytsak (2004: 66–79) and Gilley (2017b)
5. The best introduction is Golczewski (2010). Motyl (1980) is the classic text, but is now outdated.
6. Kasianov (2015) provides a good introduction by placing the *otamany* in the broader context of the civil war. Recent Western studies include Chopard (2019) and Gilley (2017a). A comprehensive recent Ukrainian work, with contributions by the country's most prominent researchers on the topic, is Arkhireis'kyi et al. (2017).
7. There is an enormous amount of literature on Makhno. The most recent and interesting works are by Schnell (see above 2008 and 2012).
8. Koval' is the founder of the Kholodnyi Iar historical club, a veritable cottage industry producing monographs on the *otamany* and republishing their memoirs. For an overview of their currently available works, see http://nezboryma-naciya.org.ua/books.php.
9. See the official website of the Verkhovna rada, http://w1.c1.rada.gov.ua/pls/zweb2/webproc4_1?pf3511=54689 (retrieved 30 June 2017).
10. Manuscript "Otaman Povstantsiv Il'ko Struk. Zi sliv Ot. Struka zapysk M.O.," Tsentral'nyi Derzhavnyi Arkhiv Vyshchykh Orhaniv Vlady ta Upravlinnia Ukrainy (hereafter, TsDAVO), f. 3504, op. 1, spr. 2, ark. 65 ob–66.
11. Agent's Report for the Political Office, 28 November 1919, Gosudarstvennyi Arkhiv Rossiiskoi Federatsii (hereafter, GARF), f. 446, op. 2, d. 45, ll. 242–43.
12. A. Taranenko, manuscript, "Vospominaniia 'Vosstanie v mestechke Gorodishche Kievskoi gubernii (9 maia 1919 g.),'" GARF f. R 5881, op. 2, d. 673, ll. 40 ob–42.
13. Andrei Vladimirov, manuscript, "Iz vspominanii atamana povstancheskogo otriada v Ukraine," GARF f. R 5881, op. 2, d. 296, ll. 35–37. The quotations are on l. 36.
14. Vladimirov, "Iz vspominanii atamana," GARF f. R 5881, op. 2, d. 296, l. 2.
15. Extract from Order No. 1 Signed by Otaman Tiutiunnyk, Commander of the Forces in the East, Tsentralnyi Derzhavnyi Arkhiv Hromads'kykh Ob'iednan' Ukrainy (hereafter, TsDAHO), f. 5, op. 1, spr. 267, ark. 129–30.
16. Order No. 2 signed by Otaman Tiutiunnyk, 15 June 1919, TsDAHO f. 5, op. 1, spr. 154, ark. 174–76.
17. Report No. 37 of the Information Section of the Tsk KPU, 12 November 1919, TsDAHO f. 1, op. 20, spr. 39, ark. 126–27.
18. Leaflet, "Zapovidi. Narodnoi povstanches'koi viiny," TsDAHO f. 57, op. 2, spr. 266, ark. 3.
19. Tiutiunnyk to Iosyp Pshonnyk, 14 January 1923, in Verstiuk, Skal'skyi and Faizulin (2011: 82–83).
20. Leaflets, "Braty—seliane!" TsDAHO f. 1, op. 18, spr. 63, ark. 12 and "Do trudovoho selianstva ta robitnykiv," TsDAHO f. 1, op. 18, spr. 63, ark. 13.

21. Leaflets, "Braty—seliane!" TsDAHO f. 1, op. 18, spr. 63, ark. 12 and "Do trudovoho selianstva ta robitnykiv," TsDAHO f. 1, op. 18, spr. 63, ark. 13.
22. Christian Rakovsky (1873-1941) was in fact a Bulgarian who spent part of his early life in Romania. He became a Bolshevik in 1918 and headed the Ukrainian Soviet government for most of the period between January 1919 and July 1923.
23. Leaflet, "Braty—seliane!" TsDAHO f. 1, op. 18, spr. 63, ark. 12.
24. "Iaka syl'na armiia otamana Zelenoho," TsDAHO f. 1, op. 18, spr. 63, ark. 30.
25. Order No.1 to the Garrison of Rzhyshchev, 30 June 1919, TsDAHO f. 1, op. 18, spr. 63, ark. 10.
26. Leaflet, "Universal," TsDAHO f. 57, op. 2, spr. 398, ark. 2. For more on Hryhor'iev's declaration of aims and condemnation of pogromists, see his "Order No. 2," 20 May 1920, TsDAHO f. 5, op. 1, spr. 265, ark. 34.
27. Leaflet, "Seliane rabochie i krasnoarmeitsy," 11 June 1919, TsDAHO f. 5, op. 1, spr. 264, ark. 116-18.
28. He may have done this to project a more statesmanlike persona. I make this argument in Gilley (2014: 120-21).
29. See for example, the "Proekt deklaratsii revoliutsionnoi postancheskoi armii Ukrainy (Makhnovtsev)," GARF f. R9431, op. 1, d. 111, ll. 3-24.
30. "Novyi Petliura," *Put' k Svodbode*, 17 May 1919. Available at TsDAHO f. 5, op. 1, spr. 259, ark. 4-8.
31. "Dnevnik Alekseia Chubenko (ad'iutanta Makhno)," in Danilov, Kondrashin, and Shanin (2000: 739).
32. "Dnevnik Alekseia Chubenko," Danilov, Kondrashin, and Shanin (2000: 739-40).
33. "Dnevnik Alekseia Chubenko," Danilov, Kondrashin, and Shanin (2000: 741).
34. For examples, see "Dnevnik Alekseia Chubenko," Danilov, Kondrashin and Shanin (2000: 739, 758, 761).
35. On these subcultures, and Ernst von Salomon in particular, see Gerwarth (2013: 57-59). The quotation is on p. 59.

References

Abramson, Henry. 1999. *A Prayer for the Government: Ukrainians and Jews in Revolutionary Times, 1917-1920*. Cambridge, MA.

Adams, Arthur E. 1963. *Bolsheviks in the Ukraine: The Second Campaign, 1918-1919*. New York.

Arkhireis'kyi, Dmytro et al. 2017. *Viina z derzhavoiu chy za derzhavu? Selians'kyi povstanches'kyi rukh v Ukraini 1917-1921 rokiv*. Kharkiv.

Chopard, Thomas. 2019. "L'ère des atamans: Politique, guerre civile et insurrections paysannes en Ukraine (1917-1923)." *20 & 21. Revue d'histoire* 2019(1): 55-68.

Danilov, Viktor, Viktor Kondrashin, and Teodor Shanin, eds. 2000. *Nestor Makhno: Krest'ianskoe dvizhenie na Ukraine 1918-1921 gg. Dokumenty i materialy*. Moscow.

Fauzlin, Iaroslav. 2011. "Iurko Tiutiunnyk i operatyvna rozrobka orhaniv DPU 'Sprava No. 39.'" In *Studii z istorii Ukrains'koi revoliutsii 1917-1921 rokiv: na poshanu Ruslana Iakovycha Pyroha: Zbirnyk naukovych prats,*" edited by V. F. Verstiuk. Kyiv.

———. 2013. "Iuryi Tiutiunnyk i radians'kyi orhany derzhbezpeky." *Problemy vyvchennia istorii Ukrains'koi revoliutsii 1917-1921 rr.* 9.

Fitzpatrick, Sheila. 2005. *Tear off the Masks: Identity and Imposture in Twentieth-Century Russia*. Princeton, NJ.

Gerwarth, Robert. 2013. "Fighting the Red Beast: Counter-Revolutionary Violence, 1917-

1923." In *War in Peace: Paramilitary Violence in Europe after the Great War*, edited by Robert Gerwarth and John Horne, 52–71. Oxford.
Gilley, Christopher. 2009. *The Change of Signposts in the Ukrainian Emigration: A Contribution to the History of Sovietophilism in the 1920s*. Stuttgart.
———. 2014. "The Ukrainian Anti-Bolshevik Risings of Spring and Summer 1919: Intellectual History in a Space of Violence." *Revolutionary Russia* 27(2): 109–31.
———. 2015. "Iurko Tiutiunnyk: A Ukrainian Military Career in World War, Revolution, and Civil War." *Journal of Slavic Military Studies* 28(2): 328–52.
———. 2017a. "Fighters for Ukrainian Independence? Imposture and Identity among Ukrainian Warlords, 1917–1922." *Historical Research* 90(247): 172–90.
———. 2017b. "Untangling the Ukrainian Revolution." *Studies in Ethnicity and Nationality* 17(3): 326–38.
Golczewski, Frank. 2010. *Deutsche und Ukrainer*. Paderborn.
Horak, V. 1998. *Povstantsi otamana Hryhor'ieva (serpen' 1918—serpen' 1919 rr.): Ist. Doslidzhennia*. Fastiv.
Hrytsak, Iaroslav. 2004. "Chomu zaznala proazky ukrains'ka revoliutsiia?" In *Strasti za natsionalizmom. Istorychni esei*, Kyiv.
Kasianov, Georgiy. 2015. "Ukraine between Revolution, Independence, and Foreign Dominance." In *The Emergence of Ukraine Self-Determination, Occupation, and War in Ukraine, 1917–1922*, edited by Wolfram Dornik, 76–132. Edmonton.
Koval'chuk, Mykhailo. 2012. *Bez peremozhtsiv: Povstans'kyi rukh v Ukraini proty bilohvards'kykh viis'k henerala A. Denikina (cherven' 1919 r.—liutyi 1920 r.)*. Kyiv.
Landis, Erik C. 2010. "Who Were the 'Greens'? Rumor and Collective Identity in the Russian Civil War." *Russian Review* 69(1): 30–46.
Motyl, Alexander. 1980. *The Turn to the Right: The Ideological Origins and Development of Ukrainian Nationalism, 1919–1929*. New York.
Rudnytsky, Ivan L. 1987. "The Fourth Universal and Its Ideological Antecedents." In *Essays in Modern Ukrainian History*, edited by Ivan L. Rudnytsky 389–416. Cambridge, MA.
Savchenko, V. 2011. *Atamanshchina. Mifi. Legendy. Deistvitel'nost'*. Kharkov.
Sereda, M. 1930. "Otamanshchyna: Otaman Bozhko." *Litopys Chervnoi Kalyny* 1.
Shatailo, Oleh. 2000. *Heneral Iurko Tiutiunnyk*. L'viv.
Schnell, Felix. 2008. "'Tear Them Apart . . . and Be Done with It!' The Ataman-Leadership of Nestor Makhno as a Culture of Violence." *Ab Imperio* 3: 195–221.
———. 2012. *Räume des Schreckens: Gewalt und Gruppenmilitanz in der Ukraine 1905–1933*. Hamburg.
Tynchenko, Iaroslav. 2007. *Ofitser'skyi Korpus Armii Ukrains'koi Narodnoi Respubliky (1917–1921). Knyha 1*. Kyiv.
Verstiuk, V. F., V. V. Skal'skyi, and Ia. M. Faizulin, eds. 2011. *Iurii Tiutiunnyk: Vid "Dviiky" do GPU; Dokumenty i materialy*. Kyiv.
Yekelchyk, Serhy. 2013. "Bands of Nation Builders? Insurgency and Ideology in the Ukrainian Civil War." In *War in Peace: Paramilitary Violence in Europe after the Great War*, edited by Robert Gerwarth and John Horne, 107–25. Oxford.

CHAPTER 3

Toward an Interactional Theory of Sexual Violence
The White Terror in Hungary, 1919–1921

Béla Bodó

The dissolution of the Austro-Hungarian Empire in the autumn of 1918 inaugurated a period of rapid change in East-Central Europe. Hungary, which emerged as one of the independent successor states to the Dual Monarchy, experienced two revolutions in ten months. The collapse of the Council Republic, founded in March 1919, and the occupation of Budapest and the eastern half of the country by the Romanian army in early August 1919, provoked a right-wing reaction. The subsequent seven months bore witness to a rapid rise in paramilitary and mob violence directed primarily against supporters of the left, poor workers, and peasants, in addition to apolitical and middle-class Jews. Political violence in the second half of 1919 and the early 1920s took the lives of between fifteen hundred and five thousand people (Fischer 1993: 863–92; Ungváry 2000: 173–203; Bödők 20011: 15–31; Katzburg 2002: 36–39). By the end of 1921, the political and military elite had been able to rein in the militias; however, isolated attacks on Jews as well as on social democratic organizations and politicians continued well into the mid-1920s. Militia violence increasingly took the form of sexual violence. Although the archives do not provide numbers or statistics, they do document incidents that allow researchers to describe the nature of this violence and to place it in a comparative context.

Sexual violence during the civil war in Hungary between 1918 and 1921 was part of a larger international trend. The rise of nationalism and separatism in the late nineteenth century posed a mortal threat to the age-old multiethnic empires in Eastern and Southern Europe. Adept in the ancient technique of divide and conquer, the political elite in Russia tolerated and often even encouraged attacks on weaker groups, like the Jews, between 1880 and 1915. Rape and other forms of sexual aggression often accompanied the pogroms (Robbers 1986; Klier and Lambroza 1992; Abramson 1999; Bartal 2005; Wells 2006; Dekel-Chen 2011). Historians attribute the gruesome murders, mutilations, and rapes committed during the Balkan Wars before 1914 both to the survival of ancient mores and customs (i.e. the violent nature of traditional peasant societies) and to the spread of modern nationalism (Clark 2012).

However, extreme violence was not confined to the less developed part of Europe. Some of the stories about German troops raping Belgian and French women may have been inventions of a sophisticated French and British campaign of misinformation aimed at destroying the reputation of the Central powers and undermining the morale of the German population (Kramer 2007: 244–45). Still others (indeed, the majority) were based on fact. Although the exact number will never be known, recent research confirms contemporaries' impression that thousands of women were raped in the first year of the war (Fogarty 2009: 59–90; Horne and Kramer 2010; Ziemann 2013: 7–24). Beside "fake news," true accounts of actual murders and mass rapes found their way into the Serbian and Austro-Hungarian press in 1914 and 1915 as well.[1] Bulgarian troops, too, committed horrendous atrocities, including sexual crimes, during their occupation of Southern Serbia between 1915 and 1916 (Hagemann and Schüler-Springorum 2002; Audoin-Rouzeau 2009).

But the worst sexual crimes seem to have taken place during the Armenian genocide in the Ottoman Empire of 1915–18. In the second phase of the Armenian genocide (after the murder of more than two hundred thousand Armenian POWs and an unknown number of male teenagers and adults in 1915), the regime in Istanbul ordered the relocation of the better part of the remaining Armenian population. During the death marches, Turkish troops, and Turkish, Kurdish, Bedouin, and Arab civilians, raped, tortured, enslaved, sold off as chattels or brutally murdered more than a million women and children (Bjørnlund 2009: 16–58). In East-Central and Eastern Europe, the tit-for-tat war between Germany and Russia and between Russia and Austria-Hungary caused enormous suffering among civilians. In many cases in Galicia and Bukovina, Russian soldiers systematically targeted Jewish and Polish women with the approval of their commanders. As a form of compensation to the local population, however, the same tsarist officers encouraged Ukrainian and Polish peasants to take out their frustration on the Jews by pillaging Jewish shops and homes, raping women, and murdering innocent civilians.

In many places, such as the city of Lemberg (present-day L'viv) and its vicinity, clashes between various army and militia units and attacks on ethnic minorities did not cease with the end of the war but continued into the early 1920s (Gerwarth and Horne 2013; Mick 2016: 137–209). World War I, as Robert Gerwarth shows in his recent book, did not end in but continued in the form of low-intensity warfare until at least 1923. Indeed, the cruelty exhibited toward civilians, particularly during the Polish-Soviet War of 1919–20, often exceeded that of the war years (Gerwarth 2017). In Soviet Russia, too, military violence both transfigured and complemented revolutionary and counterrevolutionary violence during the civil war, and claimed the lives of ten million people between 1918 and 1920 (Hagen 2018).[2] These numbers do not include the hundreds of thousands of individuals who were murdered, tortured to death, or left to die in prison by the political police during the first half of the 1920s (Ryan 2015). In the Habsburg lands, particularly in regions that were to become parts of Czechoslovakia, Yugoslavia, and Hungary, "Green" peasants pursued their own agenda of liberation (Beneš 2017: 217–41; Kučera and Hufschmied 2019: 65–83). The brutality of the "Green" cadres matched that of their Red or White counterparts: beside the pillaging of noble estates, the robbing of banks, and the raiding and demolishing of stores, houses, and farms of wealthy Jews, Hungarian peasants killed dozens of individuals and injured hundreds more in the summer and fall of 1918 (Hatos 2018: 143–265).

Sexual violence was part of the larger trend of rapidly changing sexual norms and patterns of behavior during and after the Great War. These changes were Janus-faced: their effects were simultaneously positive and negative, liberating and enslaving. The war weakened the power of the families, village communities, social classes, and peer groups to control the behavior of their members and sexual deviations. The conflict made racial, ethnic and religious, and class barriers more penetrable and the transgression of accepted norms more frequent. Sexual relations between White European men and colored women were not new; however, the public considered sexual encounters between colored men from the colonies and White European women scandalous even if they had been based on mutual consent; when they were not, as often as it may have been the case during the French occupation of the Rhineland in the early 1920s, the public reacted violently to what it considered an insult and a national disgrace. But it was not only sexual encounters between men and women of diverse social and ethnic origins that became more frequent during the war. The long military conflict, which implied men living in close quarters and developing strong emotional ties with one another, and conquering new lands and experiencing strange cultures and unfamiliar lifestyles, also favored homosexual encounters between men of different military ranks, ages, and social, ethnic, and racial backgrounds (Herzog 2011: 45–61). All these changes were tension generators. The presence of millions of Russian POWs in the Austro-Hungarian countryside, which favored sexual relations between them and local women and led to the birth of thousands of children, increased tensions in the village communities and the peasant families, even if such temporary liaisons had been consensual and benefited both parties. In the cities, women came to occupy positions in the manufacturing and service sectors, which had been traditionally the preserves of their husbands and sons. Even though the high majority of women either voluntarily gave up their jobs to the returning war veterans or, more often, were forced to surrender them, the world was never again the same after 1918. Women not only continued to occupy what used to be men's positions in the economy but also, thanks to cultural changes and the introduction of women's suffrage in most counties in Europe, such as Hungary, became socially and politically more visible after 1918, as well (Wall and Winter 1988; Grayzel 2010: 263–78). None of these developments took place without increased tensions or, often enough, open conflicts, however. In the more conservative countryside, too, changing roles, beside sexual infidelity, proved to be a major generator of domestic violence. As an extreme example of growing tensions in rural families, peasant women, led by the local midwife, poisoned with arsenic more than fifty people in the village of Nagyrév and the neighboring communities located in the backward and poverty-stricken Tiszazug region of Hungary between 1912 and 1928. The majority of victims were seriously ill and bedridden elderly whom the women, now acting as heads of their household and the controllers of the family purse, came to regard as financial and emotional burdens. The second group of victims consisted of alcoholics, husbands who brutally abused their wives, and disabled war veterans, who, like the bedridden elderly, became superfluous (Bodó 2002).

The theoretical literature on sexual violence has not only expanded in scope but also gained in sophistication since the wars in the Balkans and the Rwanda genocide in the 1990s. The first explanations, advanced by radical feminists in the 1970s, that posited that "men" used rape to enslave "women" and then keep them in the state of bondage, and that "patriarchy," in the form of obsolete family structures, harmful child-rearing practices, capitalist exploitation, male-dominated political institutions, biased legislations, and prejudiced judges, fostered violence against women and helped to cover up sexual crimes, are generally seen as sorely inadequate to explain complex events, such as group rapes and other types of sexual aggression against both men and women in war situations.[3] Instead of a monaural explanation, historical works, such as Antony Beevor's magisterial study on the final phase of the war and the behavior of Soviet soldiers, take a whole range of factors into consideration to explain Soviet brutality against German women. Among the possible explanations, Beevor considered ideological indoctrination and propaganda as the most important. By the time the Russians reached Berlin, he writes, soldiers came to regard women as rightful booty, having become convinced that their sacrifices entitled them to behave as they pleased. Rape was a response to an extreme situation, Beevor argues, and it should not be considered as a typical form of behavior of all men in peace and war (Beevor 2002). In his study of the

Russian occupation of Germany, Norman Naimark, too, lists, male aggression infused with libido drive, hate propaganda (including the demeaning depiction of German women in the Soviet press), personal experiences of suffering at home, alcoholism, the patriarchal nature of Russian and Asian societies, and the Russian sense of inferiority in relation to the West and Germany as the most important source of group rapes and other types of sexual aggression at the end of World War II (Naimark 1995: 79, 92, 108–12).

This study compares two instances of sexual violence, one pogrom and one sexual torture in prison during the White Terror in Hungary after World War I. With the help of the interactional theory of violence, advanced by American sociologist Randall Collins, the study seeks to explore the unintended (yet not necessarily unwelcomed) process of radicalization inherent in every encounter between armed soldiers and helpless civilians. The focus in this article is not on the ideology and characters of the perpetrators (bad as they were) but on the circumstance that fed their destructive drive. The thesis of this chapter hinges on the assumption that the presence of violent individuals alone does not explain extreme violence; what is needed is not only "violent individuals but [also] violent situations; and also not fearful individuals but fearful positions and situations." Violence is difficult because it goes against normal "interaction rituals," as "one has to cut out all one's sensitivity to cues of human-to-human ritual solidarity, to concentrate instead on taking advantage of others' weaknesses." However, once they are able to overcome these emotional barriers created by socialization and defended by the law, the perpetrators are set free: intoxicated by power over life and death and brought into stance by their own bodily rhythms, the perpetrators are prone to gradually raise the stakes until violence completely spirals out of control: what starts out as limited aggression, such as robbery, aimed to secure circumscribed advantages can thus easily degenerate into battery, rape, sexual torture, mutilation, and murder (Collins 2008: 8–10). What factors helped or hindered the process of radicalization during the White Terror and with what results is the subject of this chapter.

The Pogrom in Diszel

The first event discussed in this study took place in early September 1919 in the small village of Diszel, located on the shores of Lake Balaton in western Hungary.[4] The pogrom in Diszel was one of a series of attacks on Jews in the Somogy and Zala provinces during the first weeks of counterrevolution. On the morning of 9 September 1919, news of a pogrom in the neighboring spa town of Tapolca reached the small Jewish community in Diszel. The head of the local administration, the village secretary, advised Jewish leaders and their wards to leave the village for a while. The local cantor did not share the village secretary's pessimistic assessment of what might occur. Fearful that their homes and businesses would be robbed in their absence, the Jews decided to stay. Meanwhile, the village secretary visited Tapolca in the afternoon to see what was going on with his own eyes. He returned to the village around 9:00 P.M. By that time, the pogrom had begun.

At sunset, the mayor heard gunshots. Concerned about possible attacks and robberies, he distributed weapons (including hand grenades) from the local arsenal to members of the local citizens' militia. Since no professional policeman or gendarme was stationed in the small community, the mayor had nowhere else to turn. In any case, the commander of the local militia assured him of his and his men's loyalty and promised to maintain order. However, neither the militia commander nor his men kept that promise. They not only failed to quell the disturbance, but, having switched sides and being armed to the teeth, they actually led the assault. Fearful of the armed mob, which apparently regarded local administrators as "traitors" and "friends of the Jews," the mayor and his colleagues retreated into their homes. The physical abuse and destruction of private property continued for more than six hours, and the pogrom finally ended after midnight. The aftermath of the pogrom was sobering. The mob had killed nine Jews and seriously wounded an elementary school teacher, whom the perpetrators had apparently mistaken for a Jew as he passed through the village.[5] The crowd not only pillaged the houses of their victims but also demolished them. The wine that they could not drink was spilled on the ground.[6]

The mob went from house to house, stealing everything from jewelry to clothing and food, demolishing house interiors and physically attacking the residents. The Breuer family (Ignác and Mór Breuer, their wives, and their six children) left their house in the center of the village in time to find refuge in a toolshed on their farm at the edge of the village. The family was very well-to-do by local standards: Ignác Breuer owned a small mineral water bottling company as well as vineyards and orchards in Diszel and the surrounding villages. The family hid in the shed, waiting anxiously for the danger to pass. However, one of their neighbors revealed their hiding place to a seven-member detachment that had been looking for them. The militia greeted its victims with *"Pénzt vagy életet!"* (Your money or your life!) as they led the Breuers out of their hiding place. The Breuers handed over everything that they had on them, including jewelry and more than fifteen thousand crowns in cash, which was a considerable amount of money at the time. However, their compliance failed to mollify the militia men, who not only continued but also intensified the physical abuse of their victims. After half an hour of intense beatings, the leader of the militia, Kálmán Juhász, told his men to "put [the victims] out of their misery." In an attempt to escape after the first shot had been fired, Flóra, Mór Breuer's teenage daughter, broke out of the circle. Three men ran after her, and she was caught, ferociously beaten, and repeatedly raped. Meanwhile, the perpetrators killed her father and tortured her mother, mutilating her body before killing her. They also murdered Flóra's brother and uncle.[7]

The proponents of the interactional theory of violence focus on the participants' reactions to the ever-changing situation and on the interface between the participants in this human drama. In Diszel, local actors tried to assess the situation at the time and second-guess their opponents' intentions on the basis of the information available to them. As mentioned above, in order to cut through the fog of rumors, the head of the local administration and village secretary decided to pay a visit to the neighboring town. This was a fateful decision because with his departure, the main representative of the state, who was also its most feared and respected man, left the community. The leaders of the small Jewish community had misjudged the situation and the turn of events. Fearful that their neighbors and friends would pillage their property in their absence, they refused to heed the village secretary's advice to leave. The village leaders were not alone in misjudging the situation. In the early evening, the mayor and the village secretary still trusted the militia enough to distribute weapons to its members. The militia soon switched sides, however, and the men who only a few hours earlier had vowed to maintain order and protect the Jews became robbers and mob leaders themselves.

What transpired in Diszel conforms closely to the predictions of the interactional theory of violence. Crowd aggression could not be contained, and what had begun as a mere robbery soon transformed into "a grotesque carnival" and "a celebration of destruction." The mob in Diszel took a "moral holiday" (a term commonly used by the proponents of the interactional theory of violence). When robbing and pillaging no longer provided the desired thrill and entertainment, the participants raised the stakes by smashing furniture, demolishing house interiors, and setting houses and businesses on fire. In the end, the damage that they caused exceeded the value of the jewelry, clothing, and money that they had stolen.

Not only was there a progression from robbery to destruction, but physical violence also soon began to spiral out of control. The mob first attacked adults (mainly men) before manhandling children, women, and the elderly. In the end, they had killed a handicapped Jew and severely beaten an elementary school teacher merely for appearing Jewish. There was finally a shift from what Reemtsma terms *lozierende Gewalt* (localizing violence) to *raptive Gewalt* (rapturous violence) and then to *autotelische Gewalt* (autotelic violence)—that is, from a form of aggression that limits violence to the body alone to one that exploits the body of the victims as a source of sexual and aesthetic pleasure.[8] The boundaries between the three types of violence overlapped. Robbery in

Diszel gave way to vandalism and public humiliation, and light physical abuse gave way to rape. The rapists, in turn, did not stop at extorting sexual pleasure from the bodies of their victims. Rape became assimilated as part of the general mood of killing and even merged with mutilation and torture into a grotesque "killing game" (Collins 2008: 98–99).

The mob in Diszel was led by local militia men and armed outsiders. In Collins's terms, it was these "violence artists" who spearheaded the attacks by breaking down doors, smashing windows, and searching for, finding, and beginning to manhandle the victims. Armed men acted as "facilitators" similar to "non-commissioned officers in a non-hierarchic, completely voluntary, ephemeral army" (Collins 2008: 247). The foot soldiers of the riot in Diszel (civilians, women, the elderly, and teenage children) played an equally important role in the destruction. As we have seen, it was one of the neighbors who betrayed the Breuers' hiding place to the militia. The "violence artists" staged their performance on behalf of bystanders, and second-line attackers drew strength from their presence and support. The foot soldiers stole and destroyed more property than the "violence artists" who led the charge.

Looting seems to have fulfilled two functions: First, the attacks on the Jews provided an opportunity for the participants to line their pockets and vent their frustrations. Second, the looting served as "a mass recruiter and momentum-sustainer," which Collins describes as "a brilliant tactical invention, so to speak since no one invented it—since it takes a relatively useless part of the supporters and onlookers of an insurrection and turns them into activists of sorts, keeping alive the emotional atmosphere that is where the moral holiday lives or dies." Looting in Diszel functioned as "Durkheimian ritualism done for the sake of the activity itself, and as a symbolic expression of membership; the objects stolen can be nearly worthless in every other respect, but they represent one's partnership in breaking the law" (Collins 2008: 249–50).

The "violence artists" drew energy not only from the bystanders and the second-line attackers but also from the body language and reactions of their victims. The aggressors and their victims constituted a dynamic unit. Caught in "a mutual asymmetrical entrainment," they responded to each other's gestures, words, and actions. Petrified by fear and overwhelmed by the sudden appearance of heavily armed men, the Breuers could not offer any effective resistance. Their sorry state of passivity and compliance seems to have encouraged their captors to intensify the abuse; the victims' collapse seems to have fed the attackers' aggression and led them "into still more paroxysms of overkill." Once they had begun their attacks, the militia men became caught up—"self-entrained"—in their own actions. "Emotionally aroused," as if intoxicated by their "own bodily tensions and rhythms," the abusers simply could not stop manhandling their victims and stealing their watches and wallets (Collins 2008: 151).

Flóra Breuer's escape attempt interrupted this highly pleasurable exercise in total domination. Perceived as both a threat and an insult, the girl's escape could not but further infuriate and incite the aggressors. Like the beatings, Flóra's repeated rape functioned as another form of "self-entrainment" in this context, offering bodily pleasure through continuous action, reestablishing domination, and punishing disobedience. The quest for sexual pleasure and the pleasure in the pain of others merged. The gang rape represents one of the final stages in the "continuum of destruction" on which the militia had embarked in their search for the two families.

For some unknown reason, the rapists in Diszel spared the young woman's life. They did, however, brutalize her mother by cutting off her breasts (an act that could be perceived as a substitute for rape) and then killing her along with Ignác Breuer, Mór Breuer, and Mór's adult son. The perpetrators' monologue about shortening their victims' suffering by executing them was a rhetorical device used to soothe their conscience. The expression "putting the victims out of their misery" was meant to express disgust (rather than pity); it was a sign of an emotional letdown after a phase of intense pleasure and a sudden loss of interest in the badly damaged bodies of their victims rather than a manifestation of a sense of guilt or reawakened empathy. The murders simply signaled that the group had finished its business and was ready to move on and continue its hunt for the next victims.

Horror in Kelenföld

The tragedy of Mrs. Sándor Hamburger reached the British press via a report prepared by an English labor delegation that visited Hungary in early 1920.[9] The report, based on interviews with Mrs. Hamburger in Vienna, detailed her tribulations at the hands of soldiers from a battalion led by Deputy Colonel Pál Prónay. Sándor Hamburger was the brother of Jenő Hamburger, a member of the political elite, who had served as the people's commissar of agriculture during the short-lived Council Republic. Mrs. Hamburger maintained regular contact with her husband, who had gone into exile in Vienna after the collapse of the Communist experiment at the end of August 1919. The letters that they exchanged dealt exclusively with private matters, for Mrs. Hamburger had only a limited interest in politics.

At the end of January 1920, a squad of political detectives from the Prónay Battalion, led by Lieutenant György Scheftsik, had captured a courier, who was carrying among other missives letters and messages between the husband and wife. Pretending to be underground Communists, the detectives appeared at Mrs. Hamburger's flat on Sándor Péterffy Street in Budapest. They asked her to hand over all her correspondence with her exiled husband for reasons of safety and to summon her husband's closest friends in order to discuss with them how they could best leave Budapest undetected. Thus misled, the woman proceeded to summon three individuals to her home: her brother, her brother-in-law, and a family friend, Béla Neumann. Thirty-four-year-old Neumann was the secretary of a local railway workers' trade union. The officers arrested the three men and Mrs. Hamburger and transported them to the 29th Honvéd regiment's military base in Kelenföld, which housed half of the Prónay Battalion. Mrs. Hamburger was forced to leave behind her two small children, who were bedridden from influenza and remained alone without adult supervision.

In Kelenföld, the detectives locked the four detainees in a small room. In the evening, a group of officers, led by militia officers Iván Héjjas, Dénes Bibó, and György Scheftsik, began interrogating Mrs. Hamburger. First, Héjjas asked her if she had recognized him and if she had ever heard his name. Mrs. Hamburger responded that she did not know who he was. Visibly irritated, Héjjas then told her that after this night, his name would be one that she would certainly never forget. Then, he and two of his comrades began beating Mrs. Hamburger with their dog whips. After ten or fifteen minutes of abuse, they stopped the thrashing and ordered her to undress. Because Mrs. Hamburger refused to obey their order, the officers continued with the whipping. Exhausted and terrified, the victim finally yielded to the officers' demand and took off her clothes.

The officers brought in their second victim, Béla Neumann, and ordered him to rape Mrs. Hamburger. Neumann proudly declared that he would rather die than do such a thing. The frustrated officers then let loose on him, beating him with their whips even more savagely than they had Mrs. Hamburger. When their arms became tired, the officers took respite. Two of their colleagues, refugees from the Transylvanian town of Temesvár (called Timişoara in Romanian), then pulled out Neumann's teeth with a pair of pliers. Neumann fainted from pain and fear; however, after the soldiers had poured a bucket of ice water over his body, he soon regained consciousness. The officers ordered him to lick up his blood from the floor. They then castrated their victim. Heavily bleeding from his wounds, Béla Neumann lost consciousness. His body was dragged out of the room, and he died of his injuries either that very night or early the next morning. Prónay's soldiers threw Neumann's remains into the icy water of the Danube. A few days later, the corpse was found and secretly buried in an unmarked grave in the Catholic cemetery in Ercsi, a small village about twenty kilometers from Budapest. Béla Neumann's brother, Imre, received permission to exhume the remains and gave his brother a proper funeral at the end of April 1920.[10]

Mrs. Hamburger was forced to witness Neumann's torture, castration, and demise. She, too, fainted several times, but was brought back to consciousness in the same manner as Neumann. After Neumann's body had been dragged out of the room, the soldiers brought in a new male prisoner, who was unknown to Mrs. Hamburger. The officers ordered the man to undress. Mrs. Hamburger noticed the unmistakable signs of torture: his genitals were swollen from beating, and his upper body was heavily bruised. The soldiers ordered the prisoner to rape Mrs. Hamburger. At first, he also refused to obey the command, and only after repeated beating did he try to rape the defenseless woman. However, he could not physically accomplish it. Disappointed, the soldiers led the inmate back to his cell. The officers then asked Mrs. Hamburger to sit atop a heated stove. She begged them not to and screamed so loudly that the officers gave up on the idea. However, the torture session had not yet come to an end. Next, the tormentors pinned Mrs. Hamburger down to the floor and forced her to spread her legs as one of the officers stuck the handle of his whip into Mrs. Hamburgers' vagina and twisted it around several times until she screamed from pain (Mrs. Hamburger later told the members of the British labor delegation that she had bled periodically ever since the torture).

After these horrific events, Prónay's men ordered Mrs. Hamburger to put on her clothes and led her back into her cell. She was not left alone for long, though. About an hour later, soldiers dragged her into a large room filled with drunken military men. She was once again beaten and forced to undress and dance naked for the inebriated recruits. According to Mrs. Hamburger, the recruits were not as cruel as their commanding officers. They quickly lost interest in the "show" and allowed her put her clothes back on and return to her cell.

Mrs. Hamburger spent the next five weeks in captivity. For two weeks, she had to share a cell with fourteen inmates. They had no bunks and were forced to sleep on the floor covered with straw. They were not allowed to shower, change their underwear, or see a doctor. After two weeks, Mrs. Hamburger was placed in solitary confinement in a small, cramped cell in the basement. She later told the members of the British diplomatic mission that the guards, recent recruits, had treated her humanely and after a while had even shared their meals with her. Because of the torture she became seriously ill while in prison. Moreover, her solitary confinement was agonizing, and the lack of information about her sick children and exiled husband was difficult to bear.

Mrs. Hamburger's family members learned of her whereabouts from a recruit who served in Prónay's Battalion. The enlisted soldier beseeched them not to betray his identity for fear that Prónay "would kill him." Mrs. Hamburger's family and friends notified Crown attorney Albert Váry, who had been tasked by the government to look into the crimes committed by Héjjas and his men. The Crown attorney then paid a visit to Prónay in the main military prison on Margit Boulevard. The dreaded militia leader admitted that the four individuals were indeed being housed there; however, he refused to hand them over. On 23 February 1920, Mrs. Hamburger and her relatives were transported by car to Héjjas's hometown, Kecskemét, where they were handed over to the local authorities. Iván Héjjas told the local authorities that Mrs. Hamburger and her relatives were smugglers and thieves. Mrs. Hamburger did not stay in Kecskemét for long, being transferred to a prison in Budapest the next day. Thanks to pressure asserted by Váry and the civilian branch of the government, Mrs. Hamburger was finally released from captivity on 19 April 1920. Her release paper stated that she had been arrested on suspicions of espionage and kept in prison due to her support of Communism.

After her release, Mrs. Hamburger went into exile in Vienna, and it was there that she recounted the story of her tribulations to the British diplomatic mission and the émigré press. Under pressure by the British government, its only Western ally, the Hungarian government conceded that Mrs. Hamburger's story was partially based on fact and that she had endured a hard time in prison (though the government was careful to avoid the word "torture"). The individuals who completed the government's report argued that Mrs. Hamburger had only been punished for a grave transgression of prison rules because she had allegedly been caught several times having sexual intercourse with a cellmate. To prevent such a blatant breach of prison rules, the guards had allegedly moved her into a different cell. However, they said, the incorrigible Mrs. Hamburger had continued misbehaving there by seducing one of her new cellmates. In order to maintain order and standards of decency, the guards, in the end, had been forced to place Mrs. Hamburger in solitary confinement (thus giving her a punishment regularly reserved for murderers and other violent criminals).

The British diplomatic mission in Vienna found the content of the Hungarian government's report both tasteless and absurd. The members of the mission argued that Mrs. Hamburger had been too proper and too sick to engage in sexual activity in prison. The guards may have placed Mrs. Hamburger in solitary confinement as a form of punishment or because they thought that she suffered from a contagious disease that they did not want to catch.[11]

Pogroms vs. Prison Violence

In contrast to the Diszel case study, which dealt with a pogrom and crimes committed in the open, the story of Mrs. Hamburger's and her fellow victims' tribulations took place in a prison. Cut off from the outside world, concentration camps, prisons, and internment camps provide a breeding ground for all sorts of violence, including sexual attacks on women and men. Just how widespread sexual abuse in these "total institutions" must have been in Hungary after World War I can be surmised from isolated evidence. Katalin Szűcs, who had spent months in the infamous internment camp in Zalaegerszeg in 1920, told the Legal Office of the Social Democratic Party that the camp doctor had repeatedly raped her in captivity "by exploiting her situation." The doctor was not the only sexual predator in the institution. At night, drunken soldiers visited the female barracks and chose victims for their entertainment. They forced their victims to have sex in "unnatural ways" and "taught them every perversion."[12] Similar complaints about sexual violence in the internment camps in Hajmáskér were picked up by exiled Communist leaders in Vienna. Although József Pogány's contention that all but the elderly and the least attractive women in Hajmáskér were raped was most likely an exaggeration, there can be no doubt that sexual abuse was widespread in the camp.[13]

As Giorgio Agamben explains, concentration camps and prisons are situated both inside and outside the boundaries of a social and political system. They are locations where true pariahs, *homo sacers* (people who "could be killed but not sacrificed"—i.e. those whose lives and deaths have no meaning), face "sovereign powers" directly and without the protection of any intermediary. Unlimited power is exercised directly on "naked lives"—on the bodies of the detainees (Agamben 2002: 81–127). It is in these "total institutions" that "violence artists" feel truly at home. Prisons and concentration camps function as studios or laboratories, where the most dedicated killers and torturers (people whom the rest of society usually regards and despises as corrupt and sick) can realize their full potential.

Prisons and concentration camps also function as training grounds for future prison personnel and professional and experienced killers, whom Collins calls "violence artists."[14] It is there that people are seduced and manipulated, and are forced by their superiors and pressured by their comrades to transgress against social norms. Prónay's officers were masters of violence, or "violence artists," within the military prison in Kelenföld. However, regular soldiers (the recruits) acted as bystanders and trainees, and the show was in part staged for their edification. The middle- and upper-middle-class officers acted as models and instructors. Their behavior was meant to be imitated, their values internalized by the lower-middle-class and peasant recruits. However, the officers were not entirely successful. The recruits first tried to imitate their superiors' behavior by forcing Mrs. Hamburger to undress and dance for them, but they soon lost interest in her and the game. Over the next few months in the prison, regular soldiers treated Mrs. Hamburger decently, some sharing their food with her while others tried to console her in her solitude. It was in fact one of the recruits who risked his life to betray Mrs. Hamburger's whereabouts to her concerned relatives.

In Diszel, mob violence was first directed toward private property. The shift from robbery and vandalism to beating and humiliation, and then to rape and murder, was gradual. In the military prison in Kelenföld, the temporal gaps between limited and boundless violence on the one hand and between rapturous and autotelic violence on the other hand proved to be much shorter. In prison, the officers quickly gave in to "the temptation to go beyond the limit, and practice and demonstrate absolute power" (Reemtsma 2009: 133). In Diszel, the pogrom came to resemble a *Volksfest*, or carnival; the participants first went on a long journey, a "moral holiday," during which they gradually cast off all restraint before committing rape and murder. In the military prison, however, the officers acted with "malevolent frivolity" and extreme violence from the outset (Horowitz 2001: 114). In the dungeon, interrogation (i.e. the attempt to obtain new and "actionable" information) quickly gave way to beating, rape, castration, and murder as independent, primary goals. In both cases, the perpetrators underwent "self-entrainment." Caught up in their own emotions and bodily rhythms, the soldiers in Diszel and the officers in Kelenföld simply could not stop their abuse. The perpetrators also tried (with limited success) to get their victims involved in a process of "mutual asymmetrical entrainment" in order to draw the energy necessary to drive the process of radicalization forward despite their victims' gradual collapse and humiliation.

The perpetrators were "dressed to kill." Freshly shaven and sporting nice clothes, the young, healthy officers in their shining boots, with wine bottles and glasses (as well as dog whips) in hand, must have looked very different from their victims. The physical abuse, the torn clothing, the bruises on the victims' faces and bodies, and the destruction of the victims' faces were indeed meant to highlight the differences between the captors and the inmates. Like their Argentinean counterparts in the 1970s, the perpetrators of the White Terror in Budapest wanted their victims to give up, to internalize the hopelessness of their situation, and to accept their tormentors as all-powerful individuals and arbiters of life and death ("We are everything for you, we are God") (Reemtsma 2009: 104–5).

The tormentors sought absolute power at the expense of their victims. By forcing Mrs. Hamburger to sing and dance, undress, and, most importantly, to engage in sexual acts with a family friend and then with a complete stranger, the officers wanted to break Mrs. Hamburger's will and deprive her of her last shred of self-respect and dignity. However, this second case study demonstrates that "mutual asymmetrical entrainment" works only when the victim is prepared to play the assigned role. Mrs. Hamburger not only refused to admit that she had ever heard Héjjas's name (let alone that she feared him), she also refused to remove her clothes and continued to protest, scream, and reproach her tormentors. As a form of punishment, she was beaten and sexually violated, yet her tormentors failed to break her spirit. Her sorry state and dignified behavior in fact evoked the respect and pity of the regular soldiers who helped her to survive and regain her freedom.

Neumann's behavior was equally dignified and heroic. By categorically refusing to rape Mrs. Hamburger, the postal employee asserted not only his independence but also his moral superiority all while reminding the drunken middle- and upper-class officers and university students how real gentlemen should think and behave. He showed his captors a mirror in which they could recognize their insignificance and moral decay. In other words, Neumann was able use the process of "mutual asymmetrical entrainment" to his advantage. For this "crime," he had to be punished, broken, castrated, and killed.

The interactional theory of violence helps to shed light on situational variables and bring us closer to understanding the perpetrators' immediate motives and state of mind. The words and actions of the perpetrators, and, to a lesser extent, those of their victims, suggest that not only group dynamics but also interaction, progressive radicalization, and deeper, impersonal (i.e., structural) causes were at work. In their report, Hungarian government officials portrayed Mrs. Hamburger as a sexual predator who could not control her drive, a woman whose seduction of her fellow prisoners both violated prison regulations (thus posing a security risk) and morally outraged the guards and her fellow inmates. Mrs. Hamburger's image as a sexual predator was both a projection (serving to divert attention from the officers' crimes) and a temporalization of well-known anti-Semitic stereotypes that portrayed the Jewish woman as a witch, a *femme fatale*, a social outsider, and a racial alien who lacked the most important of bourgeois and Western values: self-restraint.

The officers' attempt to force Neumann to rape Mrs. Hamburger was also meant to prove that Jewish men were basically the same as Jewish women and that both represented a threat to middle-class European society. Neumann's castration represented the logical culmination of a process that had begun with his arrest and interrogation, and was the product of ethnic and religious hatred and the perpetrators' paranoia about the allegedly insatiable sexual appetite of Jewish men. When violence is perceived as language (the language of the inarticulate), torture and murder provide clues about the motives and mindset of the perpetrators, that is, what and how they thought about their victims. The officers not only ordered Neumann to lick up his own blood from the floor like a dog but also castrated him as peasants would castrate their pigs and cattle. Finally, the officers treated Neumann's remains as if his corpse were an animal carcass: they simply discarded it in the river. By denying him his last respects, the militia officers displayed their deep contempt for the deceased. In their eyes, he was not a human being but a beast; not a citizen but a *homo sacer* "who could be killed but not sacrificed."

Conclusion

This short study demonstrates the potential of the interactional theory of violence to analyze historical data tracing the unfolding of violent acts. The interactional theory of violence has its limits, however. Certain aspects of the process of violence remain hidden and require a different approach for interpretation. It cannot be used to explain, for example, why people from certain social classes (workers and poor peasants), religious groups (Jews), regions of the country (central as opposed to eastern Hungary), and types of settlements (agricultural towns and isolated farms as opposed to villages) were more likely to become victims of militia and mob violence. Collins's theory ignores the identity, culture, and mindset of the tormentors and assumes that everyone in a violent situation acts in the same manner. It does not address the issue of motives or explain national peculiarities. It does not explain, for example, why sexual violence was more common in Hungary and Soviet Russia than in Czechoslovakia in the immediate post-1918 period. Such issues are complex and require a combination of approaches (social, psychological, anthropological).[15]

The interactional theory of violence, though, helps us to understand the process of radicalization, of which rape represents one of the final stages. With the help of its basic concepts, such as "self-entrainment," "mutual asymmetrical entrainment," and "violence artists," this chapter has shown that the boundaries between different forms of violence (localizing, rapturous, and autotelic) remained fluid during the Hungarian counterrevolution. It also suggests that sexual violence was rarely planned and that rape, mutilation, and murder represented the final stages in a continuum of destruction. Physical attacks, including rape, were usually led by "violence artists" (skilled, experienced, and dedicated soldiers, war veterans, and policemen who took pleasure in the suffering of others). In the Diszel case study, "violence artists" drew their need to commit atrocities in part from their followers and from bystanders—the witnesses and foot soldiers of the pogrom. In the second case study, the followers (i.e., regular soldiers) played only a limited role, while civilian bystanders played no role at all.

In the military prison, the "violence artists" were among themselves. They used the ample time and space available to play out their fantasies and hone their methods of physical and psychological torture. Their fantasies were not original, instead they reflected class- and age-specific variations of well-known anti-Semitic stereotypes, such as the perception of Jewish women as Oriental seductresses and Jewish men as sexual predators and traders in flesh. The "violence artists'" methods of mental and physical torture were not unique. Similar but less devastating (in their impact) hazing rituals were regularly and routinely performed at boarding schools, military academies, barracks, and prisons in the Hungary of that day.[16]

Béla Bodó received his PhD from York University, Canada, in 1998. He teaches history at the University of Bonn, Germany. His latest book, titled *The White Terror: Antisemitic and Political Violence in Hungary, 1919–1923*, was published by Routledge in 2019.

Notes

1. Purseigle (2005: 10–18). Cited by Tomka (2015: 16).
2. Rayfield (2011). Cited by Bödők (2015: 91).
3. The feminist view of rape is best summarized by Susan Brownmiller's famous dicta: "Rape is nothing more or less than a conscious process of intimidation by which *all men* keep *all women* in a state of fear," and, "Rape is a crime not of lust, but of violence and power." See Brownmiller (1975: 15). Rape is a sign of successful socialization of young men in the values of patriotic society, the product of a male conspiracy, and an age-old custom practiced by sexual predators and tolerated and even encouraged by lawmakers, politicians, and the social and cultural elites. See Cahill (2001: 16–17). War, Brownmiller writes, "provides men with the perfect psychological backdrop to give vent to their contempt for women" (1975: 32).
4. The case study was also mentioned in my recent book. See Bodó (2019: 220–24).
5. Gyula Gartenbaum (thirty-eight years old), schoolteacher; Ede Löwinger (twenty-one), tinsmith; Mór Breuer (fifty-six), merchant; Berta Kohn, Breuer's wife (forty-four), housewife; Herman Breuer, Breuer's son (twenty-nine), merchant; Ignác Breuer (forty-two), mineral-water manufacturer; Bernát Singer (twenty-two), handicapped; Dávid Korein (forty-five), merchant; Jenő Strauzler (twenty-one), apprentice miller.
6. Dr. Csáky, affidavit (Jegyzőkönyv), Zalaegerszeg, 16 September 1919, cited in Németh and Paksy (2004: 69–74).
7. Flóra Breuer, deposition (Kihallgatási Jegyzőkönyv), 12 September 1919, cited in Németh and Paksy (2004: 87–88).
8. The perpetrator of localizing violence considers the victim's body merely a physical mass that has to captured, held in place, or, more often, removed and expelled. The perpetrators of rapturous and autotelic violence, on the other hand, have a strong interest in the victim's body; the former wants to possess it, while the latter wants to destroy it. The perpetrator of rapturous violence uses the victim's body to obtain sexual pleasure, whereas the perpetrator of autotelic violence sees aggression as an end in itself, and the mutilation or complete destruction of the victim's body is his main goal. See Reemtsma (2009: 110).
9. The exceptionally brutal case of Mrs. Hamburger, which drew international attention, is also dealt with in my book, Bodó (2019: 230–35), as well as by Emily Gioielli's chapter in this volume
10. Imre Neumann, deposition taken by the Legal Office of the Social Democratic Party in Budapest, 6 May 1920, PIL 658. f. 10.cs. 3. őe, 1. Kötet, Archive of the Institute for History of Politics (Politikatörténeti Intézet Levéltára [PIL]), 348–50.
11. For the transcript of the interview, see "A fehérterror Magyarországon: Az angol egyesült munkás kiküldöttség teljes jelentése, 1920 május," in Markovits (1964: 336–40). For a more tendentious account, see Pogány (1964: 246–47).
12. Katalin Szücs, deposition taken by the Legal Office of the Social Democratic Party, Budapest, 9 December 1920, PIL 658. f. 10.cs. 7 őe., Archive of the Institute for History of Politics (Politikatörténeti Intézet Levéltára [PIL]), 18.

13. "A fehérterror Magyarországon: Az angol egyesült munkás kiküldöttség teljes jelentése, 1920 május." In Markovits (1964: 115–16).
14. Mob violence is always led by small elite at the front. They are the one who throw stones, taunt the enemy, burn and smash enemy property. The violence artists stage their show for their supporters and onlookers; they stage the show for them. They draw their energy from their followers and their victims; the more their victims lose control and fall into panic, the more assertive and cruel they become. See Collins (2008: 71, 247).
15. They will be the focus of my forthcoming monograph titled *The White Terror: Antisemitic and Political Violence in Hungary, 1919–1921*.
16. For an excellent description of life in cadet schools in interwar Hungary (including hazing), see Ottlik (1976); for prewar Austria-Hungary, see Musil (2001).

Bibliography

Ablovatski, Eliza Johnson. 2004. "'Cleansing the Red Nest': Counterrevolution and Terror in Munich and Budapest 1919." PhD diss., Columbia University.
Abramson, Henry. 1999. *A Prayer for the Government: Ukrainians and Jews in Revolutionary Times, 1917–1920*. Cambridge, MA.
Agamben, Giorgio. 2002. *Homo sacer: Die souveräne Macht und das nackte Leben*. Frankfurt am Main.
Audoin-Rouzeau, Stéphane. 2009. *L'enfant de l'ennemi: 1914–1918: viol, avortement, infanticide pendant la Grande Guerre*. Paris.
Bartal, Israel. 2005. *The Jews of Eastern Europe, 1772–1881*. Philadelphia.
Beevor, Antony. 2002. *The Fall of Berlin 1945*. New York.
Beneš, Jakub. 2017. "The Green Cadres and the Collapse of Austria-Hungary in 1918." *Past & Present* 236(1): 207–41.
Bjørnlund, Matthias. 2009. "'A Fate Worse than Dying': Sexual Violence during the Armenian Genocide." In *Brutality and Desire: War and Sexuality in Europe's Twentieth Century*, edited by Dagmar Herzog, 16–58. London.
Bodó, Béla. 2002. *Tiszazug. The Social History of a Murder Epidemic*. New York.
———. 2019. *The White Terror: Antisemitic and Political Violence in Hungary, 1919–1921*. London.
Bödők, Gergely. 2011. "Vörös és Fehér: terror, retorzió és számonkérés Magyarországon 1919-1921-ben." *Kommentár* 3: 15–31.
———. 2015. "Politikai erőszak az első világháború után: Forradalmak és ellenforradalmak Magyarországon és Középeurópában." In *Az első világháború következményei*, edited by Béla Tomka, 85–108. Budapest.
Browning, Christopher R. 1992. *Ordinary Men: Reserve Police Battalion 101 and the Final Solution in Poland*. New York.
Brownmiller, Susan. 1975. *Against Our Will: Men, Women, and Rape*. New York.
Cahill, Ann J. 2001. *Rethinking Rape*. Ithaca, NY.
Clark, Christopher. 2012. *Sleepwalkers: How Europe Went to War in 1914*. London.
Collins, Randall. 2008. *Violence: A Micro-Sociological Theory*. Princeton, NJ.
Dekel-Chen, Jonothan, et al. 2011. *Anti-Jewish Violence: Rethinking the Pogroms in East European History*. Bloomington.
Fischer, Rolf. 1993. "Anti-Semitism in Hungary, 1882–1932." In *Hostages of Modernization: Studies of Modern Antisemitism 1870–1933/39*, edited by Herbert A. Strauss, 863–92. New York.

Fogarty, S. Richard. 2009. "Race and Sex, Fear and Loathing in France during the Great War." In *Brutality and Desire: War and Sexuality in Europe's Twentieth Century*, edited by Dagmar Herzog, 59-90. London.
Gerwath, Robert. 2017. *The Vanquished: Why the First World War Failed to End, 1917-1923*. London.
Gerwarth, Robert, and John Horne, eds. 2013. *War in Peace: Paramilitary Violence after the Great War*. Oxford.
Grayzel, Susan R. 2010. "Women and Men." In *A Companion to World War I*, edited by John Horne, 263-78. Chichester/Malden.
Gross, Jan T. 2006. *Fear: Anti-Semitism in Poland After Auschwitz: An Essay in Historical Interpretation*. New York.
Hagemann, Karen, and Stefanie Schüler-Springorum, eds. 2002. *Militär und Geschlechterverhältnisse im Zeitalter der Weltkriege*. Frankfurt am Main.
Hagen, William. 2018. *Anti-Jewish Violence in Poland, 1914-1920*. New York.
Hatos, Pál. 2018. *Az elátkozott köztársaság: Az 1918-as összeomlás és forradalom története*. Jaffa.
Herzog, Dagmar. 2011. *Sexuality in Europe. A Twentieth-Century History*. Cambridge.
Horne, John, and Alan Kramer. 2010. *German Atrocities 1914: A History of Denial*. New Haven, CT.
Horowitz, Donald L. 2001. *The Deadly Ethnic Riot*. Berkeley, CA.
Katzburg, Nathaniel. 2002. *Zsidópolitika Magyarországon, 1919-1943*. Budapest.
Keller, Ulrich. 2017. *Schuldfragen: Belgischer Untergrundkrieg und deutsche Vergeltung im August 1914*. Paderborn.
Klier, John D., and Schlomo Lambroza, eds. 1992. *Pogroms: Anti-Jewish Violence in Modern Russian History*. Cambridge.
Kramer, Alan. 2007. *Dynamic of Destruction: Culture and Mass Killing in the First World War*. Oxford.
Kučera, Rudolf, and Richard Hufschmied. 2019. *Zerfall und Untergang: Die Doppelmonarchie im Ersten Weltkrieg*. In *Nachbarn: Ein österreichisch-tschechisches Geschichtsbuch*, edited by N. Perzi, O. Konrád, H. Schmoller, and V. Šmidrkal, 67-80. Weitra.
Markovits, Györgyi, ed. 1964. *Magyar pokol: A magyarországi fehérterror betiltott és üldözött kiadványok tükrében*. Budapest.
Mick, Christoph. 2016. *Lemberg, Lwów, L'viv, 1914-1947: Violence and Ethnicity in a Contested City*. West Lafayette, IN.
Musil, Robert. 2001. *The Confusions of Young Törless*. New York.
Naimark, Norman M. 1995. *The Russians in Germany: A History of the Soviet Zone of Occupation, 1945-1949*. Cambridge.
Németh, László and Zoltán Paksy. 2004. *Együttélés és kirekesztés.Zsidók Zala megye társadalmában 1919-1945* (Coexistence and Exclusion: Jews in Zala County Society 1919-1945). Zalaegerszeg: Zalai Megyei Levéltár.
Ottlik, Géza. 1976. *Iskola a határon*. Budapest.
Pogány, József, ed. 1964. "A keresztény inkvizició." In *Magyar pokol: A magyarországi fehérterror betiltott és üldözött kiadványok tükrében*, edited by Györgyi Markovits, 250-3. Budapest.
Purseigle, Pierre. 2005. "Warfare and Belligerence: Approaches to the First World War." In *Warfare and Belligerence: Perspectives in the First World War Studies*, edited by Pierre Purseigle, 1-37. Boston.
Rayfield, Donald. 2011. *Sztálin és a hóhérai: A zsarnok, és akik neki gyilkoltak*. Budapest.
Reemtsma, Jan Philipp. 2009. *Vertrauen und Gewalt: Versuch über eine besondere Konstellation der Moderne*. Hamburg.

Robbers, Hans. 1986. *Jewish Polices and Right-Wing Politics in Imperial Russia*. Berkeley.
Ryan, James. 2015. *Lenin's Terror: The Ideological Origins of Early Soviet State Violence*. New York.
Theweleit, Klaus. 1987. *Male Fantasies*, 2 vols. Cambridge 1987–89; German original: Frankfurt am Main 1977.
Tomka, Béla. 2015. "Az Első Világháború Mint Történeti Korszakhatár." In *Az Első Világháború Következményei Magyarországon*, edited by Béla Tomka, 7–24. Budapest.
Ungváry, Krisztián. 2000. "Sacco di Budapest, 1919: Tábornok válasza Harry Hill Bandholtz vezérőrnagy nem diplomatikus naplójára." *Budapesti Negyed* 3–4: 173–203.
Wall, Richard, and Jay Winter, eds. 1988. *The Upheaval of War: Family, Work Welfare in Europe, 1914–1918*. Cambridge.
Wells, Theodore R. 2006. *From Assimilation to Antisemitism: The "Jewish Question" in Poland, 1850–1914*. De Kalb.
Ziemann, Benjamin. 2013. *Gewalt im Ersten Weltkrieg*. Essen.

CHAPTER 4

The Many Lives of Mrs. Hamburger
Gender, Violence, and Counterrevolution, 1919–1930

Emily R. Gioielli

On 13 May 1920 in Vienna, a woman named Mrs. Sándor [Alexander] Hamburger gave a deposition describing her arrest and torture earlier that year.[1] She recalled that on 25 January 1920, five men came to her residence, called her names, like "you stinking Jew," and arrested her, along with her brother-in-law, her brother, and another man who happened to be at her lodging.[2] They arrested her for having been in contact with communists in Vienna, but they did not have a proper warrant for her arrest. She said that she pleaded with the men to let her stay with her sick children, and even tried to bargain with them to allow her to remain with them under guard until their health improved. The men ignored her pleas, and she was "dragged away" while they performed a house search, illegally seizing many of her belongings. After recounting the circumstances of her arrest, she began to describe her experience of brutal, sexualized torture, which Béla Bodó has also referenced in his contribution to this volume.

She was taken, along with the men with whom she had been arrested, to the Kelenföld barracks, where members of the Prónay officers' detachment were quartered. The Prónay detachment was one of many White Officers' militias that formed in response to successive revolutions in Hungary following the November 1918 Armistice: the social democratic government of Mihály Károlyi and the radical communist regime helmed by Béla Kun. Members of these militias embraced an array of counterrevolutionary ideas ranging from legitimism to royalism, "traditionalism" to right radicalism, and violently targeted those groups that they held responsible for the political, economic, social, and military crises facing the country, including all "leftists" as well as Jews, feminists, and peasants. These militias were responsible for many of the acts of violence associated with the White Terror in Hungary from 1919 to 1922 (Bodó 2004, 2010a, 2011a, 2011b).

Immediately upon her arrival at the barracks, Mrs. Hamburger was questioned, during which the interrogators called her "bolshevik hore, Jewish hore, hore of the Roumanians [sic]. . . . If you shall not tell everything about the people's commissaries, then we shall shoot you. 'You shall die you hore,' etc."[3] Mrs. Hamburger said she knew nothing about the people's commissars, and after hours of questioning (she said they began around 12:30 P.M.), they removed her from the interrogation room.[4]

After the room filled with officers, she was brought back in, and they began to torture her. They forced her to undress, constantly insulted her when she refused, and beat her until she complied. She was beaten so badly that according to her description, she could barely stand, especially because she was already weak because of menstruation. After this, she was thrown on a bed as two officers forced her legs apart and "dishonoured" her with the handle of a whip, what she termed "terrible [animal] tortures." The torture went on, and she was forced to undress and dance for them while they beat her with a piece of wood with nails in it. She begged for them to stop, but they refused, telling her "You shall die you Jewish hore [sic]." One of the men she was arrested with, Béla Neumann, "an honourable and good man," was brought up from the cell, and officers ordered him to rape her. When he refused, they beat and castrated him. After more dancing and beatings, another man, whom she described as Jewish and beaten "half dead", was brought in and also ordered to rape Mrs. Hamburger. They beat his genital organs and tortured him until he got on top of her, despite being physically unable to perform any sexual act.

After this, she was ordered to dance for them again, and finally, more than twelve hours after her torture began, she, her brother, and Mr. Neumann were taken into a room for the night. One of the officers eventually came down and asked her about her last wishes, to which she replied that she wanted to see her children. This encounter led to taunts like, "It is right that the wife of a people's commissary suffers we shall bring her husband from Vienna, hang him up, and then you will be released . . ."[5]

After nearly a month of incarceration, on 20 February 1920, she and two of the men she was arrested with were taken to Kecskemét, a city in central Hungary. They did not stay there long and were driven back to the barracks at Kelenföld, where they were told that they were going to be executed. Finally, her relatives' discovered her whereabouts and consulted with an attorney and the foreign missions active in Budapest. The case against the three was transferred to the Budapest criminal courts, and they were physically transferred to a prison where they were treated better by the civil prison authorities. The three were released from prison on 19 April 1920.[6] At the time she gave her testimony in May 1920, Mrs. Hamburger was in Vienna and still very ill as a result of the injuries sustained during her incarceration.

The testimony above was *personally* given by Mrs. Sándor Hamburger, a woman born in Gyöngyös in 1890. She had two children (different numbers appear in different sources), and was an official in the state sick benefit bureau, according to some sources.[7] She knew how to read and write and had at least a primary school education, according to her prison record, which also identified her as Jewish.[8] Her testimony to the delegation does not indicate her self-identification as a Jew, although a narrative attributed to her from 1920 does indicate self-identification as Jewish, and her place of birth, Gyöngyös, was notable for its large Jewish population (Hajnal 1920: 9). Her husband was a veteran of World War I and was active in leftist politics, as was his brother Jenő Hamburger, a physician and commissar of agriculture in the Kun regime. Like thousands of others, they had escaped to Vienna after the collapse of the Hungarian Republic of Councils (also known as the Hungarian Soviet Republic) in August 1919.[9] This government had embarked on a program of radical sovietization following the negotiated transfer of power from Károlyi to Kun in March 1919. They also organized a Hungarian Red Army to recapture historical Hungarian lands that were to be ceded to Hungary's neighbors. The regime enjoyed some early military victories, but its domestic policies alienated the population, and its foreign policies provoked a reaction by Entente powers. By the summer of 1919, a counterrevolutionary movement formed, and the Romanian army (allies of the Entente) invaded, reaching Budapest in August. When the Councils government collapsed, a new counterrevolutionary regime took power. In response to political persecutions by the new government, an estimated one hundred thousand leftists like the Hamburger brothers fled the country and took refuge in Vienna (Bodó 2010b: 704; Bodó 2011a: 133).

The Case of Mrs. Hamburger

At first glance, what happened to Mrs. Hamburger and those arrested with her appears to be a horrific but nevertheless fairly unremarkable story of sexualized violence during a postwar period of political crisis in a small state in Europe's east. In other words, it stemmed from what many might consider to be a "normal" outcome of the political, social, and regional context. As Béla Bodó's contribution explains, sources across the continent from the period suggest that sexualized and gendered violence against women *and men* was fairly common during the post-Armistice violence in Hungary and Central Europe more broadly (Gerwarth 2011: 122–36); such acts included rape with and without objects, compulsory gynecological exams of inmates, beatings intended to hurt the fetuses of pregnant women, genital mutilation, and the sexual extortion of female relatives who came to provide food and clothing to prisoners.[10] Further, some of these practices, notably compulsory vaginal exams for certain groups of female prisoners, predated the war and were not unique to Hungary.[11]

However, the story of Mrs. Hamburger is more than just a graphic illustration of the complex politics of sexual violence during the Hungarian counterrevolution. Her story traveled far in the interwar period, due in large part to the report from a British Labour Party and Trades Union Congress delegation that visited Central Europe in the spring of 1920. This narrative became a symbol to those persons and groups, including many in the non-Comintern left, who were opposed to the Entente governments' response to postwar violence against leftists and democrats in Hungary and the broader region. Yet the story of Mrs. Hamburger also shows women's individual experiences and agency—and the limits to it—during this period of crisis. Consequently, it reveals the complex relationship between gender and counterrevolutionary violence, as well as the role that gender and women played in producing competing discourses between the labor movement and the Entente democracies concerning international security and diplomacy in the early interwar period.

The case of Mrs. Hamburger and the story of its dissemination positions it within the broader history of atrocity stories, which became an important tool that all belligerent powers used during the Great War and which continued into the "smaller" wars and conflicts that followed the 1918 Armistice. The modern iterations of atrocity stories emerged at the end of the nineteenth and early twentieth centuries and came into their own as a means to shape public opinion and mobilize both civilians and soldiers during World War I. As ever more people were integrated into the political system, it became necessary to win them over, and atrocity stories became an important part of the tool kit for winning, or perhaps conquering people's hearts and minds through demonizing images of the enemy and the threat they posed (Gullace 1997: 716).

Much of the scholarship that has appeared on the subject and time period relates to the information wars between Great Britain and Germany, and turns on a variety of questions including the veracity of atrocity claims, the role of interwar pacifists in discrediting atrocity literature, and, as historians such as Alan Kramer and John Horne have shown, the effects of such stories on the perspectives of those who fought—that is, atrocity propaganda as a mobilization factor (Laswell 1927; Ponsonby 1928; Kramer and Horne 1993, 2002). While this chapter takes up some of these questions, it pays special attention to the centrality of gendered and sexual violence in the content of such atrocity stories and the role this played in both international and domestic politics throughout war-torn Europe. In addition, Ruth Harris's scholarship on the transformation of meaning assigned to gendered images of suffering in France over the course of the war and Nicoletta Gullace's exploration of sexual violence and international law raise important questions regarding these issues—in particular, how to communicate more technical and abstract principles to the public and investigate the sexual ambiguities caused by war and social upheaval (Harris 1993; Gullace 1997).

In shifting focus away from the conflict between the Great Powers and the traditional periodization to the "wars after the war," this chapter also pays attention to issues less apparent in the studies above: international hierarchies between more and less powerful states; international politico-humanitarian engagement that had blossomed during the war; and on the Eastern Front, the shift from the larger war to smaller, often internal conflicts between different internal and external political factions on the left and right that extended beyond the 1914–1918 periodization (Dogan 2014). These factors must be taken into consideration when considering the use and impact of atrocity stories from the long World War I period in East-Central Europe. In tracing the origins and dissemination of the story, it also builds on the scholarship of Eliza Ablovatski, who has positioned the story within the larger history of memory of post-Armistice revolutions in Central Europe (Ablovatski 2005). Yet, the story of Mrs. Hamburger demonstrates the overlapping processes of policy-making, memory-making, and reconstructing social and diplomatic hierarchies in Europe following years of war and political upheaval.

The Story of Mrs. Hamburger Spreads

Reports of atrocities and repression against leftists—a catch-all term for democrats, social democrats, socialists, communists, trade unionists, and feminists—and Jews leaked out of Hungary following the collapse of the Hungarian Soviet Republic. In the polarized political atmosphere of the time, stories and rumors about atrocities on the left and right flew around and were easily dismissed as propaganda. Thus for many outside of Hungary, the primary source of "trusted" information about conditions in Hungary was the February 1920 *Report on the Alleged Existence of "White Terror" in Hungary*, which consisted of documents composed by official British Diplomatic Mission representatives stationed in Budapest.[12] This report was filed with Parliament and stated unequivocally that there was no White Terror in Hungary, that stories to the contrary of this finding were exaggerations, and that any violence was understandable given the brutality of the Soviet revolution, and, in any case, such violence was controllable.[13] British Labour leaders were unsatisfied with these conclusions, which contradicted all of the information they received from exiled Hungarian socialists and the secretary of the International Socialist Bureau. The Labour Party also heard that the Italian Socialist Party sent a delegation to investigate but that it had been deported for "spreading lies" about the counterrevolutionary government. Thus, Labour officials wanted to see what was actually happening in Hungary.

The post-Armistice years were an important period of transition for the British Labour Party because it was becoming a more cohesive institution and a major player in British politics (the first Labour government was 1924). Part of this transition entailed the formulation of a foreign policy as a way of demonstrating the party's ability to govern. British Labourites were also seriously engaged with the revival of a non-Comintern socialist international and sought to (re)build stronger, transnational connections with other labor parties that also sought the restoration of a non-Soviet socialist internationalism. Consequently, members of the British Labour Party and the Trades Union Congress wrote to the Hungarian government and received an invitation by the minister of the interior to send representatives to Hungary in the spring of 1920. The Labour Party, in cooperation with Camille Huysmans, the secretary of the International Socialist Bureau, took them up on the offer, organizing a delegation to Hungary and Vienna in the spring of 1920.[14]

In Hungary, the British Labour delegation investigated the conditions of prisons and internment camps, and they also went to Vienna to meet with exiled leaders of the Hungarian labor movement. Through their Hungarian contacts, the delegation met and interviewed other escapees who fled the violence in Hungary. The British Labourites were cognizant of the challenges facing them as outsiders who had to rely on the Hungarian regime for access to points and people of interest. They were also aware that people would be reluctant to testify about their treatment for fear of reprisals, as well as the shame associated with acts of violence perpetrated against them by the regime and the White militias. In light of this, the delegation included a woman named Mrs. Williams, "who rendered valuable assistance in dealing with the evidence of female witnesses," which suggests the group's relative sophistication concerning how to approach different groups in order to get the most accurate picture of conditions in Hungary. While a draft of the report includes an express mention of Mrs. Williams's contributions, the final version does not mention that a woman was part of the delegation, much less that she played a key role in helping the delegation gain access to female victims of violence who were not eager to share their experiences with an all-male committee.[15] These concerns help account for the delegation's heavy reliance on the materials gathered and curated by exiled leftists like Vilmos Böhm, who helped British Labour representatives conduct interviews with Hungarian émigrés/refugees in Vienna, and Ernő Garami.[16] Mrs. Hamburger was one of these interviewees.

Exiled Hungarian leftist leaders in Vienna already knew about her experience in the custody of the Prónay detachment and told their British contacts about it.[17] The British delegation had been in regular contact with their Hungarian ideological "brothers," who sent them letters and translated clippings from newspapers about conditions in Hungary. On the basis of these materials, the British delegation composed a "to-do" list for their investigatory mission, the goal of which was to find out whose version of recent Hungarian history—their leftist comrades' or the official government delegation's—was true. The goal of reinvestigating incidents they had read about in the press and in official reports is important because the Labour delegation was operating in a context in which truth, especially when it came to violence and atrocities, was regarded as a partisan and national issue.[18] To be sure, the delegation had a domestic and international political agenda; but they played the role of "doubting Thomas," as their itinerary suggests that they wanted to see what was happening with their own eyes before treating it as fact. Thus, the list the delegation compiled included examining notable incidents, such as a mass killing committed by the Héjjas detachment in the Orgovány forest outside of Kecskemét in Transdanubia. This execution included people who had already been imprisoned for what appear to have been political reasons, as well as others, many of whom were Jewish, who were taken off a train as they were traveling. The delegation also planned to visit several prisons, gaols, and internment camps and collect materials on irregular judicial proceedings. The case of Mrs. Hamburger was a top priority for the delegation; it was mentioned twice on their four-page "Programme."[19] According to the final report published by the Labour Party and filed with Parliament, the delegation interviewed Mrs. Hamburger twice for a total of four hours. Out of the roughly twenty-five-page report, her story takes up three pages. The British Labour delegation's description of Mrs. Hamburger's experience would become the standard, but not the only, account of her torture.

According to her signed statement, Mrs. Hamburger gave her testimony to the Labour Delegation on 13 May 1920 in Vienna, but references to what happened to her and the male prisoners also appear in other depositions, including a secondhand account by the brother of Béla Neumann, one of the men tortured with Mrs. Hamburger.[20] The final draft of the Labour delegation's report submitted to the Parliament argued that the arrest of Mrs. Hamburger and the other men stemmed from the trickery of officers associated with Iván Héjjas. Militia soldiers detained and, it seems, killed, a courier carrying letters from both Mrs. Hamburger's husband and brother-in-law in Vienna to family in Budapest. A member of the detachment proceeded to deliver the letters to her on 21 January 1920 under the identity of the original courier, who was well known in the exile community in Vienna. The disguised officer directed her to prepare herself and her friends to flee to Vienna, but at the prearranged meeting time, she and four others were arrested and taken to the Kelenföld barracks, leaving her sick children behind. The Labour narrative recounted Mrs. Hamburger's rape and torture, as well as the torture of the other men, and noted that she was released from the royal prison in Budapest on 19 April

1920, where she was being held on charges of "Bolshevik activities."[21] The original prisoner log held in the Budapest Municipal Archives confirms that this was the recorded basis for her arrest, and although the court records from the period are incomplete, there are no other files on her case in the criminal courts or files of the royal prosecutor, which seems to confirm her description of the events surrounding her arrest and incarceration.[22]

According to the Labour report, the Labour delegation requested information from the Hungarian government regarding the case of Mrs. Hamburger and her fellow inmates, but the government provided no written documentation on the case, which is borne out in the archival record of the delegation's visit to Central Europe. Rather, according to the Labour report, Hungarian government officials confirmed her imprisonment to British diplomatic officials in Budapest (*not* the Labour delegation, which received the information secondhand, and likely verbally) but stated that the physical injuries she received were punishments for her voracious sexual appetite, which she satiated with male cellmates.[23] Thus, the beatings she received were a form of "discipline."[24] However, in the narrative, the Labour delegation disputed this "semi-official" explanation on the basis of logistics and Mrs. Hamburger's character. Firstly, they argued that placing women and men in cells together violated the operating norms they observed, as even in the most crowded conditions, segregation on the basis of gender was maintained. Further, the report said that even if men and women were held together because of overcrowding, there would have been more than two people in a cell, and thus no opportunity to engage in sexual intercourse. Secondly, the report argued that the story did not ring true because Mrs. Hamburger "appears to be a respectable woman of good education," a "quiet, unassuming, and a highly respected woman, and [the delegation] was informed by all who knew her that she possessed a moral character beyond reproach."[25]

The British Labour delegation's narrative about Mrs. Hamburger's arrest and torture (as opposed to Mrs. Hamburger's testimony) was reprinted in full in social democratic newspapers across Austria and in one of the reports produced by the American Jewish Joint Distribution Committee's representative Joseph Marcus, who copied the Labour delegation's narrative about Mrs. Hamburger verbatim in 1921.[26] The American magazine *The Nation* also addressed the British delegation's report, but it did not specifically mention Mrs. Hamburger, referring only to stories of torture "of a peculiarly revolting character," and the *American Israelite*, an American Jewish newspaper, also mentioned the delegation's report, though it did not quote from it.[27] The Labour narrative also appeared in the 1922 book published in French titled *Quand Horthy est Roi* (When Horthy is king), written and compiled by Robert Tarcali. This book focused on the persecution of and atrocities perpetrated against Jews in Hungary and was Tarcali's response to a book titled *Quand Israel est Roi* (When

Israel is king), published in Paris a year earlier, which had asserted an idyllic portrait of Eastern European Jewish life. The delegation's narrative also traveled to Latin America via journalist and political activist J. C. Mariategui, who included the incident in a lecture he gave on revolutionary events in Europe in the Student Federation Hall of the People's University in Lima, Peru, in the summer of 1923 (Tharaud and Tharaud 1921; Tarcali 1922; Mariategui 1923).

In July 1920, approximately one and a half months after the British Labour delegation released their report, Eugen Hajnal published a fifty-two-page book in German and Hungarian about Mrs. Hamburger, replete with a cover by Marcel Vértes, an artist who published other political illustrations, notably several depicting the suffering of and sexual violence against women during the White Terror (these have different captions in different publications) (Hajnal 1920).[28] Hajnal's book, published in Vienna, contained a narrative attributed specifically to Mrs. Hamburger, and it was censored in Hungary, along with many other anti-Horthy publications. But there is no doubt that at least a couple of copies trickled into the country.[29] It presented a slightly different narrative of Mrs. Hamburger's experience in captivity, but this version of events does not seem to have circulated very widely beyond a few mentions in Jewish publications (Harden 1921). The latest mention of Mrs. Hamburger's story I have been able to locate thus far appears to be famed sexologist Magnus Hirschfeld's inclusion in the 1930 German-language edition of *Sittengeschichte des Weltkrieges* (translated as the "Sexual history of the World War") (Hirschfeld 1930: 347–49).[30] He included a summary of the British Labour report's narrative, as well as Vértes's illustrations.

From all of these sources, different versions of the torture of Mrs. Hamburger exist: her own and other witnesses' and relatives' testimonies, including that of Imre Neumann, the brother of Béla Neumann, and what appears to be a deposition filed by Jénő Poósz (or Pósz), one of the other men arrested with Mrs. Hamburger; there was the narrative produced by and published in the Labour delegation's official report, which was based on testimony but included key interpretative changes; and the lengthier Hajnal narrative, which I will not address in this chapter.[31] Each highlighted a different dimension of the violence. In Mrs. Hamburger's personal testimony, she emphasized the effects of the violence on her family and her modesty, recalling her pleas to stay with her sick children and her efforts to remain clothed, until the severity of beatings made it impossible for her to refuse the soldiers' orders to undress and dance. She placed the humiliating acts she was compelled to perform in the context of the extreme violence, recalling her resistance to sexual assault throughout her testimony.[32] For Mrs. Hamburger, it was both connections to and the alienation from family (children, relatives who could visit and provide her with fresh clothing and underwear) and her resistance to sexual shame that appear as themes throughout her description. She identifies herself as a devoted mother and wife who had had no direct links to communism and did done nothing to deserve her classification as a "hore," much less the violence she experienced.

Likewise, Imre Neumann's account emphasized familial connections by recounting the experience of his younger brother. From information he received from others imprisoned with the group, he learned that his brother Béla declined to assault Mrs. Hamburger, despite the officers' death threats and sexualized torture that followed his refusal to assault the woman. Imre Neumann's deposition includes information regarding his and other prisoners' relatives interactions with various authorities as he attempted to identify and bury his brother's body, which had been found floating in the Danube near the town of Ercsi. He described his search for his brother and his attempt to exhume his body from a Catholic cemetery to give Béla, a "Jewish man," a proper burial.[33]

In contrast, the narrative presented in the British Labour delegation's report emphasized Mrs. Hamburger's ties to the labor movement and personal characteristics that should have prevented the violence against her. It noted at the beginning that Mrs. Hamburger's husband was a political refugee in Vienna and her brother-in-law was a people's commissar and a "known communist." It also included the charges against her, as recorded in her prison records: "bolshevist activities" (Bodó 2011a: 9–10).[34] Similar to her testimony, the Labour narrative emphasized her efforts to resist assault. For those who had access to the report of the Joint Distribution Committee, the American Jewish relief agency, the story of Mrs. Hamburger was *implicitly* identified as an example of anti-Jewish violence since it was included in their report, but her testimony to the Labour delegation and the Labour narrative do not address her Jewishness explicitly. In Hajnal's book (and the discussion of it in the *American Hebrew & Jewish Messenger*), the anti-Jewish dimensions of the torture are discussed and emphasized: the officers involved in her torture identified Mrs. Hamburger as a Jewess, and their explicitly anti-Semitic songs and insults toward the woman were recounted in far more detail than the scant mention of them in her testimony to the Labour delegation (Hajnal 1920).[35]

I would argue that aside from Mrs. Hamburger's original testimony of the events, the Labour delegation's account is the most influential narrative about this episode of violence for two reasons. First, in this period, when opponents dismissed all stories of atrocities as propaganda, the British provenance of this account lent it a legitimacy that other contemporary reports of White Terror circulating in Europe could not claim to possess. This legitimacy had much to do with the unequal power relations between Great Britain and the postwar Habsburg successor states, and the belief or hope among many Hungarians of different political stripes was that it was still possible to alter the direction of the Peace Treaties, or at the very least, leave open the possibility of future treaty revision.[36] Second, this perceived legitimacy coupled with the internationalism of the Labour Party permitted the Labour report to travel across the world, which helps explain why the delegation's narrative made it into nonlabor sources, like the Joint Distribution Committee's report. Consequently, the Labour Party's narrative became the standard account of Mrs. Hamburger's experiences.

The Significance of Mrs. Hamburger's Case

But while it is possible to trace the transmission of Mrs. Hamburger's story, the question remains: What does it reveal about the White Terror in Hungary? And why was Mrs. Hamburger so important then, especially to the labor movement?

Perhaps most importantly, after interviewing her, reviewing corroborating evidence (the statement concerning Jénő Poósz), and making further inquiries into the incident, the Labour delegation was convinced that the torture of Mrs. Hamburger actually happened.[37] For the Labour delegation, her story was incontrovertible evidence that atrocities against leftists were taking place in Hungary. Although, according to both her testimony and the Labour delegation's narrative, she herself did not personally participate in communist politics, she was connected to leftist politics through her husband and brother-in-law. Therefore, like many women at the time who were arrested in connection to their male relatives' political activities, she was conceptualized as a victim of political violence, even if she did not consider herself politically active.[38] This formulation of women's political identities contradictorily made women visible as political victims while simultaneously denying or severely weakening their political agency, whether it be as activists or as witnesses, advocates, or intercessors on behalf of their families, friends, and communities.[39]

Another factor in the dissemination of the Labour delegation's narrative very likely had to do with the ability to depict Mrs. Hamburger as the ideal victim and the officers as the perfect perpetrators. As such, her story could be used to exemplify the horrific nature of the White Terror as a devoted mother, a loyal wife, and a "well-educated," "respectable," "soft-spoken" woman whose "moral character was beyond reproach." She was also legally innocent, having never been brought up on formal charges in a court (although incomplete, the court records do not indicate that a formal case was ever brought against her), and she herself was not a communist or leftist, even if her relatives were. In short, there were no ambiguities surrounding her claim of victimhood. On the other hand, the report presented the perpetrators of the attack against her and her associates as elites who sat on top of the social hierarchy as ethnically Hungarian, Christian, military men (Stiehm 1983: 367–76). However, the implicit idea presented in the British Labour report (and in other sources from the period critical of the Hungarian counterrevolutionary regime) was that this elite status was dependent on chivalric masculine ideals, which these officers severely violated, along with the rule of law.[40] Furthermore, however dubious the content and notwithstanding the lack of written record, the Hungarian government's indirect response to their inquiries about Mrs. Hamburger confirmed to the Labour delegation that the Hungarian state and the counterrevolutionary militias were in cahoots.[41] This was because even if Hungarian government officials were not responsible for her injuries, the state had knowledge of what had happened to her and had taken over her case during the final weeks of her incarceration.

Considering all the evidence, the Labour delegation was convinced that Mrs. Hamburger was trustworthy and that the story was true. In addition to her testimony and her "respectability," the delegation was armed with confirmation from the deposition concerning Jénő Poósz as well as the secondhand, "semi-official" confirmation from the Hungarian government that Mrs. Hamburger experienced harsh treatment during her incarceration. There were no impediments, no ambiguities to her claims of victimhood. Thus, if this story, along with the others included in the report—and many more left out—was true, it meant that the first report filed by the British diplomatic mission in Budapest, which declared that there was "no White Terror in Hungary," was false, and the Labour report stated this in its conclusions (Bodó 2011a: 24). The Labour report also declared that British government representatives' denial of the White Terror, coupled with the Entente's and especially the British diplomatic mission's refusal to intervene in Hungary to stop violence, made these countries responsible ("morally if not legally," a phrase borrowed from the letters they received from their Hungarian comrades) for the continuation of the White Terror.[42] Further, Labourites claimed that the unwillingness to intervene was not based on the Entente governments' genuine commitment to state sovereignty but rather on the anticommunist character of the Hungarian regime. To the Labour delegation, this meant that the Entente was propping up an illiberal and undemocratic regime in Eastern Europe.

In order to make this critique through the story of Mrs. Hamburger, the labor movement mobilized norms that presumed the exemption of women from political violence (Elshtain 1991: 95–406; Sjoberg 2006: 890; Sjoberg 2010: 53–68). While a reader could easily justify or even dismiss persecution of revolutionary young men who actually were involved in militias and political organizations seeking political and class overthrow, it was not so easy to overlook violence against a "well-educated," respectable, morally virtuous, and apolitical mother and wife of a veteran. Mrs. Hamburger's story helped "prove" that the political regime in Hungary was deviant and illegitimate, that it was not a source of stability but was guilty itself of upsetting social order in

Hungary. By extension then, the Entente was helping to perpetuate disorder and violence instead of stabilizing and securing East-Central Europe. While this critique of Western intervention in the region is familiar to those who work on the period, the story of Mrs. Hamburger, and the Labour delegation generally, helps illuminate the role that gender played in helping produce and set patterns of anticommunist discourse and intervention that would remain influential for the next seventy years or so.

The final question, then, is what does Mrs. Hamburger's story tell us about the White Terror today? First, the story and its dissemination shows how gender, class, ethnic, political, and even global hierarchies overlapped in the interpretations of violence during the Hungarian White Terror and counterrevolution in ways that show the persistent salience of norms that rested on the presumed exemption of *certain* women from violence. Mrs. Hamburger's story was not powerful because it portrayed sexualized violence against a woman. It was powerful because it described sexualized violence against a woman who, on every level, according to the narrative presented by the Labour delegation, was not a legitimate victim of violence.

Conversely, the behavior of the militias toward her and the response of the Hungarian government combatted this exemption. They did so by linking her—at least on the level of discourse—to women who did not fall under exemption. In her narrative of events, this is captured neatly when the soldiers call her a "Bolshevik whore, Jewish whore, and whore of the Romanians."[43] In one fell swoop, Mrs. Hamburger became the free-loving, radical, working-class communist woman whose primary political motivations were promiscuity; the traitorous woman who slept with the enemy; and the fecund Jewish woman and/or Jewish prostitute.[44] Through the mobilization of stereotypes of working-class, Jewish, and wartime women's sexuality, what emerges is a gendered version of the conceptualization of the interconnectedness of Jewishness, communism, and defeatism.[45]

Second, the experience of Mrs. Hamburger and its interpretation by others shows the complex and contradictory effects that violence had on gender and social relations. On the one hand, the nature of the sexualized violence perpetrated against Mrs. Hamburger served to reinforce Christian male supremacy, reimpose "traditional" class and gender hierarchies, and exclude Jews through the simultaneous mobilization of assumptions about working-class (female) promiscuity, Jewish women's fertility and Jewish men's insatiable sexual appetites, and women's and Jews' lack of full bodily autonomy (Crenshaw 1991: 1241–99; Collins 1998: 917–38). On the other, counterrevolutionary supporters who railed against the communist and feminist destruction of traditional society played a key role in undermining Mrs. Hamburger's family, as their persecution against leftists drove her husband into exile, thereby requiring her to become—or remain—the breadwinner. She was not at all unique in this regard. Counterrevolutionary violence and repression forced Mrs. Hamburger and thousands of other women to continue in or take up roles traditionally reserved for men prior to the Great War.[46] Counterrevolutionary violence actually perpetuated or initiated the disintegration of many working-class and Jewish families and households in Hungary.

The story of Mrs. Hamburger exemplifies these contradictions. By sharing her experience of torture with the Labour delegation, she played an active role in the short-lived and ultimately unsuccessful attempt by the international labor movement to intervene in Hungary, "before the treaty is signed."[47] In other words, in a small window of time when the future of Hungary and its borders did not seem to be quite so fixed (judging from the language used in sources), Mrs. Hamburger's story was part of a last-ditch effort by Hungarian leftists and their "brother parties" in Europe to alter the course of politics and peace. As such, it was not simply an element of the memory produced about the early post-Armistice chaos in Hungary by the European left in the early interwar period; it was a dimension of formal, albeit failed, political advocacy efforts.[48] Thus, while it is tempting to regard the outcome of Hungary's political crises with an air of inevitability by the time the report was published in May 1920, the Labour delegation's investigation serves as a reminder of the perceived fluidity of political conditions and diplomacy during this chaotic period.

Mrs. Hamburger's narrative also provides a window into the process of constructing an atrocity story, a term I use neutrally to categorize contents as opposed to the source or accuracy of a story. Most significantly, it shows us that she and other women played significant roles in producing it: she by telling her story in public, and British and other Hungarian women by assisting the delegation with its investigation. To be sure, the Labour delegation provided her with a platform, chose the story as one of many, and reframed and interpreted it in certain ways through a slight subversion of the maternal narrative often emphasized in such Atrocity Stories more broadly (Gullace 1997: 714–47; Grayzel 1999: 50–58). But Mrs. Hamburger was not a passive object, she was an active subject. Never mind that the polarized domestic and international political context, coupled with approximately six years of propaganda that heavily featured sexual violence, made this sensational story easier to disregard as either a "normal" part of war or a politicized story concocted by the left, thus rendering her and others, both female and especially male victims of sexual and nonsexualized violence, invisible.

The effects of violence on gender hierarchy went deeper. The presumed exemption of Mrs. Hamburger from violence on the basis of her gender, social status, personal comportment, and morality that lay at the base of the Labor movement's narrative fundamentally undermined the presumption that women were serious political actors that could be legitimate targets of political violence. While Mrs. Hamburger denied her personal involvement in leftist politics, many women did participate in actual revolutionary activities or complied with the orders of the revolutionary Republic of Councils (Hungary) of 1919.[49] Further, the Labour report's emphasis on her attempt to preserve her "honor" also affirmed the assumptions about proper sexual comportment and suggested that working-class women who did not conform to the standards of a bourgeois respectability would not enjoy similar immunity from violence (Zimmermann 1999: 183; Davidson and Hall 2001; Stauter-Halsted 2009: 564–66; Wingfield 2013: 571). In so doing, it rendered invisible the sexualized violence against women who were not (characterized) like Mrs. Hamburger, as well as most violence against men that had the potential to destabilize gender hierarchies, particularly penetrative sexual acts perpetrated by men against men. Such incidents were known to the Labour delegation, but they were not included in the final report, which only mentioned genital mutilation, like the castration of Béla Neumann, and naked beatings of men.[50] However, unlike the commentary on Mrs. Hamburger, the Labour report offered no discussion about the unacceptability of these acts against men. No elaboration on the men's education, class, or moral comportment was needed to identify these acts as severe violations. A man's right to full bodily autonomy was assumed by the Labour delegation, although even these assumptions regarding men were not universal and were often shaped by ethnicity.[51]

As evidenced by their actions, the White militias and the counterrevolutionary regime rejected the premises of women's exemption from violence. Their torture of Mrs. Hamburger challenged the immunity of women from violence, justifying their violence on the basis of their victims' supposed embrace of radical and/or traitorous politics. Moreover, the government's explanation of violence rested on the idea that certain women, because of their gender, class, and political and ethnic identities (which were inseparable), did not enjoy bodily autonomy or, more pointedly, that certain women were always available for or always sought after sex. Therefore, as demonstrated by the militia's insults, Mrs. Hamburger's ascribed Jewishness, along with her connection to Hungary's military enemies and to communism, all of which were indicative of a "deviant" sexuality, meant that she was sexually available; from the perspective of the government, her alleged promiscuity (her "misconduct" with other male prisoners) could be used to confirm her political loyalties. It is important to be suspicious of justifications of this sort, as it was clear that the violence was intended specifically to discipline and humiliate women *as* women. However, both justifications rested on a perversely ironic logic that women were political actors and therefore that violence against them could be considered legitimate.

Conclusion

What emerges from this analysis of the story of Mrs. Hamburger is a pair of contradictions. Through their response to violence, the labor movement, which very cautiously embraced a politics of (future) emancipation for women, emerged as a defender of a norm of violence that rested on traditional ideas of women's roles and spheres of activity as outside of politics. Conversely, through violence, many of those persons and groups who supposedly sought to restore traditional social/gender hierarchies undermined one of the very foundations on which these hierarchies rested: protection of the vulnerable and the restriction of violence to social equals.

Finally, the proliferation of Mrs. Hamburger's story internationally demonstrates the symbolic significance of (sexualized) violence against *women* in international relations in the long World War I period. That women's bodies play important symbolic roles in nationalist and military conflicts is not a novel idea.[52] In fact, probably the most iconic imagery of World War I had to do with sexual violence against women (the "rape of Belgium").[53] Indeed, the case of Mrs. Hamburger demonstrates a great deal of continuity with the war. During World War I, sexual violence against women and female distress were common features of wartime publicity and propaganda, and all of the belligerent powers used such stories and imagery to promote the justness of their war effort and their national suffering. Across national contexts, these various national efforts featured women in idealized roles, especially as mothers, although Mrs. Hamburger's maternal role was not heavily emphasized in the Labour delegation's report (Gullace 1997; Grayzel 1999; Healy 2004). Her story is also part of a wider pattern of sexual violence in the revolutionary struggles across Central and Eastern Europe at the time (Figes 1998; Wrobel 2003; Gerwarth 2012). Indeed, both the woman as victim and the dangerous woman were important features of both revolutionary and counterrevolutionary publicity in Hungary, such as anti-alcohol campaigns of the Kun regime and counterrevolutionary fears about communist "free love," as it was women who stood to become the primary beneficiaries of social, political, and sexual emancipation.[54]

In retelling the story of Mrs. Hamburger, this article shows that the sexually violated female body was an important symbol for the international labor movement's efforts to challenge the political legitimacy of the new regime in Hungary and to attack the moral authority of the Entente democracies who were in charge of building the "New Europe." In other words, women's bodies were symbolically valuable for both nationalist as well as internationalist politics.

As a researcher, the challenges of writing the story of Mrs. Hamburger leave me with simultaneous feelings of satisfaction and discomfort. While it seems clear that Mrs. Hamburger wanted to testify to what happened to her, what remains uncertain is how many people she wanted to know. That is, did Mrs. Hamburger realize her story would be instrumentalized, or more strongly, exploited around the world for political and even humanitarian purposes in the interwar period? This has not been an easy question for me to answer, in part because her voice in the historical record on this subject thus far appears to exist solely in her deposition to the British Labour delegation. But whether she realized and welcomed it or not, Mrs. Hamburger became a symbol of the missed opportunity of the Entente to democratize the successor states of Eastern Europe. Her experience, as narrated by the Labour Party, also demonstrated the moral consequences of replacing one idea of European civilization, however imperfect (representative democracy) with another (anticommunism).

Acknowledgments

I would like to thank the English-Speaking Union of Cincinnati, Ohio, the American Council of Learned Societies, the American Jewish Archives, Imre Kertész Kolleg, and the College of William & Mary for their generous support of this research. I would also like to thank the editors of this volume for their careful reading of this manuscript, as well as Susan Zimmermann, Paul Hanebrink, and Melissa Feinberg for reading various versions of this manuscript.

Emily R. Gioielli is a Research Fellow at Pasts Inc., Center for Historical Studies at Central European University. She is also on the editorial teams of *East Central Europe* and the *Hungarian Studies Review*. She specializes in the history of women, gender, and sexuality in East-Central Europe and the history violence. Her article "'Home Is Home No Longer': Political Struggle in the Domestic Sphere in Post-Armistice Hungary, 1919–1922," published in *Aspasia: The International Yearbook of Central, Eastern, and Southeastern European Women's and Gender History*, was awarded Honorable Mention for the Mark Pittaway Best Article Prize from the Hungarian Studies Association. She has also published in *Polin* and the *Cultures of History Forum*. She previously was a fellow at Imre Kertész Kolleg Jena and was an ACLS East European studies fellow.

Notes

1. Protocoll of Mrs. Alexander Hamburger and Mrs. Elizabeth Kunfi, 13 May 1920, LP/HUN/5/46-18.i-iv, Labour History Archive and Study Centre, People's History Museum and Archives, Manchester, England (Document collection hereafter referred to as LHA).
2. According to one source, by the time Mrs. Hamburger was arrested, she and her children were living in the coatroom of a Budapest café. See Harden (1921).

3. Protocoll of Mrs. Alexander Hamburger and Mrs. Elizabeth Kunfi.
4. Protocoll of Mrs. Alexander Hamburger and Mrs. Elizabeth Kunfi.
5. Protocoll of Mrs. Alexander Hamburger and Mrs. Elizabeth Kunfi.
6. Prison Record of Mrs. Sándor Hamburger, VII.102.a-fogoly-1920-1570, Budapesti Királyi Büntetőtörvényszéki Fogház iratai, Fogolytörzskönyvek, Budapest Fővárosi Levéltár (hereafter BFL).
7. Prison Record of Mrs. Sándor Hamburger, VII.102.a-fogoly-1920-1570, BFL; Hajnal (1920); Harden (1921). Although I have traced her story in multiple archives in Hungary, Austria, Great Britain, and the United States, I have not yet been able to find her given name.
8. Prison Record of Mrs. Sándor Hamburger, VII.102.a-fogoly-1920-1570, BFL. As a source her prison record should be used carefully, as there is no other official record affiliated with her time in prison. There is a record of her in the database of the criminal courts, but the file simply has her name and her brother-in-law's scrawled on the outside of the folder. Her name does not appear anywhere else in the file.
9. No name, "Protocoll," LP/HUN/5/46/17.i.-ii, LHA.
10. On sexual extortion of relatives, see Statement by István Végh to Social Democratic Party Legal Aid Office (hereafter SDP), May 4, 1920, pg. 345, Fond 658, Allag 10, Dossier 3, Politikatörténeti Intézet Levéltár (collection hereafter abbreviated PIL); Statement by Mrs. Mihály Hegedűs to SDP, May 11, 1920, pg. 357, PIL; Joseph Marcus, "Is There White Terror in Hungary," pg. 39, June 5, 1921, doc. 220562, folder 151.4, Records of the American Jewish Joint Distribution Committee of the years 1919–1921, New York Collection, American Joint Distribution Committee Archives (hereafter cited as JDC); on vaginal exams as punishment, see Marcus, "Is There White Terror in Hungary."
11. Women engaged in or suspected of prostitution were subjected to gynecological exams to prevent the spread of venereal diseases. Working-class women were generally the most vulnerable to these types of charges as it was women in the lower classes who often turned to prostitution in times of economic hardship. Moreover, the working classes were associated with sexual and/or familial relationships that did not conform to bourgeois standards of morality. Because of the revolutions, the working classes broadly were politically suspect, and "deviant" sexual behavior was politicized. For discussions of the regulation of prostitution including so-called "sanitary exams" in Budapest, Vienna, as well as partitioned Poland, see Zimmermann (1999: 183); Stauter-Halsted (2009: 570); Wingfield (2013: 571). See also Walkowitz (1980); Spongberg (1997); and the recently published Wingfield (2017).
12. Report on the Alleged Existence of "White Terror" in Hungary. London: His Majesty's Stationery Office, 1920.
13. Report on the Alleged Existence of "White Terror" in Hungary. London: His Majesty's Stationery Office, 1920.
14. Letter from Camille Huysmans to William Gillies, April 26, 1920, LP/HUN/1/15, LHA.
15. Draft of Report, LP/HUN/2/8.i, LHA. Other women, both Hungarian émigrés/exilees and British leftists were also concerned about increasing the visibility of women who were victims of atrocities at the hands of White militias. Rózsika Schwimmer, famed feminist and pacifist, wrote to women in the British Independent Labour Party for assistance in launching an investigation by women for women in Hungary. See Rózsika Schwimmer to Mrs. Despard, Mrs. Snowden, and Mrs. Charles Buxton, 31 March 1920, Box 65, Folder 1, Edith Wynner Papers, Archives and Manuscripts Division, New York Public Library (hereafter referred to as NYPL). In addition to the woman

who accompanied the Labour delegation, other women, Hungarians as well as British and American aid workers active in Central Europe, also served as sources for the delegation.
16. See especially files LP/HUN/4-5 concerning the Labour delegation's journey to Hungary, LHA.
17. I have not yet found correspondence mentioning her in the files of the Labour Party. However, the itinerary the delegation drew up prior to their departure included investigating Mrs. Hamburger's story.
18. See Horne and Kramer (2001), a magisterial study of German atrocities during World War I. In the case of White Terror, this partisan stance may be summed up by an article in *Neue Zurcher Zeitung* from 23 August 1920, which claimed that "White Terror is entirely an invention of émigrées in Vienna."
19. No author, "Programme," LP/HUN/5/46/4.i-iv, LHA.
20. No name, "Protocoll," LP/HUN/5/46/17.i.-ii, LHA; Statement by Imre Neumann to SDP May 6, 1920, pg. 348, PIL.
21. British Joint Labour Delegation to Hungary, *The White Terror in Hungary* (London: 1920), 10.
22. Prison Record of Mrs. Sándor Hamburger, VII.102.a-fogoly-1920-1570, BFL.
23. British Joint Labour Delegation to Hungary, *The White Terror in Hungary* (London: 1920), 10.
24. British Joint Labour Delegation to Hungary, *The White Terror in Hungary* (London: 1920), 10. See also "A fehérterror Magyarországon: Az angol egyesült munkás kiküldöttség teljes jelentése, 1920 május," in Markovits (1964: 336–40).
25. See also "A fehérterror Magyarországon: Az angol egyesült munkás kiküldöttség teljes jelentése, 1920 május," in Markovits (1964: 10–11).
26. The British Labour Delegation's full report, translated into German and Hungarian, appeared in Social Democratic and leftist newspapers across Austria. For example: "Der weise Terror in Ungarn," *Salzburger Wacht* (Salzburg), 24 June 1920, 3; "Der weise Terror in Ungarn," *Arbeiter Zeitung* (Vienna), 23 June 1920, 1–3; "Der weise Terror in Ungarn," *Arbeiterwille* (Graz), 25 June 1920, 2–3; "Az Angol Küldöttség jelentése," *Bécsi Magyar Ujság* (Vienna), 23 June 1920, 6. Articles based on the report also appeared in the Austrian press. See "Die Folterqualen der Frau Hamburger," *Wiener Sonn- und Montags Zeitung* (Vienna), 14 June 1920, 4; Marcus, "Is There White Terror in Hungary."
27. "British Labour and the Hungarian Terror," *The Nation* 111 (July–December 2010): 53. The article printed in *The Nation* came from the *Daily Telegraph* (London), 7 June 1920. The story also reappears in 1922 in an article by Emmanuel Urbas, "The White Terror in Hungary," *American Israelite* (Cincinnati, Ohio), 19 October 1922.
28. Marcel Vértes was an illustrator whose images on the White Terror appeared in the leftist Hungarian-language paper *Bécsi Magyar Ujság* in May and June 1920. His images of White Terror were highly gendered. See "Spring," *Bécsi Magyar Újság* (Vienna), 20 May 1920; Marcel Vértes, "The Pain of Transdanubia," *Bécsi Magyar Újság* (Vienna) 22 May 1920; Marcel Vértes, "Because It Will Be the Grand and Lovely Thought for Hungarian Women," *Bécsi Magyar Újság* (Vienna) 26 June 1920. These images also appeared in Tarcali, *Quand Horthy est Roi*, 15, 50, 54. In addition to Vértes's images, the other famous images on the White Terror were produced by Mihály Biró in a book titled *Horthy: The White Terror in Hungary under the Horthy Regime*. Two of the twenty images appear to depict events related to the story of Mrs. Hamburger: "Rape" and "The Beasts!," the latter of which portrays castration. This published collection, while censored in Hungary and in Austria, traveled with its creator Mihály Biró, who re-

printed the images in Argentina in 1946. The images were about the size of postcards, and there is conflicting information if they were postcards. See Graphic Witness, "Visual Arts and Social Commentary," retrieved 17 July 2016 from http://www.graph icwitness.org/contemp/biro.htm. See also Katrin Pokorny-Nagel and Michael Diers, *Pathos in Red* (Nürnberg: Moderne Kunst Nürnberg, 2011).
29. Minisztertanácsi jegyzőkönyv, napirend pontok 25, 22 August 1924, Magyar Országos Levéltár (hereafter MOL), W szekció, Miniszteritanácsi könyv, K27, 1924, retrieved 16 July 2016 from https://www.eleveltar.hu/web/guest/bongeszo?ref=TypeDeliverab leUnit_825d691a-9f6d-4fa6-8116-a0f25c14e2dc&tenant=MNL.
30. The book was also translated into English. Not all editions included the illustrations. For example, Hirschfeld (1941: 335–36).
31. Protokoll in connection with Mr. Eugen Poózs (no date) LP/HUN/5/46.17.i-ii, LHA.
32. Protocoll of Mrs. Alexander Hamburger and Mrs. Elizabeth Kunfi.
33. Statement by Imre Neumann to Social Democratic Party Legaid Aid Office, 6 May 1920, 658 fond 10 csoport 3. őe, pp. 348–350, PIL.
34. Her prison record confirms that the basis of her arrest was "bolshevist activities." Prison Record of Mrs. Sándor Hamburger, VII.102.a-fogoly-1920-1570, BFL.
35. Although Hajnal's book suggests that the author/compiler had personal letters and testimony from Mrs. Hamburger, I am cautious about the role Hajnal played in shaping the narrative, and I do not know the provenance of his sources, especially since there is a strong literary quality to it. This is not to invalidate the material contained in the book but rather to approach it with care as a narrative about Mrs. Hamburger's experiences, as opposed to her direct testimony.
36. H. N. Brailsford, Advisory Committee on International Questions, "Memorandum on the White Terror in Hungary," LP/HUN/2/6/1.i, LHA; Letter from Ernő Garami to Frederick Kuh, n.d., LP/HUN/2/7.iii, LHA; Letter from William Gillies to J. J. Davies, 27 January 1920, LP/HUN/1/6, LHA; Letter from Camille Huysmans to Arthur Henderson, 8 January 1920, LP/HUN/1/1/iii, LHA; Letter from Camille Huysmans to ?, 24 November 1919, LP/HUN/3/2, LHA; Letter from Ernő Garami to Camille Huysmans, 30 December 1919, LP/HUN/3/4.i-ii, LHA; Letter from Ernő Garami to Camille Huysmans, 16 October 1919, LP/HUN/3//3.i-ii, LHA; Letter from Camille Huysmans to British Labour Party, 26 February 1920, LP/HUN/3/7.
37. There is a small paper trail for Mrs. Hamburger's case. While the court records from the period are incomplete, there is no arrest record or case log in the records of the criminal courts, although there is a prison log that includes very little personal data—including her given name at birth (*lanyanév*). The paucity of sources confirms the information provided by the delegation in their report. Two depositions beyond Mrs. Hamburger's exist, that of Jénő Poósz and Imre Neumann, the brother of Béla Neumann. I have, as yet, been unable to locate medical records for Mrs. Hamburger in either Hungary or Vienna or the Hungarian government's explanation about Mrs. Hamburger's imprisonment. It is unclear whether both delegations received the response verbally or just the Labour delegation. Two additional accounts from the period are related secondhand, one of which seems to strongly mirror the British Labour delegation's report, albeit with some added details. Bodó's article includes a more full accounting of these details as they focus on the interaction of the perpetrators and victims that reflects the content of these sources.
38. There are many examples of this explanation for women's imprisonment. For example, see Sándor Lestyán, "Mi történik a budapesti foghazakban?" *A Világ*, 17 October 1919; n.a., "In the Woman's Prison in Budapest," LP/HUN/5/46/13, LHA.

39. For a more thorough analysis of women's political activities during the post-Armistice period in Hungary, see Gioielli (2015), especially chapters 3 and 4.
40. Letter from Frederick Kuh to William Ewer, 30 April 1920, LP/HUN/1/24.i, LHA; Frederick Kuh, "England and the White Terror," *The Liberator*, July 1920, 43. See also Oskar Jászi, *Revolution and Counter-revolution* (London: P.S. King & Son, LTD., 1924), 159–61.
41. The British Labour Report states that they did not receive any written confirmation, partial or otherwise, from either the Hungarian government or the British diplomatic delegation, which was the recipient of the government's response to the inquiry regarding Mrs. Hamburger. There is no evidence of this confirmation in the records of the Labour delegation, and thus far I have not been able to locate such a response in the British national archives, although more research is needed with regard to this issue. It may be that the diplomatic delegation also received their response verbally, in conversation with Hungarian officials.
42. For example, Letter from Vilmos Böhm to Labour Party, 8 February 1920, LP/HUN/1/9.i, LHA.
43. Protocoll of Mrs. Alexander Hamburger and Mrs. Elizabeth Kunfi.
44. Associations between Jews and prostitution, both in terms of traffickers and women trafficked, were well established by the 1910s. Jewish Association for the Protection of Girls and Women, "Jewish International Conference on the Suppression of the Traffic in Girls and Women, 1910 London, Official Report" (London: Wertheimer, Lea & Co., 1910). See Bristow (1982); Graetz and Cwikel (2006: 25–58); Vyleta (2007); Wingfield (2011: 291–311); and Stauter-Halsted, (2009: 567–69).
45. These ideas later become crystallized as the *Dolchstoßlegende* (stab-in-the-back) and Judeo-bolshevism. See Ablovatski (2010: 473–89).
46. Given that her husband was a veteran of the war, Mrs. Hamburger, like many other women across Europe, already had quite a bit of experience managing on her own over the previous five years. I have written about this further in my dissertation. See also Healy (2004); and Davis (2000).
47. See Letter from Vilmos Böhm to the International Socialist Bureau, 14 February 1920, LP/HUN/3/9.i-ii; Report, "Responsibility on the Entente Powers Respecting the Political Persecutions in Hungary," n.d. LP/HUN/1/10.iv.
48. Eliza Ablovatski has explored the British Labour report within the context of collective memory and "counter-memory" of the revolutions in Hungary and Germany in the post-1919 period. However, the goal the report was to effect policy change. Moreover, for the thousands of people whose cases were winding their way through the court system or who were imprisoned or interned, the conceptualization of events as genuine "revolutions" had a profound impact on their ability to make certain legal claims and defenses. See Ablovatski (2005; 2006: 86).
49. See my forthcoming manuscript, "Homefront, Commune, Horthyland."
50. Statement by József Dündek to SDP, 19 December 1919, pg. 115, Fond 658, Allag 10, Dossier 3, PIL; "A Magyar Texas," *Az Ember* (Vienna), 17 January 1920. The statement of Dündek recounts his subjection to "sexually immoral acts" by officers, who later summoned his wife to visit and "made love" to her in front of him, despite her "vigorous refusal of him." His experience was reported in the Viennese Hungarian-language paper *Az Ember*, but the emphasis in the story was placed on the rape of Dündek's wife in front of him, rather than his own rape. The Labour delegation had knowledge of this material. See also Bodó (2011a: 9).
51. See also Bela Bodó's chapter in this volume.

52. Feminist scholars of international relations and anthropology have been discussing the connection of gender to international security and nationalism since the late 1970s and early 1980s. Notable examples of this theoretical approach are Stiehm (1983: 367–76); Anthias and Yuval-Davis (1989); Peterson (1992); Siefert (1994: 54–72); Sjoberg (2006: 889–910).
53. The "rape of Belgium" and the imagery associated with this conceptualization of the German occupation of the Lowlands is probably the most famous, but sexualized violence and/or gendered violence appeared in pamphlets, posters, and newspapers of all the belligerent powers. Hirschfeld's *Sittengeschichte des Weltkrieg* contains a compilation of many images produced during the war that portray sexualized and gendered violence by the military enemy. Other interesting collections of these types of posters may be found collected in the online exhibition "Sexuality during the War," *The First World War and the End of the Habsburg Monarchy*, retrieved 15 September 2016 from http://ww1.habsburger.net/en/stories/sexuality-during-war.
54. Examples of communist imagery may be seen in "Alkohol és Prostitucio az Emberiség gyilkosai," 1919, Museomap, Retrieved 17 July 2016 from http://www.museumap.hu/record/-/record/display/manifestation/oai-aggregated-bib4121052/ad3799b8-7934-4283-beef-e88576ed8e58/0/24/3/6/titleOrder/asc. For examples of anticommunist imagery and discourse, see Kovács, "Ezek marasztaltál a Románokat," Museomap, retrieved 17 July 2016 from http://www.museumap.hu/record/-/record/display/manifestation/oai-aggregated-bib4119523/6ea9f190-a378-44f9-84d2-cf6cfac76afe/72/24/3/103/titleOrder/asc; Tormay (1923: 198, 281; Tormay (1924: 41–42, 53–54).

References

Ablovatski, Eliza. 2005. "'Cleansing the Red Nest': Revolution and White Terror in Munich and Budapest, 1919." PhD diss., Columbia University.
———. 2006. "Between Red Army and White Guard: Women in Budapest, 1919." In *Gender and War in Twentieth-Century Europe*, edited by Nancy M. Wingfield and Maria Bucur, 70–95. Bloomington, IN.
———. 2010. "The 1919 Central European Revolutions and the Judeo-Bolshevik Myth." *European Review of History/Revue europeenne d'histoire* 17(3): 473–89.
Anthias, Floya, and Nira Yuval-Davis. *Women, Nation, State*. New York. 1989.
Bodó, Béla. 2004. "Paramilitary Violence in Hungary after the First World War." *East European Quarterly* 38(2): 129–72.
———. 2010a. "Iván Hejjas: The Life of a Counter-revolutionary." *East Central Europe* 37(2–3): 247–79.
———. 2010b. "Hungarian Aristocracy and the White Terror." *Journal of Contemporary History* 45(4): 703–24.
———. 2011a. "The White Terror in Hungary, 1919–1921: The Social Worlds of Paramilitary Groups." *Austrian History Yearbook* 42: 133–63.
———. 2011b. *Paramilitary Violence and Anti-Semitism in Hungary, 1919–1921*. Pittsburgh.
Bristow, Edward W. 1982. *Prostitution and Prejudice: The Jewish Fight against White Slavery, 1870–1939*. Oxford.
Collins, Patricia Hill. 1998. "The Tie That Binds: Race, Gender, and US Violence." *Ethnic and Racial Studies* 21(5): 917–38.
Crenshaw, Kimberlé. 1991. "Mapping the Margins: Intersectionality, Identity Politics, and Violence against Women of Color." *Stanford Law Review* 43(6): 1241–99.

Davidson, Roger, and Lesley A. Hall. 2001. "Introduction." In *Sex, Sin, and Suffering: Venereal Disease and European Society since 1870*, edited by Roger Davidson and Lesley A. Hall, 1–14. New York.

Davis, Belinda J. 2000. *Home Fires Burning: Food, Politics, and Everyday Life in World War I Berlin*. Chapel Hill, NC.

Dogan, Çetinkaya, Y. 2014. "Atrocity Propaganda and the Nationalization of the Masses in the Ottoman Empire during the Balkan Wars (1912–13)." *International Journal of Middle East Studies* 46(4): 759–78.

Elshtain, Jean B. 1991. "Sovereignty, Identity, Sacrifice." *Millennium: Journal of International Studies* 20(3): 395–406.

Figes, Orlando. 1998. *A People's Tragedy: The Russian Revolution, 1891–1924*. London.

Gerwarth, Robert. 2011. "Sexual and Non-Sexual Violence against 'Politicised Women' after the Great War." In *Sexual Violence in Conflict Zones from the Ancient World to the Late Twentieth Century*, edited by Elisabeth Heinemann, 122–36. Philadelphia.

———. 2012. "Fighting the Red Beast: Counter-Revolutionary Violence in the Defeated States of Central Europe." In *War in Peace: Paramilitary Violence in Europe after the Great War*, edited by Robert Gerwarth and John Horne, 62–71. Oxford.

Gioielli, Emily R. 2015. "'White Misrule': Terror and Political Violence during Hungary's Long World War I." PhD thesis, Central European University.

Graetz, Naomi, and Julie Cwikel. 2006. "Trafficking and Prostitution: Lessons from Jewish Sources." *Australian Journal of Jewish Studies* 20: 25–58.

Grayzel, Susan. 1999. *Women's Identities at War: Gender Motherhood, and Politics in Britain and France during the First World War*. Chapel Hill, NC.

Gullace, Nicoletta F. 1997. "Sexual Violence and Family Honor: British Propaganda and International Law during the First World War." *American Historical Review* 102(3): 714–47.

Hajnal, Eugen. 1920. *Der Fall der Frau Hamburger*. Wien.

Harris, Ruth. 1993. "The 'Child of the Barbarian': Rape, Race and Nationalism in France during the First World War." *Past & Present* 141(1): 170–206.

Healy, Maureen. 2004. *Vienna and the Fall of the Habsburg Empire: Total War and Everyday Life in World War I*. Cambridge.

Hirschfeld, Magnus. 1930. *Sittengeschichte des Weltkrieges*. Leipzig.

———. 1941. *The Sexual History of the World War, From Reports Collected by the Institute for Sexual Science*. New York.

Horne, John, and Alan Kramer. 1993. "German 'Atrocities' and Franco-German Opinion, 1914: The Evidence of German Soldiers' Diaries." *Journal of Modern History* 66(1): 1–33.

———. 2001. *German Atrocities: A History of Denial*. New Haven, CT.

Jászi, Oskar. 1924. *Revolution and Counter-revolution*. London.

Laswell, Harold. 1927. *Propaganda Technique in the World War*. London.

Peterson, V. Spike. 1992. *Gendered States: Feminist (Re)Visions of International Relations*. Boulder, CO.

Ponsonby, Arthur. 1928. *Falsehood in War-Time*. London.

Siefert, Ruth. 1994. "War and Rape: A Preliminary Analysis." In *Mass Rape: The War against Women in Bosnia-Herzegovina*, edited by Alexandra Stiglmayer, 54–73. Lincoln, NE.

Sjoberg, Laura. 2006. "Gendered Realities of the Immunity Principle: Why Gender Analysis Needs Feminism." *International Studies Quarterly* 50(4): 889–910.

———. 2010. "Women Fighters and the 'Beautiful Soul' Narrative." *International Review of the Red Cross* 92(877): 53–68.

Spongberg, Mary. 1997. *Feminizing Venereal Disease: The Body of the Prostitute in Nineteenth-Century Medical Discourse*. New York.

Stauter-Halsted, Keely. 2009. "Moral Panic and the Prostitute in Partitioned Poland: Middle-Class Respectability in Defense of the Modern Nation." *Slavic Review* 68(3): 557–81.

Stiehm, Judith Hicks. 1983. "The Protected, the Protector, the Defender." *Women and Men's Wars*, edited by Judith Hicks Stiehm, 367–76. Oxford.

Tarcali, Robert. 1922. *Quand Horthy est Roi*. Paris.

Tharaud, Jérôme, and Jean Tharaud. 1921. *Quand Israel est Roi*. Paris.

Tormay, Cecile. 1923. *An Outlaw's Diary: The Revolution*. London.

———. 1924. *An Outlaw's Diary: The Commune*. London.

Harden, Maximilian. 1921. "Jew-Baiting." *American Hebrew & Jewish Messenger* 7. New York City.

Vyleta, Daniel M. 2007. *Crimes, Jews and News: Vienna 1895–1914*. New York.

Walkowitz, Judith R. 1980. *Prostitution and Victorian Society: Women Class, and the State*. Cambridge.

Wingfield, Nancy M. 2011. "Destination: Alexandria, Buenos Aires, Constantinople: 'White Slavers' in Late Imperial Austria." *Journal of the History of Sexuality* 20(2): 291–311.

———. 2013. "The Enemy Within: Regulating Prostitution and Controlling Venereal Disease in Cisleithanian Austria during the Great War." *Central European History* 46(3): 568–98.

———. 2017. *The World of Prostitution in Late Imperial Austria*. Oxford.

Wrobel, Piotr. 2003. "Seeds of Violence: The Brutalization of an East European Region, 1917–1921." *Journal of Modern European History* 1(1): 125–49.

Zimmermann, Susan. 1999. "Making a Living from Disgrace: The Politics of Prostitution, Female Poverty and Urban Gender Codes in Budapest and Vienna, 1860–1920." In *The City in Central Europe: Culture and Society from 1800 to the Present*, edited by Malcolm Gee, Tim Kirk, and Jill Steward, 175–97. London.

CHAPTER 5

"A Little Murderous Party"
Poland after World War I in the Works of Joseph Roth

Winson Chu

In the summer of 1920, Soviet Russian troops were advancing deep into Central Europe and were on the cusp of crushing the Polish army. Twenty-five-year-old Joseph Roth was then a reporter for the *Neue Berliner Zeitung* and sending frequent dispatches from the front back to Germany. Roth expressed his pessimism about the Polish nation-state's ability to survive and was troubled by the escalation of violence against civilians as army discipline collapsed. He related how deserters and isolated units joined together in what had degenerated into a war of plunder (*Bandenkrieg*) (Roth 1989a: 311). Above all, Roth was dismayed that roving bands of Polish soldiers were attacking Polish Jews. Although he was not an eyewitness, he repeated information on 5 August 1920 that Poles had instigated "a little murderous party" (*ein kleines Mordfest*) in Suwałki (Roth 1989b: 320). He also relayed the murder of sixty Jewish families in Grodno, describing how Polish soldiers in "tried and tested method" had "blinded seventeen Jewish men, cut off the breasts of women, and raped minors" (Roth 1989b: 320).

Roth, the future renowned novelist, is commonly associated simultaneously with a cosmopolitan and universalist outlook as well as his nostalgia for the world before 1914. Born in Brody in multiethnic Galicia in 1894, Roth studied in Vienna before serving in the Habsburg army during World War I. After the war, Austria became a republic and Galicia became part of independent Poland. Roth returned to Vienna to work as a journalist before moving to Berlin in 1920 and then to France after Hitler's accession to power in 1933. He died in Paris in 1939 from the effects of alcoholism.

Roth's biography suggests a unique ability to communicate the complicated history and sensitivities of marginalized peoples in Eastern Europe. The scholarship on Roth has focused on the discovery of his Jewish roots, his cosmopolitanism, and his romanticization of the Habsburg Monarchy (Jakubów 2012; Le Rider 2012). Roth's fiction writing is often framed in terms of a search for identity, and he is seen as instrumental in shaping the myth of a supranational Galician homeland (Ignasiak 1987: 73; Lughofer 2011: 79). The painful loss of the Habsburg fatherland was encapsulated in his most famous works, the novel *Radetzkymarsch* (1932) and the short story "Die Büste des Kaisers" (1934).[1] At the same time, Roth is known for his profound hatred of Prussian militarism (Lazaroms 2013: 20–21).

While Roth's body of work generally remains critical of nationalisms and of right-wing violence, this article argues that Roth embraced various strands of thinking about the East that catered to prevailing German views on Poland. A new look at his journalistic writings on military and paramilitary violence after World War I reveals not just a lingering attachment to the Habsburgs but also nearly unwavering support for Germany's interests when they ran contrary to those of the fledgling Polish state. In his accounts, Roth deployed national stereotypes that undermined Polish national claims while privileging German ones. His portrayals of Polish malaise and violence thus appear at odds with his reputation as a "multicultural" author and his own avowals to communicate a sympathetic view of the East. At the same time, his war reporting also challenged negative stereotypes of Russia and romanticized the Soviet experiment.

Between Polish Nation-Making and German-Centric Narratives

As could be expected in travel literature generally, Poland served as a mirror for Roth to investigate the past and future of Central Europe. Especially the purported multicultural harmony in which Poles, Jews, and others once lived together informed deeply Roth's view of growing nationalism in the region. His own Jewish heritage and his sense of displacement in the current world played a role here, too, as Ilse Lazaroms notes: "The millennial exile of the Jews, it seems, carried on undisturbed in the East. Almost without exception, Roth portrayed the Galician landscape and its people sympathetically" (Lazaroms 2013: 34). While this sympathy was true for his belletristic works, there is also a need to assess his early journalistic writings more closely. For much of the 1920s, Roth worked in Berlin as a reporter for left-liberal German newspapers, including the tone-setting *Berliner Börsen-Courier* and the less-established *Neue Berliner Zeitung*. He later also worked for the somewhat more conservative *Frankfurter Zeitung*, Germany's most famous paper.[2] During this time, Roth wrote several articles and essays from Poland. The steady discovery and republication of these feuilletons and articles from his Berlin years have allowed for new interpretations of Roth's later works. For example, Nicole Frank has uncovered many articles written by Roth in the *Neue Berliner Zeitung* and *Berliner Börsen-Courier* in her dissertation analyzing the content of Roth's early journalism (Frank 2007: 14, 181). These will be discussed later in relation to Roth's views on Poland.

"Polish themes" were especially important and often appeared in Roth's works (Koprowski 1989: 13; Bartoszewska 1999: 63; Bartoszewska 2005: 117).[3] His first novel, *Hotel Savoy* (1924), takes place in an unnamed city but is generally recognized to be set in the Polish industrial city of Łódź.[4] Several scholars have investigated Roth's views of Poland and its people in his journalistic and literary writings (Forst-Battaglia 1979; Mazur 1979; Lipiński 1990; Bartoszewska 1995; Kaszyński 1995; Dzikowska 1997; Bartoszewska 1999; Lipiński 2000). These travel reports from the late1920s tend to be positive and sympathetic toward Poland (Dücker 2003: 159). The Polish writer Józef Wittlin was a good friend and remarked upon Roth's love for Poland (Bartoszewska 1999: 63). The Polish Germanist Krzysztof Lipiński has even asked if Roth could be considered a Polish author (1990: 191). Maria Kłańska gives a more nuanced account and distinguishes between Roth's views of Poles and his views on the country (Kłańska 1996: 565). Outside of Poland, the scholarly treatment of Roth's writings on that country during the 1920s remains sparse. David Bronsen's monumental biography of Roth from 1974, for example, leaves out much of his experience in Poland. Indeed, Bronsen's chapter on Roth's early journalism does not include his experience from the Polish-Soviet War, which will be discussed below (1974). Jon Hughes, who has investigated Roth's works in the 1920s, likewise does not examine his works on Poland in detail (Hughes 2006: 7). There is a need to take his views on Poland seriously, however, since Roth at least considered himself "partially Polish."[5] As will be shown below, Roth even believed he should defend Polish honor against those who would denigrate Poland's name.

Yet many of Roth's writings offer a very critical view of Poland, and it remains worthwhile to ask how Roth may have shared and perpetuated negative stereotypes regarding Poland. Here, Roth's critique of Alfred Döblin (1878–1957) in regard to the latter's portrayal of Poland reveals Roth's own conflicted views when writing on the East. Born in Prussian Stettin, Döblin was—like Roth—based mainly in Berlin in the 1920s, and he published his best-known novel, *Berlin Alexanderplatz*, in 1929. As with Roth, much of the scholarship on Döblin has focused on his search for a lost Jewish identity (George 2002). There were other similarities between the two writers. Both championed a form of Jewish assimilationism and were wary of Zionism.[6] While skeptical of the mysticism associated with Chasidism, they also idealized the Eastern European Jews (*Ostjuden*) as a source of salvation and rejuvenation for Western Jews.[7] Unlike Roth, however, Döblin was already an established writer when he went to Poland in the fall of 1924. Döblin's travels were published soon thereafter as *Reise in Polen* (literally Journey *in* Poland, but often translated as Journey *to* Poland) (1991). In the book, Döblin declared himself to be a "friend of the Polish people" during an encounter in Vilnius with a Lithuanian woman who spoke poorly of the Poles (Döblin 1991: 131; George 2002: 346). No one, it would seem, could doubt Döblin's good intentions vis-à-vis Poland.[8]

Roth, however, reviewed Döblin's *Reise in Polen* in the *Frankfurter Zeitung* in January 1926 and found the book (and Döblin) to be condescending to the Poles. Roth noted that someone with Döblin's ability should have been more careful in avoiding sweeping generalizations (*Pauschalschilderungen*) that depicted "dirty hotel rooms, pests, and the lack of sewers." Roth chastised Döblin's "chutzpah" and his Western European "civilizational arrogance"; his "atavisms" merely propagated French, British, and German stereotypes of Eastern peoples. Roth was especially critical of Döblin's portrayal of Polish women as having "broad foreheads," "low-set noses," and "wide and fleshy mouths," as well as their overly done makeup and seductive dress. Roth wondered if Döblin would have written the same in Paris where women were similarly powdered and likewise wore light-colored and suggestive stockings. Roth used these alleged biases to compare Döblin to other shallow works on the German borderlands that also used the trope of "dangerous Polish women" who knew how to use "Cupid's arrows" to subdue German men. Roth rhetorically asked "whether Döblin is allowed to describe Poland in the year 1925 in the same manner that Tacitus described the Germanic tribes in the first century A.D." (Roth 1990: 533).

Thus, Roth stated the obvious—that Döblin's *Reise in Polen* revealed more about the author than about Poland itself. Not only did Roth believe that there was nothing new to be learned in Döblin's book, but, worse, he felt that the work might be confused with others that had more dubious, right-wing origins. At the same time, Roth criticized the book for its ethnocentrism, proposing that *Reise in Polen* should have been named "Reise zu den Juden" (Journey to the Jews). Here, Döblin's purported obsession with the Jews had led to a search for the exotic, including the so-called "Wunderrabbi." Roth thereby conjured the specter of Orientalism within German-Jewish culture: "For the Western European the Eastern Jewish world is less accessible than for instance India." For Roth, Döblin's desire to discover the Eastern brethren was both patronizing and dangerous because it failed to capture the nuances of Jewish life. The biggest threat, it seemed, was the reductionism of national thinking that had gripped Western European Zionists. According to Roth, such thinkers were seeking to "degrade a rich world into a nation" (Roth 1990: 535). Roth clearly thought of himself as better informed than Döblin on Jewish and Polish affairs, and he used the opportunity to position himself against what he saw as Döblin's national essentialism (Friedrich 1984: 94–96). Given his roots in the region, the languages he spoke, and his declared sympathies, Roth should have easily avoided Döblin's sweeping negative generalizations in his own work on Poland.

The Polish-Soviet War, 1920

Yet a cursory glance at Roth's earliest writings on independent Poland seems to indicate an even more critical and perhaps no less Orientalizing view of Poland than that of Döblin. As a correspondent for the *Neue Berliner Zeitung* during the Polish-Soviet War in July and early August of 1920, Roth described the rout of Polish forces near the then–East Prussian town of Lyck (now Ełk). In these reports, Roth portrayed Poland as a defeated and seemingly illegitimate state and society. In particular, he initially had little faith in newly independent Poland's ability to survive. Among the soldiers streaming westward, he recounted, only a few were wounded, and many appeared drunk. Roth concluded that Polish units must have retreated without resisting the enemy. He surmised that the leadership of the Polish officers, many of whom had probably once served in the third-rate Austrian reserve army (*Landsturm*), was "extraordinarily poor" (Roth 1989c: 303). Even the presence of French military aides could not prevent small Russian detachments from routing larger Polish forces (Roth 1989a: 310). The words "flight" (*Flucht*) and "to flee" (*fliehen*) peppered Roth's accounts, and the headline of one article proclaimed, "The Polish Northern Army Destroyed: Encirclement and Penetration of the Front—Panic-Stricken Flight of the Poles—Capture of Important Towns by the Russians" (Roth 1989d: 304). Roth saw the collapse of the Polish army despite French help as a reflection of the "inner weakness" of Poland. He was sure that the Polish army, pressed against Prussia's eastern border, would never recover (Roth 1989a: 310–12). Roth believed—or wanted to believe—that only an armistice could save the Polish troops from a bitter fate (1989a: 312).

Having closely examined Roth's reports from the Polish-Soviet War, Maria Kłańska is one of few scholars to find Roth to be unsympathetic to Poland. She concludes that "it is beyond doubt" that Roth had "at this time at least a contemptuous and mistrustful attitude toward the reborn Polish state" (1996: 549). Yet Roth seemed to have misgivings about the Polish people as well, especially as discipline began to dissolve and Polish soldiers attacked the Jewish population. Roth relayed a Russian officer's statement that Polish soldiers had plundered and initiated a pogrom in Suwałki, the event that Roth later called "a little murderous party" mentioned at the beginning of this chapter (Roth 1989b: 320). Since non-Jewish civilians were also targeted by these bandits and since the Russians had not implemented the much-feared socialization policies, according to Roth, "Jew and Christian" alike were happy about the stability that the Soviet army had brought with them (Roth 1989b: 320). Roth seemed to suggest that grassroots enthusiasm for an independent Poland after a century of foreign subjugation was not a given.

The Soviet Russian enemy, however, was greatly romanticized in Roth's articles. The Russian soldiers appeared to him to be well armed, well trained, and in high spirits. Perhaps a reflection of his own political tendencies, Roth remarked that the Soviet forces were an antimilitaristic people's army, whereby the soldiers were "not drilled, but disciplined" as well as "not bullied, but trained." The men ate together with their officers; they behaved correctly and could not be bribed (Roth 1989b: 316–18). Roth barely concealed his adoration for the cultural refinement of one multilingual Russian officer, emphasizing that he was a "convinced socialist," not a communist (1989d: 308). Roth also accepted at face value the officer's claim that the Russians had no interest in crossing the border into Germany and no orders to do so: "In Deutschland haben wir nichts zu suchen!" (1989d: 307).

In contrast to his reports on how the Polish military and paramilitary units raped and pillaged Jews, Roth noted that the Russians had banned all acts of anti-Semitism. In one account, he witnessed how the new Soviet order had even managed to reconcile long-standing enemies: a Jew who offered to sell his belt to a Cossack met only a smile and a polite refusal rather than a lashing with the infamous Cossack whip, the *nagaika*. Given the history of Cossack anti-Semitism and tsarist oppression of the Jews, Roth thus depicted succinctly how the Soviet project had already fostered a great leap forward in tolerance. Roth remarked that there was a disproportionate number of Jews in the Russian army: his source (*Gewährsmann*) estimated on average twelve Jews in every "sotnie" (military unit based on one hundred men) (Roth 1989b: 318). For Roth, the Red Army was progressive and free of anti-Semitism, while the Polish side treated Jews cruelly. The great power of Soviet Russia thus seemed to provide the order needed for a continuation of multicultural coexistence.

Here it is clear that Roth was badly misinformed about the good behavior of the Red Army. On the same day (30 July) on which Roth repeated the Red Army officer's claim of a Polish pogrom against Jews, the Soviet writer and war correspondent Isaac Babel recorded in his diary that Cossacks were plundering Polish and Jewish towns (Babel 2003: 240). He also recorded countless instances in his diary and in his "Red Cavalry" stories about how Russian soldiers murdered Polish prisoners of war (Babel 2003: 130–31, 192–95). The acts of violence against Jews, including murder, seemed to increase as the Russians retreated in late August 1920, and Poland's Jews were quickly disabused of any better treatment under Soviet rule. Babel described how a Jew who had once looked toward Soviet rule now only saw "Yid-killers" (Babel 2003: 276). Cossack troops may have done much of the killing, but the disillusioned Babel laconically admitted that "[w]e too are Cossacks" (Babel 2003: 279). Yet Roth did not relate any such incidents of Soviet atrocities in his reports from the front.

Besides the aforementioned Russian officer's assurance that Russia had no designs on Germany, Roth stressed the strength of anticommunist forces in Germany: "They won't come to East Prussia. They can't come to East Prussia. The swastika is much too strong in East Prussia" (Roth 1989b: 321). At this time, the swastika was not exclusive to the fledgling Nazi movement and was used by various right-wing movements that rejected liberal democracy and the Weimar Republic (Evans 2003: 174). Among these groups were the *Freikorps*, the paramilitary units that sprang up across Germany at the end of the war, but especially in the occupied and contested eastern territories. The *Freikorps* became synonymous with the rise of different ultranationalist, anti-Semitic, and violent subcultures that developed across Central Europe (Gerwarth 2012: 65).

After having brutally repressed the Latvian population in 1919, a large number of these irregular troops withdrew to East Prussia (Sauer 1995: 883, 896). There, they gathered for the next expected battle against a possible Bolshevik invasion. Roth encountered many of these hardened fighters on his way to and from the front in Poland in the summer of 1920. Despite his antagonism toward the *Freikorps*, Roth depicted the German paramilitary units as disciplined. Still, their willingness and desire to resort to violence was omnipresent in his articles. Roth described a menacing encounter with a right-wing paramilitary on a train ride from Insterburg (today Chernyakhovsk). The man, a "young blond person" talking through the open compartment window, was handed a barely concealed weapon from an accomplice on the platform. In a dispute over a seat, another passenger insinuated that the paramilitary could be mistaken for a Jew, although it was obvious that he was "certainly a German man." The *Freikorps* soldier retorted that he would not tolerate the insult. As they disembarked from the train after reaching Königsberg, Roth brushed against the coat pocket of the "swastika hero," who was holding an ammunition box. Roth noted that there was at least one gun in the coat (Roth 1989b: 321–22). The weapons and the escalated confrontation of fellow passengers portended the internecine violence that was to come in Germany. As this last vignette makes clear, Roth seemed to worry more about right-wing paramilitaries than about the Soviet troops approaching Germany's eastern border.

Yet the Polish-Soviet War and *Freikorps* violence were not the only issues that concerned Roth at this time. As part of the Wilsonian moment after World War I, a plebiscite was held on 11 July 1920 to determine whether the East Prussian regions of Warmia and Masuria were to belong to Germany or Poland. Writing from Lyck in early August 1920, Roth reported that only seven people from the town had voted for Poland. He claimed that even nationally conscious Poles preferred belonging to Germany for economic and pragmatic reasons (Roth 2007c: 284–85). Leaving East Prussia shortly before Józef Piłsudski's decisive victory against the Soviet Russian army during the so-called Miracle on the Vistula on 15 August 1920, Roth was obviously wrong about Poland being finished. His ambivalence about Polish designs on Germany's eastern borderlands would eventually overshadow his concerns about German paramilitary violence in the next borderland contest.

Upper Silesia, 1921

Roth wrote again on Polish affairs in the context of the Silesian Uprisings. According to the Treaty of Versailles signed in June 1919, the fate of Upper Silesia was also supposed to be decided by plebiscite. As James Bjork has noted, the local population was given only an "either-or" choice of remaining in Germany or becoming part of Poland. With so much at stake, paramilitary violence flourished in this region. In the First Silesian Uprising of August 1919, the attempted takeover of the region by Polish insurgents was suppressed by the German *Freikorps* and regular military units. In August 1920, shortly after Roth reported the near collapse of Poland during the Soviet invasion, thousands of Germans angered by the news of French aid to Poland demonstrated in the streets of Kattowitz (Gerwarth 2016: 193). The false report that Warsaw had fallen to the Russians led to widespread violence and the murder of several Polish officials. This incident initiated the Second Silesian Uprising, in which some fifty thousand Polish paramilitaries effectively gained control over eastern Upper Silesia. A deal brokered by the French-dominated Inter-Allied Commission gave Polish nationalists greater influence over Upper Silesian police forces in the leadup to the plebiscite in March 1921. In return, Polish paramilitary units were demobilized (Tooley 1997: 77–79, 182–90; Bjork 2009: 216–18; Polak-Springer 2015: 29–31).

When the Inter-Allied Commission contemplated partitioning Upper Silesia following the plebiscite, in which almost 60 percent voted for Germany, Polish nationalist militias once again tried to occupy as much of the region as possible. This Third Silesian Uprising that began on 3 May 1921 was the last and largest of the outbreaks of violence in the region. This uprising was very much a hybrid war in which the Polish state supported an insurgency abroad with thousands of troops while maintaining the guise of a popular uprising by local Silesians (Polak-Springer 2015: 32–33). It culminated in a *Freikorps* victory over the Polish insurgents around the hilltop monastery at Annaberg in late May 1921. In October 1921, the Supreme Council of the Paris Peace Conference went ahead with the partition of Upper Silesia, with Poland gaining the smaller but heavily industrialized eastern part around Kattowitz (Gerwarth 2016: 201).

Roth traveled to Upper Silesia to report on the conflict, but he himself could not escape succumbing to the patriotic mood. Roth disparaged Polish nationalism while being blind to his own prejudices for Germany. In his article "The Right to Upper Silesia," published shortly after the bloody clashes around Annaberg, Roth countered the demographic and economic arguments of Polish nationalists and dismissed the idea that Poles had been oppressed and forcefully Germanized during the Wilhelmine period. Roth noted that if Germany had really tried to Germanize Upper Silesia in the past, then they would have undoubtedly succeeded, but the German government had instead left the language issue up to the people. The linguistic diversity of Upper Silesia, it seemed to Roth, was actually proof of German benevolence and tolerance (Roth 1989e: 568).

In recognition of a phenomenon that scholars have recently called "national indifference," Roth did concede that the average Upper Silesian may not have known the nationality to which they belonged. At the same time, he suggested that the local people had clear national preferences.[9] For Roth, Germanization in Upper Silesia was the result of voluntary social mobility since "industry, science, and trade are German." He noted that there were 109 German newspapers in Upper Silesia with 372,000 subscribers, and only 16 Polish newspapers with 102,000 subscribers. In contrast to this passive Germanization in Upper Silesia, Roth explained that the Polish state was forcibly Polonizing the German minority elsewhere in Poland's newly acquired territories (Roth 1989e: 568). In this way, Roth indicated that Poland—in contrast to Germany—could advance its culture only through brute methods that threatened minority communities. Roth's reasoning echoed the official German position on this matter (Gerwarth 2016: 200–201).

Yet it was likely that his reporting was colored by his own belief in Germany's superior cultural achievements and their inherent attraction to the people of Central Europe. In circular reasoning, Roth justified Germany's right to Upper Silesia with its essential Germanness. He claimed that even the casual observer could see the "German physiognomy" of the land. While Sosnowice (Sosnowiec, in the former Russian partition) was marked by flat barracks and huts, the neighboring German-ruled city of Kattowitz had "all the achievements of modern civilization. No wonder then that the population has leaned toward Germandom" (Roth 1989e: 568). Roth's language connected primitivity, naïveté, and lack of education with Polishness. Giving Upper Silesia to Poland would have been a waste: Roth claimed the Poles would not have been able to run industry without German workers anyway, playing on the trope of Polish incompetence in political and socioeconomic matters. Although he did not use the term *polnische Wirtschaft* (Polish economy), the contrast between German Kattowitz's modernity and Slavic Sosnowice's dilapidated state conjured the cliché that the Poles were unable to make significant progress if left to themselves. Above all, Upper Silesian industry was necessary for German survival, and German rights trumped Polish desires. Roth thus insisted that Upper Silesia should remain part of Germany regardless of its ethnic composition: "We *must* keep Upper Silesia. And even if all our other claims were unfounded, the fact alone that Germany needs Upper Silesia more than any other country ought to let us keep it" (Roth 1989e: 569–70). Such statements actually echo the spiteful discourse about the "lousy East" that Roth accused Döblin of trafficking in just a few years later (Roth 1990: 533).

In another piece published the following day in the *Berliner Börsen-Courier*, Roth began on a more reflective note that saw both sides as victims of an economic struggle. He pondered how a poor Polish writer and he, a poor writer in Germany, would remain enemies for eternity because they both needed affordable Upper Silesian coal to heat their homes in winter. Yet the article then returned to a negative assessment of Poland or Polish nationalism. As during the Polish-Soviet War in 1920, he implied once again that savagery and barbarism existed mainly on the Polish side. Roth recalled that he was inspired in the town of Rost to visit the ruins of a hilltop castle that had belonged to the family of poet Joseph von Eichendorff, implying here the Germanness of the landscape. Lost in nostalgia for his student days, Roth very nearly forgot that he was in a war zone. He was quickly brought back to reality by the sight of a Polish soldier climbing the hill after him. Roth did not describe any dialog in the encounter but only the demeanor of the Polish soldier, who appeared to swagger in his own self-importance and sense of national heroism: "And he hates me because I am a German." Roth, who was unarmed, assumed it would have been counterproductive to explain to the Pole why his hatred of him was wrong, for the soldier would have had no other response than to simply raise his rifle, aim at Roth's head, and pull the trigger (Roth 1989f: 571–72). Here, it is telling how Roth himself assumed the guise of the "German" in the story, and his own belief that reason would not work on the Pole in itself reveals the national-essentialist thinking that had taken root at the time.

At the same time, Roth largely ignored the activities of the *Freikorps* paramilitaries who were not just fighting the Polish insurgents but also spreading anti-Semitic ideas (Sauer 2008). They fostered a culture of violence and feuding that resulted in the murder and disappearance of hundreds during the Upper Silesian unrest (Sauer 2002: 15–16). Given the ambivalence toward German paramilitaries in his writing from less than a year before in Poland and East Prussia (Roth 1989b: 321–22), Roth's apparent support here for the German forces may seem surprising at first. After all, the few scholars who have examined Roth's journalistic writings from the Upper Silesian conflict tend to understand Roth in contradistinction to German hostility toward Poland in the interwar period and World War II. Nicole Frank's 2007 dissertation, for example, uses two previously undiscovered articles by Roth on the Upper Silesian conflict for the *Neue Berliner Zeitung*. In her interpretation, these pieces are "conspicuously positive" and have an "amazingly Poland-friendly position" despite being published in a German newspaper: the Germans *Freikorps* appear "aggressive" (*kampfbegeistert*), while the Polish soldiers were portrayed as "peaceful" (*friedlich*) (Frank 2007: 131–32).[10]

Roth does indeed present a less emotional and one-sided view in these articles uncovered by Frank: for example, Roth relativizes Polish excesses by saying that plundering was part and parcel of war, and he writes how Poles distributed captured booty to civilians. Yet a closer look at the sources does not support Frank's interpretation that Roth was somehow praising Polish paramilitaries on their friendly and capable administration of the civilian population (Frank 2007: 131–32). Roth was rather recounting how Polish authorities were treating civilians with little consistency: sometimes they distributed confiscated goods to civilians, and at other times they arrested Germans arbitrarily. Local government was working, but Roth's word choice ("Behörden, selbst die von den Polen eingesetzten, funktionieren") hints that the Polish success here was an exception to the rule (Roth 2007a: 288). Moreover, Roth did not necessarily present the Polish soldiers as peaceful, but instead he showed that the force operating under Polish national activist Wojciech Korfanty was in dissolution. Roth claimed that many such troops (*Korfanty-Soldaten*) had deserted and could be found working peacefully in agriculture (Roth 2007a: 288). Regarding the Polish officers, Roth merely claimed that their behavior was "superficially quite friendly" (Roth 2007a: 287).

Roth tended to highlight the poor morale and discipline of the Polish militants, in a sense rehashing the stereotypes he had used during the Polish-Soviet War from a year before. The lack of Polish trenches is thus not a sign of less aggression on their part, as Frank suggests (2007: 132). In Roth's report, the Poles preferred not to expend the effort to build them ("Die Polen arbeiten im Gegenteil sehr wenig mit Schützengräben und begnügen sich mit der Aufstellung von Posten und kleineren Patrouillen auf den Wegen, die zu den besetzten Städten führen") (Roth 2007a: 288). Here, Roth was actually denigrating Polish military ability. Despite their overwhelming force of well-fed and well-equipped men, the Poles remained in disarray and were not able to launch an offensive to drive out the Germans. At best, this was a backhanded compliment that remained anchored in the trope of *polnische Wirtschaft*, indicating here that the Poles did not know how to run an army and did not know how to win battles. Poland's insurgent army, it seemed, was very Polish in the widespread German understanding—superficial and lazy.

Frank argues that Roth was denouncing German aggression with his remark on the omnipresence of Iron Cross medals (Frank 2007: 132). Yet Roth intended to say that all *Freikorps* volunteers, despite their motley uniforms, proudly wore their awards for heroism. It was a nod toward the better morale on the German side in contradistinction to Poland's forces. Moreover, the Germans were the ones on the "defensive" yet steadily improving according to Roth. There may have been some bad apples in the *Freikorps*, but a new commander, General Karl Höfer was working to remove unsavory and rowdy elements (Roth 2007a: 288). Tellingly, Roth also regularly used the terms *Insurgenten* and *Aufständische* (rebels) to delegitimate the Polish cause, while the German *Freikorps* were mostly referred to as *Freiwillige*, connoting their voluntary answer to the call to arms to defend the country. Indeed, Roth appeared displeased that the French general Henri Le Rond had called the *Freikorps* "German insurgents" (Roth 2007b: 287). As if to refute Le Rond's mischaracterization of the German side, Roth described the public administration (*Ordnung*) of the *Freikorps* as "exemplary" (*musterhaft*) (Roth 2007a: 287).

Roth was also clear on whom the locals preferred. When the Weimar government started to demobilize the *Freikorps* units, it caused great displeasure among the Upper Silesian civilians (Roth 2007a: 288). Roth in a sense anticipated the wider crisis here, whereby the disarming of the *Freikorps* in Upper Silesia would play out in a second "stab in the back" myth. As James Bjork and Robert Gerwarth have suggested, one of the legacies of the Silesian Uprising was the belief that the Weimar Republic had somehow failed the German fighting man and the German people in 1921 just as the socialists had done in 1918 (Bjork and Gerwarth 2007: 384–85). Frank's newly recovered articles, even if milder in their assessment of the Poles, do not change the trajectory of Roth's other works that culminated in his aforementioned execution fantasy by a Polish militant. Indeed, they seem to fit his previous pattern of upholding German official policy and national claims against those who considered a different national future for the region. Some German activists had begun to search for a peaceful solution by creating an autonomous Upper Silesia under Polish rule, but Roth belittled them as "allegedly German personalities" (Roth 2007a: 287).

What then drove Roth to write in this manner, and what do the reports from the two postwar conflicts tell us about his times? It is likely that the starting point for his apparently pro-German and pro-Soviet positions was a recognition of the danger that nationalisms posed after the collapse of the Central European empires. Roth was writing for a German audience that was still reeling from pain and anger after World War I, and as a "winner" of the war, Poland was part of the Versailles treaty system that many blamed for unfairly punishing Germany. Roth despised all kinds of violence in his war pieces and he remained suspicious of Germany's right-wing paramilitaries, yet the German forces could not help but look better than the Polish militants in the precarious political constellation after the war. Roth's devotion to Germany's moral right during the Upper Silesian conflict thereby crossed political camps. The *Neue Berliner Zeitung* and the *Berliner Börsen-Courier*, both liberal democratic newspapers, catered to widespread nationalist viewpoints, especially vis-à-vis Poland. Ceding a patriotic stance on the Polish question to the *Freikorps* and the far right would possibly endanger the opportunities that educated German speakers like Roth, a Jewish immigrant from provincial Austrian Bukovina, enjoyed. The danger, however, was that he may have inadvertently furthered the interwar myth of the Annaberg struggle, which posited the *Freikorps* spirit against purported enemies to be found not just abroad but also in Berlin and among nationally indifferent opportunists in Upper Silesia (Bjork and Gerwarth 2007: 374).

Conclusion

Roth's depiction of Poland in his war reporting from 1920 to 1921 reveals his deep skepticism about Poland's ability to function as a state and society. Rather than seeing these East-Central European countries within the hopeful Wilsonian moment of national self-determination, Poland was portrayed as both a crippled country and a threat to German interests. His writings might even appear on the surface to be part of a wider German discursive paradigm about Eastern European backwardness. Yet Joseph Roth was not a German nationalist who shared in National Socialist and *völkisch* concepts, as Wolf Marchand provocatively suggested in 1974 (Marchand 1974: 1; Hughes 2006: 7). His position vis-à-vis Poland was embedded in a broader critique of the post-Habsburg order and the new nationalisms in Central Europe after World War I. Although his own political views may have changed, Roth constantly abhorred nationalist jingoism and sought a more respectful understanding of the East.

Roth's portrayal of Soviet Russia as the epitome of progress and tolerance in his war reporting shows especially the complicated and contradictory perceptions that he, like many other Germans, shared toward the East. His sympathetic rendering of Russia and the communist regime may not have been in line with contemporary German mainstream opinion in 1920–1921, but his representation of Poland as an unstable *Saisonstaat* was. Roth's dismissal of the Soviet Russian threat could hence be understood as a reaction to perceived Polish nationalist overreach following World War I. Yet his views on both countries became more nuanced as he did more travel reporting, especially during an extended trip in 1926 to the Soviet Union, which could not be covered here.

Above all, his stance against nationalism deepened as his writing career developed in the early postwar period. He began working for the party organ of the Social Democratic Party, *Vorwärts*, in July of 1922 and contributed regularly to the *Frankfurter Zeitung* in 1923 (Frank 2007: 18, 36). In the fall of

1923, he wrote *Das Spinnennetz* as a serial for the Viennese socialist paper, the *Arbeiter-Zeitung* (Rosenfeld 2001: 16–19). The immediate tensions with Poland had died down, but domestic turmoil was building over the Ruhr crisis. As Robert Gerwarth notes, Roth deftly understood the growing threat posed by the German paramilitary right in this work (2012: 52–53; 2016: 123–24). Roth's story centers on Theodor Lohse, a demilitarized officer who joined a secret military organization bent on overthrowing the Weimar Republic. Yet it was a wide cross-section of society that came to Lohse to become informants, including the crippled Upper Silesian veteran named Klatko (Roth 1967: 55). Perhaps the maimed fighter stood for the injury done to Upper Silesia during the violent conflict that Roth had witnessed. As in his earlier war reporting, Roth recognized that the bitterness of the Wilsonian promise of national self-determination had divided the Central European borderlands. The early postwar battles over Germany's eastern borders had subsided, and Roth now focused on how fear of the enemy within flourished across a broken German society.

Winson Chu is associate professor of modern Central European history at the University of Wisconsin–Milwaukee. Dr. Chu completed his PhD at the University of California, Berkeley. His monograph, *The German Minority in Interwar Poland*, was published by Cambridge University Press in 2012 and received a Fraenkel Prize commendation by the Wiener Library in London. As a 2020–2021 Humboldt Research Fellow at the Center for Holocaust Studies in Munich (Leibniz Institute for Contemporary History, IfZ), Dr. Chu is working on how locals serving in the Kriminalpolizei (German Criminal Police, Kripo) in the Central Polish city of Łódź/Litzmannstadt facilitated the Holocaust.

Notes

* All translations are mine unless otherwise noted.
1. Eva Raffel compares Roth's loss of the monarchy with the loss of his own father. See Raffel (2002: 17, 21).
2. For a thorough account of the Berlin press scene and Roth's journalism, see Frank (2007: 17–36).
3. My thanks to the Research Library of the Herder-Institut in Marburg for providing a copy of this document. Also cited in Bartoszewska (1999: 63; 2005: 117).
4. *Das Spinnennetz* appeared serially in the Vienna *Arbeiter-Zeitung* in late 1923 and was not published as a book until 1967, but Roth himself claimed that *Hotel Savoy* (1924) was his first novel. See Rosenfeld (2001: 16–23).
5. Roth's remarks here appeared in Polish as "jestem poczęści Polakiem." See T. N. Hudes, "Legitymista Joseph Roth," *Wiadomości Literackie*, 15 March 1936, 3. My thanks to the Research Library of the Herder-Institut in Marburg for providing a copy of this document.

6. On Roth's assimilationist views, see Raffel (2002: 19–26).
7. For an early view on the wartime Eastern encounter with so-called "Ostjuden" as salvation for German Jews, see Landauer (1915).
8. One Polish author describes Döblin as a writer with "friendly intentions" toward Poland (*ein freundlich gesinnter Schriftsteller*). See Załubska (1976).
9. On the salience of national indifference in Central Europe, see Zahra (2010). On the question of national indifference in Upper Silesia, see Bjork (2009); Polak-Springer (2015); Karch (2018). For other works on Upper Silesia, see also Tooley (1997); Michalczyk (2011). On the contested memory of Upper Silesia, see Haubold-Stolle (2008); Demshuk (2014).
10. Both documents from the *Neue Berliner Zeitung* are reprinted on pages 286–88 in Frank (2007).

References

Babel, Isaac. 2003. *Red Cavalry*. New York.
Bartoszewska, Irena. 1995. "Józef Roth i Polacy." In *Polonia i przyjaciele Polski w Austrii*, edited by Władysław S. Kucharski, 185–92. Lublin.
———. 1999. "Józefa Rotha działalność publicystyczna na przykładzie 'Listów z Polski." In *Polska—Austria: Drogi porozumienia*, edited by Krzysztof A. Kuczyński, Aleksander Kozłowski, and Bonifacy Miązek, 57–64. Łódź.
———. 2005. 'Łódź i sprawy polskie w twórczości Josepha Rotha.' In *Wizerunek Łodzi w literaturze, kulturze i historii Niemiec i Austrii*, edited by Krzysztof A. Kuczyński, 109–18. Łódź.
Bjork, James E. 2009. *Neither German nor Pole: Catholicism and National Indifference in a Central European Borderland*. Ann Arbor, MI.
Bjork, James, and Robert Gerwarth. 2007. "The Annaberg as a German-Polish *Lieu de Mémoire*." *German History* 25(3): 372–400.
Bronsen, David. 1974. *Joseph Roth: Eine Biographie*. Cologne.
Demshuk, Andrew. 2014. *The Lost German East: Forced Migration and the Politics of Memory, 1945–1970*. New York.
Döblin, Alfred. 1991. *Journey to Poland*. New York.
Dücker, Burckhard. 2003. "Joseph Roths Reiseberichte aus Osteuropa: Sowjetunion, Albanien, Polen." *Estudios filológicos Alemanes* 2: 143–61.
Dzikowska, Elżbieta. 1997. "Ein 'Schwabe' aus Brody: Zum journalistischen Werk Joseph Roths." In *Begegnungen: Facetten eines Jahrhunderts; Helmut Kreuzer zum 70. Geburtstag*, edited by Doris Rosenstein and Anja Kreutz, 22–27. Siegen.
Evans, Richard J. 2003. *The Coming of the Third Reich*. New York.
Forst-Battaglia, Jakub. 1979. "Joseph Roth und Polen." In *Österreichisch-polnische literarische Nachbarschaft. Materiały z konferencji (Poznań 30.11.–2.12.1977)*, edited by Hubert Orłowski, 105–8. Poznań.
Frank, Nicole. 2007. "'Mich zu fixieren, ist unmöglich': Schreibstrategien von Joseph Roth; Eine Analyse neu entdeckter Zeitungsartikel aus seiner Berliner Zeit 1920 bis 1923." PhD diss., University of Freiburg/Fribourg (Switzerland).
Friedrich, Dorothea. 1984. *Das Bild Polens in der Literatur der Weimarer Republik*. Frankfurt am Main.
George, Marion. 2002. "Auf der Suche nach der verlorenen Identität: Alfred Döblins 'Reise in Polen' (1926)." In *Ein weiter Mantel: Polenbilder in Gesellschaft, Politik und Dichtung*, edited by Andrea Rudolph and Ute Scholz, 339–52. Dettelbach.

Gerwarth, Robert. 2012. "Fighting the Red Beast: Counter-Revolutionary Violence in the Defeated States of Central Europe." In *War in Peace: Paramilitary Violence in Europe After the Great War*, edited by Robert Gerwarth and John Horne, 52–71. Oxford.

———. 2016. *The Vanquished: Why the First World War Failed to End*. New York.

Haubold-Stolle, Juliane. 2008. *Mythos Oberschlesien: Der Kampf um die Erinnerung in Deutschland und in Polen 1919–1956*. Osnabrück.

Hughes, Jon. 2006. *Facing Modernity: Fragmentation, Culture, and Identity in Joseph Roth's Writings in the 1920s*. London.

Ignasiak, Detlef. 1987. "Karl Emil Franzos und Joseph Roth als galizische Schriftsteller. Bemerkungen zur Problematik der literarischen Landschaft." In *Galizien—Eine literarische Heimat*, edited by Stefan H. Kaszyński, 65–75. Poznań.

Jakubów, Marek. 2012. "Alles Österreicher? Galizier-Figuren bei Joseph Roth und Andrzej Stasiuk." In *Joseph Roth—Zur Modernität des melancholischen Blicks*, edited by Wiebke Amthor and Hans Richard Brittnacher, 139–50. Boston.

Karch, Brendan. 2018. *Nation and Loyalty in a German-Polish Borderland: Upper Silesia, 1848–1945*. New York.

Kaszyński, Stefan H. 1995. "Der Kampf um Mitteleuropa: Joseph Roth als Reporter im polnisch-bolschewistischen Krieg." In *Österreich und Mitteleuropa: Kritische Seitenblicke auf die neuere österreichische Literatur*, edited by Stefan H. Kaszyński, 63–75. Poznań.

Kłańska, Maria. 1996. "Österreich und Polen im Leben und Schaffen Joseph Roths." *Studia austro-polonica* 5: 535–65.

Koprowski, Jan. 1989. "Józef Roth, Polska i Polacy." In *Kierunki. Tygodnik Społeczno-Kulturalny Katolików* 34, no. 33 (13 August 1989): 13.

Landauer, Gustav. 1915. "Ostjuden und Deutsches Reich." *Der Jude: Eine Monatsschrift* 1: 433–39.

Lazaroms, Ilse Josepha. 2013. *The Grace of Misery: Joseph Roth and the Politics of Exile, 1919–1939*. Boston.

Le Rider, Jacques. 2012. "Arbeit am Habsburgischen Mythos: Joseph Roth und Robert Musil im Vergleich," In *Joseph Roth—Zur Modernität des melancholischen Blicks*, edited by Wiebke Amthor and Hans Richard Brittnacher, 19–28. Boston.

Lipiński, Krzysztof. 1990. "Joseph Roth als 'polnischer' Autor: Seine Übersetzungen und seine Rezeption in Polen." In *Joseph Roth: Interpretation—Kritik—Rezeption; Akten des internationalen, interdisziplinären Symposions 1989, Akademie der Diözese Rottenburg-Stuttgart*, edited by Michael Kessler and Fritz Hackert, 191–200. Tübingen.

———. 2000. "Die 'fremde' Heimat: Polen in den Reiseberichten Joseph Roths." In *Auf der Suche nach Kakanien: Literarische Streifzüge durch eine versunkene Welt*, edited by Krzysztof Lipiński, 103–14. St. Ingbert.

Lughofer, Johann Georg. 2011. "Joseph Roth—ein Schriftsteller der Hybridität oder der Reinheit der Kulturen." In *Joseph Roth: Europäisch-jüdischer Schriftsteller und österreichischer Universalist*, edited by Johann Georg Lughofer and Mira Miladinović Zalaznik, 79–86. Boston.

Marchand, Wolf R. 1974. *Joseph Roth und völkisch-nationalistische Wertbegriffe: Untersuchungen zur politisch-weltanschaulichen Entwicklung Roths und ihrer Auswirkung auf sein Werk*. Bonn.

Mazur, Ewa Maria. 1979. "Die sogenannten polnischen Motive bei Joseph Roth." In *Österreichisch-polnische literarische Nachbarschaft: Materiały z konferencji (Poznań 30.11.–2.12.1977)*, edited by Hubert Orłowski, 109–12. Poznań.

Michalczyk, Andrzej. 2011. *Heimat, Kirche und Nation: Deutsche und polnische Nationalisierungsprozesse im geteilten Oberschlesien (1922–1939)*. Cologne.

Polak-Springer, Peter. 2015. *Recovered Territory: A German-Polish Conflict over Land and Culture, 1919–1989.* New York.

Raffel, Eva. 2002. *Vertraute Fremde: Das östliche Judentum im Werk von Joseph Roth und Arnold Zweig.* Tübingen.

Rosenfeld, Sidney. 2001. *Understanding Joseph Roth.* Columbia, SC.

Roth, Joseph. 1967. *Das Spinnennetz.* Cologne and Berlin.

———. 1989a. "In den Wäldern von Augustowo." *Neue Berliner Zeitung—12 Uhr Blatt*, 31 July 1920. In *Joseph Roth Werke 1—Das journalistische Werk 1915–1923*, edited by Klaus Westermann, 309–12. Cologne.

———. 1989b. "Die Rote Armee." *Neue Berliner Zeitung—12 Uhr Blatt*, 5 August 1920. In *Joseph Roth Werke 1—Das journalistische Werk 1915–1923*, edited by Klaus Westermann, 315–22. Cologne.

———. 1989c. "Jagd auf die fliehenden Polen," *Neue Berliner Zeitung—12-Uhr-Blatt*, 30 July 1920. In *Joseph Roth Werke 1—Das journalistische Werk 1915–1923*, edited by Klaus Westermann, 303–4. Cologne.

———. 1989d. "Die polnische Nordarmee vernichtet: Umfassung und Frontdurchbruch—Panikartige Flucht der Polen—Einnahme wichtiger Orte durch die Russen." *Neue Berliner Zeitung—12-Uhr-Blatt*, 30 July 1920. In *Joseph Roth Werke 1—Das journalistische Werk 1915–1923*, edited by Klaus Westermann, 304–8. Cologne.

———. 1989e. "Das Recht auf Oberschlesien: Polen und Deutsche—Zeitungswesen—Korfantys Agitation—Polen als Absatzgebiet." *Neue Berliner Zeitung—12-Uhr-Blatt*, 28 May 1921. In *Joseph Roth Werke 1—Das journalistische Werk 1915–1923*, edited by Klaus Westermann, 567–71. Cologne.

———. 1989f. "Oberschlesien." *Berliner Börsen-Courier*, 29 May 1921. In *Joseph Roth Werke 1—Das journalistische Werk 1915–1923*, edited by Klaus Westermann, 570–73. Cologne.

———. 1990. "Döblin im Osten." *Frankfurter Zeitung*, 31 January 1926. In *Joseph Roth Werke 2—Das journalistische Werk 1924–1928*, edited by Klaus Westermann, 532–35. Cologne.

———. 2007a. "Den Polen gegenüber! Strengste Grenzabsperrung—Auflösung des Freikorps—'Wie im Jahre 1914'—Defensive der Deutschen. Telegramm unseres Sonderberichterstatters Joseph Roth." *Neue Berliner Zeitung—12-Uhr-Blatt*, 27 May 1921. Reprinted in Nicole Frank. 2007. "'Mich zu fixieren, ist unmöglich': Schreibstrategien von Joseph Roth; Eine Analyse neu entdeckter Zeitungsartikel aus seiner Berliner Zeit 1920 bis 1923," 287–88. PhD diss., University of Freiburg/Fribourg (Switzerland).

———. 2007b. "Die Engländer als Stadtschutz in Oberschlesien: Telegramm unseres Sonderberichterstatters Joseph Roth." *Neue Berliner Zeitung—12-Uhr-Blatt*, 26 May 1921. Reprinted in Nicole Frank. 2007. "'Mich zu fixieren, ist unmöglich': Schreibstrategien von Joseph Roth; Eine Analyse neu entdeckter Zeitungsartikel aus seiner Berliner Zeit 1920 bis 1923," 286–87. PhD diss., University of Freiburg/Fribourg (Switzerland).

———. 2007c. "Die Stimmung in Ostpreußen, Kampf der Parteien—Monarchismus—Der Streik in Königsberg—Die "Nationalbolschewisten"—Wie Grenzorte abstimmten. Von unserem Sonderberichterstatter Joseph Roth. Lyck, 2. August." *Neue Berliner Zeitung*, 3 August 1920. Reprinted in Nicole Frank. 2007. "'Mich zu fixieren, ist unmöglich': Schreibstrategien von Joseph Roth; Eine Analyse neu entdeckter Zeitungsartikel aus seiner Berliner Zeit 1920 bis 1923," 284–85. PhD diss., University of Freiburg/Fribourg (Switzerland).

Sauer, Bernhard. 1995. "'Vom Mythos eines ewigen Soldatentums': Der Feldzug deutscher Freikorps im Baltikum im Jahre 1919." *Zeitschrift für Geschichtswissenschaft* 43: 869–902.

———. 2002. "Gerhard Roßbach—Hitlers Vertreter für Berlin: Zur Frühgeschichte des Rechtsradikalismus in der Weimarer Republik." *Zeitschrift für Geschichtswissenschaft* 50: 5–21.

———. 2008. "Freikorps und Antisemitismus in der Frühzeit der Weimarer Republik." *Zeitschrift für Geschichtswissenschaft* 56: 5–29.

Tooley, Hunt T. 1997. *National Identity and Weimar Germany: Upper Silesia and the Eastern Border, 1918–1922*. Lincoln, NE.

Zahra, Tara. 2010. "Imagined Noncommunities: National Indifference as a Category of Analysis." *Slavic Review* 69: 93–119.

Załubska, Cecylia. 1976. "Polen nach dem I: Weltkrieg in den Augen eines deutschen Schriftstellers." *Studia Germanica Posnaniensia* 5: 29–35.

CHAPTER 6

Suicide Discourses

The Austrian Example in an International Context from World War I to the 1930s

Hannes Leidinger

Introduction

As a starting point, it may be useful to mention the ongoing scientific debates about what can be called "material" or "objective" reality, both generally and in the particular field of historical research on the history of suicide. One should take into consideration what sociologist Jack D. Douglas tried to stress when he analyzed the development of cultures and societies using statistics. For him, it was important to keep in mind that figures, numbers, and rates "reflect discourses and values underlying them" (Goeschel 2009: 3). Similarly Michael MacDonald and Terence R. Murphy, authors of the influential book *Sleepless Souls: Suicide in Early Modern England* (1990) found it "unhelpful," and in a way misleading, "to calculate a suicide rate and engage in quantitative approaches, especially towards suicide" (Goeschel 2009: 2–3; cf. MacDonald and Murphy 1990). Instead, they focused on changing cultural and societal meanings of "depression" and "self-destruction," on the textual construction of suicide, and on the assumptions underlying suicide statistics (Goeschel 2009: 2–3; cf. Leidinger 2012: 17–18). From another point of view, the medievalist historian Alexander Murray tended to support those scholars who stressed individual motivations for self-destruction and, ultimately, the need for freedom of action of the individual (Murray 1998: 9–11, 22–24).

In a recently published study, Norman J. W. Goda came to a different conclusion. He pointed out that "suicide rates correlated in various ways with broader trends" (cf. Goda 2010). Buttressed by studies of the consequences of unemployment—above all during the world depression of the 1930s—and by the results of investigations by the World Health Organization, he found that the hypothesized links between suicide and unemployment rates could be corroborated in detail (Leidinger 2012: 227–29). Without totally thrusting aside the cultural and "constructivist" approaches, Goda emphasized the necessity of a multifaceted methodology in his review of Christian Goeschel's *Suicide in Nazi Germany* (2009: 3). Goeschel himself had pointed out that "we need to combine both schools, the statistical and the cultural," by which he meant that there are, as he put it, "three different ways of approaching the study of suicide: the discursive, the social, and the individual." But Goeschel noted that these were "not simply different methods that should be juxtaposed to each other. Rather than that, there is an interpenetration of all three," because "suicide is not simply a discourse; we also need to pay attention to practice" (Goeschel 2009: 4).

The "Communal Experience"

It was exactly this perspective that turned the work of the French sociologist Émile Durkheim into a milestone in academic and scientific discussion. Using the debate about suicide, among other subjects, to found modern sociology (Durkheim 1983: 17–22), Durkheim rejected the age-old condemnation of suicide as a sin from a theological standpoint, considering it "a most private and impenetrable human act" and advancing the idea that it is the ultimate product of illness or "timeless frailties" (Goeschel 2009: 1–3).

Durkheim's rejection of what had been the common medical wisdom up to the late nineteenth century influenced the habilitation thesis authored in 1881 by the future president of Czechoslovakia, Tomáš G. Masaryk, although Masaryk's analysis employed much vaguer terms and classifications. Durkheim's famous book, *Le suicide* (Paris 1897) was written more concisely, against a backdrop of unease with modernity in its various forms. His book presented a model of suicide as the result of socially determined structures. He distinguished three forms of suicide: egoistic self-destruction, resulting from the suicidal person's lack of social integration; altruistic suicide, which he believed to stem from a desire to die for the cause of society; and anomic suicide, which he understood as the consequence of a complete upsetting of norms and values (Leidinger 2012: 73–74; cf. Masaryk 1881: 234–39; Besnard 2002: 83).

Apart from the possibility that military operations could call forth acts of heroism as expressions of altruistic self-sacrifice, it has to be said that Durkheim's models were not much discussed at the time. Only a specialized magazine, *Das Österreichische Sanitätswesen* (Austrian public hygiene) mentioned *Le suicide* at the end of October 1912, in a bibliography of "suicide themes."[1] At the same time, there was much more intense interest in Durkheim's "suicide theories" in Russia (Morrissey 2011: 202–4). Newspapers in the Danube monarchy, such as the *Wiener Zeitung* and *Pester Lloyd*, referred to the "prominent Parisian professor" only with regard to the new scientific discipline of sociology, along with its methods, its theory of collective consciousness and its emphasis on social entities as opposed to individual phenomena. Durkheim's research on suicide was not even mentioned in margin notes.[2]

World War I and its aftermath contributed to a general neglect of Durkheim, his adherents, and his students, several of whom fell victim to the war (Pickering 2002: 9–11; cf. Lukes 1973; Besnard 2000: 9–46). *Le Suicide* only began to be thoroughly studied by scholars in quite a few countries, including Austria, in the second half of the twentieth century. It must be admitted that his interpretations were inconsistent and inappropriate in light of developments during and after World War I. For instance, his concept of anomic suicide did not correlate with a comparatively low rate of suicide in Austria during the revolution there in 1918–1919 (Leidinger 2012: 487).

On the other hand, there is a connection between Durkheim's theories and the decline of suicide rates as a result of an alleged improvement in social integration in wartime. During World War II, psychiatrists praised the "great communal experience" of mobilization and military conflict. Of course, during the war, frontline soldiers could easily commit suicide by exposing themselves to enemy fire, but such cases would not necessarily be recorded as suicide (Durkheim 1983: 227–31; Leidinger 2012: 189–99).

It is obvious that the boundaries are blurred when one tries to define acts, methods, and reasons for "self-killing." But do we have any proof of the "absorption theory" advanced in Ursula Baumann's book *Suicide from the 18th to the 20th Century* (Weimar 2001)? There Baumann states that the "masculine aggression" (leading to higher rates of "male suicide" in peacetime) will be "absorbed" by the "official acceptance" of violence in the course of regular military operations (2001: 325).

Let us have a closer look at the Austro-Hungarian statistics. According to several quantitative evaluations, suicide rates in the territory of what became the Austrian Republic dropped throughout World War I, decreasing from twenty-six to seventeen suicides per hundred thousand inhabitants (Leidinger 2012: 486–87). Parallel to this result, studies of seven of the most populous parishes in Styria showed similar trends. Between 1914 and 1918, only five suicides were registered there, compared to eighteen from 1919 to 1921, seventeen from 1922 to 1924, and thirty-three from 1925 to 1927.[3] Viennese statisticians, like René M. Delannoy, took it for granted that wartime causes a general "downward movement" in suicide figures. Delannoy stressed the fact that even female suicide rates fell, inferring a general effect of war as "the great communal experience" (Delannoy 1927: 14–17). Some international experts even noted enhanced social solidarity in neutral countries after the beginning of hostilities in 1914. Several contemporary studies confirm these theories.

According to them, reported suicides decreased about 1.6 percent in the Netherlands, roughly 10 percent in Finland, more than 14 percent in Switzerland and about 30 percent in Norway and Sweden (Gruhle 1940: 28; Leidinger 2012: 189).

Contrarily, suicide statistics from Spain show the opposite trend, with a 57 percent increase in suicides after July 1914. When research into the World War II period is considered as well, there is no absolute certainty that stronger social coherence leads to fewer cases of suicide. Notwithstanding different methods of recording suicides in different countries and epochs, as well as the lack of reliability of international and diachronic comparisons, it has to be stated that the decline in women's "world-weariness"—as Delannoy put it—was "not so intensive." German studies went even further. Hamburg officials, for instance, could not see the slightest decrease in female suicide. On the contrary, they registered an increase, as did their colleagues in Prussia (Leidinger 2012: 186–87).

More telling statistics confirm at least parts of Baumann's "absorption theory." A book published in 1937 by physician Raphael Weichbrodt compared quantitative analyses of suicides in the German army before 1914 to those from 1914 onward. Weichbrodt came to the conclusion that the average suicide rate amounted to 43.2 per 100,000 soldiers between 1903 and 1914, but only 14.3 during World War I (Weichbrodt 1937: 118). Unfortunately, we do not have any comparable data for Austria-Hungary because the War Ministry in Vienna, at least for 1917–1918, was ordered not to report suicides or lethal accidents separately in the military death statistics.[4]

There existed other approaches to the connection between wider social conditions and suicide besides Baumann's "absorption theory," Durkheim's view of the dynamics of social integration, and the idea held by some scholars that military conflicts were not only increasing social solidarity but also providing a "distraction from the burdens of everyday life." A more differentiated assessment of the whole problem emerges if one distinguishes possible hidden suicides on the front lines from those attributable to general world-weariness among males in the "hinterland." It is exactly this point of view that caused René Delannoy to advance his original theory. Noting that the male population did not decline in Vienna during the war because refugees sought shelter and soldiers were stationed in the Austrian capital, Delannoy calculated a decrease of 35 percent in male suicides for the years between 1914 and 1918 (Delannoy 1927: 14–15).

In general, it was not completely unlikely that male suicide rates would decrease least in belligerent countries and—according to many statistics—above all in Austria. Like Delannoy, some journalists were also convinced that "world-weariness" had receded into the background during the "great seminal catastrophe." In any case, the *Neues Montagsblatt* (New Monday paper) concluded, "During the war the frequency of suicides dwindled of course, apart from the fact that nobody had time to focus on individual voluntary death amid a widespread dying-off."[5]

Quantification of Changing Discourses

Apart from painstakingly compiling and interpreting suicide statistics, studies of how the media linked suicide and world-weariness bring about more telling results. Under conditions of censorship, it goes without saying that the "unpatriotic act" of suicide was not a focus of press coverage after the assassination of the heir to the Austrian throne in Sarajevo. Suicide discourses ceded their key role as a component of discussions and critiques of modernity to an "optimistic collective feeling for the fatherland" and the subordination of the individual to the interest of the emperor, the nation, and the people(s).

Reports and even short articles regarding suicide disappeared almost completely from the pages of newspapers. The Social Democratic Party's paper *Arbeiter-Zeitung* (Worker's journal) informed the reader about thirty-two "successful" and fifty-six "failed" cases of suicide in January 1914, as well as twenty-eight successful and twenty-nine failed in June 1914. In October and November of the same year, only short reports were published that mentioned two suicides and five attempted suicides. Other newspapers presented similar figures. The *Illustrierte Kronen-Zeitung* (Illustrated crown-daily), which in the peaceful days of the "fin de siècle" was full of headlines and stories dealing with "individual tragedies," published thirty-three detailed articles on suicides on its front page between May 1913 and May 1914. During the same months in the years 1915 and 1916, the "*Krone*" only focused on six similar "tragedies" (Leidinger 2012: 186f).

A slight increase in news reports of suicides can be observed in the second half of the war, whereas the opposite trend persisted in other kinds of publications. For instance, fewer discourses about the phenomenon of suicide and scientific studies of the theme were published at that time. Though far from being complete, an international bibliography of "world-weariness and suicide" compiled in 1927 listed 228 specific titles from the 1870s, nearly 400 in the 1880s, 366 in the 1890s, close to 800 in the first decade of the twentieth century, and 340 within the time span of 1911 to 1913. Also, according to this bibliography, 291 publications focused on the theme from 1921 to 1927. Against this, two-thirds of the 155 works published between 1914 and 1920 were issued in the last months before the outbreak of the world war. Notwithstanding the weaknesses of such quantitative analysis, a general trend is obvious. Along with published statistics on suicide, public discourses on the subject faded away during wartime and the immediate postwar years. In spite of the fact that the discourse and the "reality" of suicide did not always correlate, debates about "world-weariness" and the "dark sides of modernization processes," which reflected the danger to individuals in problematic institutions such as schools and barracks, clearly reached their maximum on the eve of World War I (Leidinger 2012: 97, 184).

Suicide discourses, however, were still important means of social, economic, political, and artistic criticism, above all in the second half of the 1920s. Worldwide economic depression, ideological rifts, and the tensions of the interwar period boosted interest in the topic in the early 1930s. Suicide then again lost significance for the public due to the consequences of World War II, especially in belligerent countries. Even before that, authoritarian and totalitarian rule tended to suppress reporting of "individual weaknesses," "forms of dissatisfaction," and negative aspects of life (Baumann 2001: 370; Goeschel 2009: 69; Morrissey 2011: 350–52).

Quantitative analyses confirm that the discourse patterns of the second half of the nineteenth century still existed in the 1920s. Thus, publications that addressed suicide reflected a long fin de siècle. Special bibliographies and press coverage followed the same patterns. For example, the *Arbeiter-Zeitung* gave maximum attention to "world-weariness" stemming from social and living conditions before 1914 but published only four articles relevant to the theme in March 1919, and no more than three in January 1922. On the other hand, renewed interest in the topic of suicide arose in later years, when the *Arbeiter-Zeitung* reported on fifty-four attempted and completed suicides in January 1925, thirty-four in January 1928, forty-nine in January 1930, and forty-eight in January 1931. A remarkable decrease was apparent afterward, when the Social Democratic Party's newspaper reduced its coverage to nine short notices in June 1932 and seven in January 1934. When we look at the editorial policy of this moderate leftist party organ shortly before it was prohibited in 1933–1934, we cannot blame the "corporative state" with its Catholic political design, propaganda, and censorship endeavors as the only reason for the obvious decline in suicide discourses. Even the Austrian tabloid press, despite its intense interest in "personal and human tragedies," reduced its reporting on suicide topics in the years before the *Anschluss* (Leidinger 2012: 100–101).

Some experts add that certain shifts, and the ups and downs of different suicide discourses, were accompanied by new forms of presentation and a changing media reality. Austria was in many ways a good example of these developments, which transcended borders. At least twenty-nine silent movies produced between 1920 and 1924 in the Alpine republic turned to the theme of suicide. Many other countries were also busy with novels, short stories, poems, and stage plays about self-murder. In Austria, stories about suicides by students continued prewar criticism of contemporary public education well into the 1920s (Leidinger 2012: 98, 372).

Forms of Instrumentalization

Contrary to the lower figures for reported suicides, and the reduced interest in the subject in the general press, specialist magazines, and expert publications from 1914 to roughly 1924, several political groups tried to use "self-murder" for their own ends. After 1918, for instance, scholars in the footsteps of Durkheim believed that times of uncertainty, upheaval, revolution, "chaos," disorder, and economic hardship must inevitably lead to rising "world fatigue." Nationalist circles went even further, characterizing certain cases of suicide as the consequences of the Central Powers' failure and defeat. Shooting oneself was interpreted as an act of patriotism consistent with military tradition and "honor." German "victims" like the scientist Richard Semon and Karl von Schirach, the older brother of the man who later led the Hitler Youth, both of whom killed themselves in November and December of 1918 respectively, were presented as embodiments of "Germany's misfortune" (Goeschel 2009: 11).

Similar "destinies" were reported and discussed. One woman, for example, told a medical doctor in close contact with psychoanalyst circles about her cousin's decision to voluntarily end his life. Receiving more information about the family, the doctor came to the conclusion that the man in question identified the German Empire with his mother, father, and a beloved professor, most of whom had passed away in the previous years.[6]

The notion of a "fatherless society" emerged among experts, especially among those who adhered to deep psychological and psychoanalyst interpretations. At the same time, newspaper articles fostered a depressive mood among those who felt defeated. The *Salzburger Volksblatt* (Salzburg people's daily) and the *Neue Wiener Tagblatt* (New Vienna daily) published short articles about ordinary soldiers, but above all about former officers who killed themselves because of "deplorable living conditions after the armistice."[7] A "nerve specialist" stated in March 1919 that the Hungarian upper class was "afflicted by a certain melancholia." Although it was widespread among Budapest's "elite," this depression, brought about by the "circumstances of the present time" had "not cause[d] a suicide epidemic so far," the specialist concluded (Leidinger 2012: 203).

The debate continued throughout the 1920s. "World-weariness" as a consequence of the Trianon treaty, for instance, was on the mind of journalists. According to the protocols of the parliament in Budapest, the Hungarian prime minister, István Bethlen, took it for granted that the Hungarian army's officer corps had started to "turn away from life." Comparable press coverage in Germany and Austria resulted in inquiries into a special "world fatigue" among the citizenry and above all among the soldiers of the defeated countries. Statisticians stressed the fact that the German Reichswehr and the

Austrian Federal Army had average suicide rates of 1.24 per thousand men in 1921 and 2.8 per thousand in 1924, while at the same time, the U.S. and French armed forces reported lower figures, roughly 0.3 per thousand or less (Leidinger 2012: 203, 354).

Social Democrats (SD) referred to these figures in the Berlin Reichstag and pointed out that the war had drastically changed the collective mentality. They worried that the "value of human life" did not much count for those who were "accustomed to take up weapons in cases of conflict," as one of the SD representatives stated.[8] He recommended the convening of a parliamentary investigatory commission to seek more information about the mental state of soldiers in the postwar society.[9] Politicians, particularly those on the left, demanded details about maltreatment and suicides, especially among the rank and file of Austrian troops. A special parliamentary commission for military matters began its work in spring 1925. By the early 1930s it became clear that—despite continuing conflict between the left and the right that escalated into the "Austrian Civil War" of 1934—suicides were not the result of the then-current ideological debates. Most of the "individual tragedies" that were investigated were not attributable to political rivalries. A nebulous "youth crisis," consisting of family disputes, lovesickness, social ineptness, and alcohol consumption, prompted party activists to act with caution and to refrain from unambiguously blaming politics (Leidinger 2012: 353, 356–64). This of course applied to the more or less moderate "movements" as opposed to the radical parties. After 1918 in Germany and Austria, both Communists and National Socialists attacked the political establishment, placing the blame for suicides directly on the Alpine republic and the "Weimar system" (Goeschel 2009: 22, 28).[10]

Explanations and Theories

It goes without saying that the polemics of political extremists did not (always) concur with statistics and scientific deliberation. In particular, before the mid-1920s, public debates suffered from the attempts of "Bolsheviks" and right-wing groups to denounce their political opponents and the ruling parties by scandalizing and making political capital out of the "social reasons for world fatigue." The "communal experience" only partially helped to explain the comparatively low suicide rates in the ten years after 1914. Some experts pointed out that (young) men in particular were distracted by unrest and societal rupture from 1918–1919 onward (Goeschel 2009: 15).

Even among left-wing groups, eugenic ideas influenced discussions about the meaning of the war and its consequences. The discussions focused on the need to save "the best and bravest part" of society during wartime, and not its "degenerate weaklings and malingerers" (Leidinger 2012: 193f). In this connection, a disconcerting letter from Ignaz Brand, the founder of the *Volksbuchhandlung* (The people's bookshop) in the Gumpendorferstraße, to his Social Democratic Party colleague Ferdinand Skaret, was published in May 1916, just before he committed suicide. Brand informed Skaret that a person should not "stay" any longer than seventy years on Earth, because the "continuation of life" after that birthday is "worth nothing." At the outbreak of the war, Brand decided to "prolong his life" because of his "concern for the fate of the relatives" in the course of the "enemy's invasion." After the "Russian retreat," he was so dismayed by the increasing shortages in the Danube monarchy that he came to the conclusion that it was time for him—as a "useless eater"—to pass on.[11]

On the other hand, the *Arbeiter-Zeitung* published a slightly different statement later on. "Vienna's inhabitants," the newspaper editorialized in 1930, "waited for a reward after so many years of suffering, hunger, fighting, distress and bereavement, after the end of the era of revolution and hyperinflation. But when they realize that there is eventually no happiness possible, and no return to the peacetime of 1913, strong hopes turn into disillusion, despair, and the readiness to throw away their lives."[12]

At that time, experts presented and defended theories that were either unconvincing or that led to great controversies. For instance, rather questionable statements were made positing close links among neurosis, wartime experiences, and diminished neurotic symptoms and suicide against the backdrop of the military conflict (Leidinger 2012: 190–91). As a matter of fact, thousands of suicides that were recorded—among other places—in Austro-Hungarian hospitals gave evidence of a sharp *increase* in "hysteria," "nervousness," "paranoia," "nightmares," "trembling," "shivering," and "shell shock."[13] Quite a few medical doctors at the beginning of the twentieth century considered their patients to be "neurasthenic by nature" or, in many more cases, simply unwilling to fight (Leidinger 2012: 191).

Electroshock "therapy" was advocated by the German physician Fritz Kaufmann and applied to alleged malingerers.[14] This led to new cases of suicide and to an investigation by the War Ministry, as reported by Karl Kraus in his famous book *The Last Days of Mankind* (1918). The "Kaufmann method" was endorsed by the Austrian psychiatrist Emil Redlich, regimental medical doctor Martin Pappenheim, and many others, but it eventually fell into disrepute with the authorities of the Habsburg army (Hofer 2004: 321; Eissler 2007: 124–36).

At the same time, new explanations for wartime neuroses were badly needed in order to avoid inadequate treatment of patients suspected of being "weaklings," seditionists, or cowards simply committed to "self-preservation." The military's general interest was to keep up military readiness and was impacted by a controversy among German scholars about the very existence of traumatic neuroses. The "trauma theory," promoted by the Berlin neurologist Hermann Oppenheim, theorized a distinct diagnosis resulting from the direct physical and psychic effects of traumatic events. It evoked skepticism and objections among his colleagues. Most Austrian experts agreed with those other German experts. As Surgeon-Major Erwin Stransky stated, "The majority of psychiatrists and neurologists viewed such symptoms as hysterical or psychogenic reactions, thus locating the source of the pathology in the subject's mind and not in any external traumata" (Lerner 2003: 79–103, 84).

Meanwhile, such attempts at finding an explanation, as well as the "Kaufmann struggle" and the "Oppenheim controversy," offered a chance for new scientific movements to take root. Behind the scenes of a conference for physicians held in Baden near Vienna in October 1917, many scholars still welcomed Kaufmann's "electro-" or "farad-therapy." But critical decision-makers in the highest ranks of the Habsburg military bureaucracy started to show—although reticently—some sympathy with Sigmund Freud and his adherents (Hofer 2004: 325–26, 358–60, 366).[15]

However, much to the confusion of the military leadership and his foreign audience, Freud himself began to turn away from his original thoughts about self-inflicted deaths. Before 1914, members of his psychoanalytical circle agreed upon the theory that suicide emerged from the traumatic loss of a beloved "object." Though Freud was never fully satisfied with this idea, it took him years to reassess his psychoanalytic theory of suicide, taking into consideration the wartime experience. After four years of bloodshed, his former "libido theory" did not seem convincing to him anymore. The horror of the war led Freud to a new concept, a "death drive" or "death drives" that he explained in his books *Beyond the Pleasure Principle* (1920) and *Civilization and Its Discontents* (1930). From a basically "positive, common-sense" psychology, "Freudianism"—as affected by World War I—became a gloomy and more skeptical way of thinking, centered around a primary human tendency to aggressiveness, dissolution, and "transformation of organic into inorganic order" (Leidinger 2012: 199–200).

In the long run, however, the "thanatomania" concept, derived in part from Freud's work with returnees from the front lines who repeated or reenacted traumatic experiences, had only a moderate influence on the practical work of psychoanalysis. Oppenheim's theories were taken more seriously after World War II and the Vietnam War, until "post-traumatic stress disorder" was included in the American Psychiatric Association's diagnostic manual of mental disorders in 1980 (Leidinger 2012: 209–10).

Shortly after the end of the Great War, in the 1920s, most experts, including even Sigmund Freud to some extent, believed that nervous symptoms would disappear with the end of life-threatening situations, and the "peacetime self," as Freud put it, would recover. From such a perspective, "war hysterics" after 1918 were considered to be "liars, swindlers and pseudo-querulous." Nevertheless, they were often as not judged not to be simulating but to have fallen ill as a kind of survival strategy amid adverse conditions (Lerner 2003: 83, 87).

Normally, it was not easy for veterans with psychiatric disabilities to get pensions or any other support for their ailments. This was even more true because of the continuation of certain strands of prewar medical thinking, such as faith in the "healing power of the iron bath" and of war as "reinvigorating bodies and minds" and "remasculating a nation grown weak and effeminate" (Lerner 2003: 91). Against this backdrop, the "sentimental culture of death" was "supplanted by the hardened and cynical notion of 'life in death.'" This inverted approach to general trauma characterized the mindset of the long fin de siècle.[16]

Other discourses confirm the thesis that interest in the causes of suicide revived after the caesura of 1914–1918. Activities and debates regarding suicide prevention are good examples of that interest. Places welcoming those who were "life-tired" were founded in Vienna in the late 1920s and early 1930s by different churches and ideological groups such as the "Ethical Community" and "Freethinker Circles." These groups reflected the general tendencies of the previous four or five decades (Leidinger 2012: 417–20). New York hosted the first "telephone counselling" in 1895, and "Anti-Suicide Bureaus" under the auspices of the Salvation Army offered completely confidential advice to depressed people and potential suicides from 1906. Austrian newspapers like the Christian Social Party's *Reichspost* (Empire post) informed their readers about the new institutions in 1913. At nearly the same time, similar "offices" and "associations" opened in Berlin and Vienna (*Reichspost* 3 January 1913: 2; Wedler 2000: 89–100, 90). In 1921, the *Neues Morgenblatt* (New morning paper) and the *Reichspost* announced the establishment of dispensaries for "world-sickness and weariness."[17] Spurning the old Christian condemnation of suicide, the *Reichspost* opposed its criminalization and referred to roughly 50 percent of all cases of "world-weariness" as a sort of illness, such as "incurable melancholia." The "Anti-Suicide Bureaus" of the Salvation Army, according to the *Reichspost*, used "psychoanalytic methods," but not "those currently fashionable among certain Viennese medical doctors," rather the "good old holy confession."[18]

Sigmund Freud, who was the target of the newspaper's gibe, stressed the importance of his own notions and "discoveries" in the late nineteenth century in the following words:

> The terrible war that is just over has been responsible for an immense number of such maladies—to which the name "traumatic neurosis" is attached—and at least

has put an end to the inclination to explain them on the basis of organic injury to the nervous system due to the operation of mechanical force.... The patient has so to speak undergone a psychical fixation as to the trauma. Fixations of this kind on the experience which has brought about the malady have long been known to us in connection with hysteria. Breuer and Freud stated in 1893 that hysterics suffer for the most part from reminiscences. In the war neuroses, observers... have been able to explain a number of motor symptoms as fixation on the factor of the trauma. (Freud 2009: 7–8)

All in all, even current literature comes to comparable conclusions. Heated debates about shell shock, for instance, did not result in new scientific insights, methods, or diagnoses. Rather, they reactivated, modified, and—more than anything else—privileged psychiatric and psychological notions, techniques, and practices that already existed before the war (Leidinger and Moritz 2013: 177).

Conclusion

Freud's *Beyond the Pleasure Principle* and *Civilization and Its Discontents* introduced innovative theories, albeit the "death drive" remains highly controversial for many psychoanalysts (Quinodoz 2005: 193). Additionally, and more or less as a marginal note, Freud offered another promising perspective and interpretation when he stated, "A severe injury inflicted at the same time by the trauma lessens the chance of a [war] neurosis arising ... so far as the term has any significance apart from a reference to the occasion of the appearance of the illness" (Freud 2009: 24). As he opened up new fields of conjecture, Freud put his finger on possibilities for neutralizing or mitigating psychic diseases caused by physical and mental suffering.

Apart from that, and in part contrary to the idea that the statistical incidence of neurosis and of suicide rise and fall together, the assumption of a "lower level" of "world fatigue" and suicide is only strengthened by Durkheim's thesis of a link between enhanced social integration in wartime and the decline of "world-weariness."

At the same time, the reliability of the general trends mirrored in various statistics—above all when the same bureaucratic practices for compiling cases and rates are used—indicate the "reality" of suicide and the importance of social and economic influences as causative factors. There are good reasons to question the reality of "absorption," "social integration," and similar psychological theories. But statistics suggest that they in fact hold validity for the era of World War I and to some extent for the first half of the 1920s (Goeschel 2009: 18). This of course applies even more to suicide discourses, which receded into the background for approximately a decade after 1914.

The "seminal catastrophe" of war until 1918 represented a hiatus or "time out" but marked no specific final break with regard to suicide and suicide discourses. Press coverage, scientific explanations, statistics, and a "real changing will to life" in diverse societies, countries, and cultures at varying times are clearly reflected in the discourse patterns of the long fin de siécle from about 1870 to approximately the 1930s. Prewar discussions and interpretations re-emerged in the 1920s, along with tendencies to exploit the problem of suicide for ideological reasons.

From a political point of view, mental diseases and "world fatigue" were seen as an unwanted burden hindering postwar reconstruction and, in the 1930s, endangering military preparedness. Concern with the patriotic community and its "defensive capacity" marginalized the respective debates.

To conclude, basically two different consequences were obvious:

On the one hand, patriotic and military principles—combined with the harsh treatments of the patients—condemned the "weaknesses," fears and nightmares of soldiers in particular and of a whole war generation in general. These resolute attitudes—together with the media neglecting the theme or adopting a negative framing of it—excluded mentally impaired, depressed, and world-weary individuals from the national collective. Apart from single relief campaigns for "life-tired individuals" before and after World War I, there were hardly any exceptions. For example, the overwhelming majority of physicians worked in line with the military commands too.

On the other hand, the decisive social reaction—mirrored above all by the behavior of the authorities, the press coverage, and even the endeavors of medical experts—stood in contradiction to the lack of terminological clarity and the uncertain results of scientific research. Controversial standpoints drew on incompatible explanations for the interaction between the body and the psyche. What is more, neurologists, psychologists, and psychiatrists could not even agree upon the fact that a phenomenon like "war neurosis" or something akin to "post-traumatic stress disorder" caused an increase or a decrease of suicidality. The same applies to other analyses. The scientific findings are not clear. It would be untrustworthy to make crystal clear what the studies were achieving. Yet, the past debates—for instance with a view to the statistics and explanations of absorption theories—still function as a stimulation for future research work.

Hannes Leidinger serves as a visiting professor, lecturer, and associated researcher at the Universities of Vienna, Salzburg, Berne, and Budapest. He is the head of the Viennese branch of the Ludwig Boltzmann Institute for Research on the Consequences of War and member of the Commission for Military History and Military Monuments of Historical Importance at the

Austrian Federal Ministry of Defence, head and member of various research projects, curator of several exhibitions, and author of numerous publications on Austrian history and the development of Central and Eastern Europe in the nineteenth and twentieth centuries.

Notes

 1. *Das österreichische Sanitätswesen* 24(43), 24 October 1912, 1275.
 2. *Wiener Zeitung* 48, 27 February 1908, 16; *Wiener Zeitung* 274, 29 November 1912, 8; *Pester Lloyd* 145, 20 June 1909, 19.
 3. Quantitative analysis by the author, based on sources from the following parishes "with roughly 13,000 Catholics": Graz——Hl.Blut, Graz——St. Peter, Graz——St. Leonhard, Graz——Kalvarienberg, Leoben——Waasen, and Leoben——St. Xaver. Another parish taken into account, Graz——St. Andrä, counted about thirty-four thousand "souls" in the investigation period. The mentioned documents are preserved in the archive of the diocese of Graz.
 4. Comments regarding the compilation on the mortality of Austro-Hungarian soldiers in the years of 1914 to 1917.
 5. *Neues Montagblatt* 2, 3 January 1921, 5.
 6. Heinrich Mengg, "Gespräche mit einer Mutter über Selbstmord," *Zeitschrift für psychoanalytische Pädagogik* III. Jg., folder 11-13, subfolder "Selbstmord," August–October 1929, 344–55, 344.
 7. *Salzburger Volksblatt* 120, 27 May 1919, 5; *Neues Wiener Tagblatt* 72, 14 March 1919, 10.
 8. Parliamentary Commission of the Social Democratic Party, Report 1925, Federal Ministry of Military Affairs, Zl. 851, Austrian State Archives/Archives of the Republic.
 9. In this connection, see also the latest research on postwar military violence, particularly that committed by war veterans. Cf. Gerwarth and Horne (2012).
10. Sources for Austria, among many others: Die Rote Fahne no. 683, 6 August 1921, 7; and no. 12, 14 January 1931; Der Kampfruf no. 11, 29 November 1930, 1; no. 3, 17 January 1931, 1, 5; no. 13, 28 March 1931, 2; no. 19, 9 May 1931, 5; no. 31, 1 August 1931, 1; and no. 3, 20 February 1932, 1.
11. *Ilustrierte Kronen-Zeitung*, 17 May 1916, 7.
12. *Arbeiter-Zeitung*, 7 August 1930: 6.
13. Rosenhügel Mental Home, Vienna, Medical file nos. 3176, 3178, 3179, 3190–3192, 3195, 3200, 3212, 3216, 3222, 3224, 3225, 3227, and 3259, Austrian State Archives/War Archive.
14. The suspicions of medical doctors, neurologists, psychologists, psychiatrists and many other experts derived from a multitude of reports regarding "self-mutilation." See, for instance, Expert Reports on Self-Mutilations (Medicines, Toxins, etc.), file nos. 21-106, 21-111, 21-119, 21-130, 21-133, 21-142, 21-146/2, 21-153, 21-153/2, 21-155, 21-156, 21-167, 21-168, 21-175, 21-180, 21-183, 21-184, 21-184, 21-185, 21-187, 21-201, 21-207, 21-208, 21-209, 21-211, 21-212, 21-221, 21-222, 21-224, 21-225, 21-227, 21-249, 21-251, and 21-256, War Ministry/Dep. No. 14, Box 2243, Austrian State Archives/War Archive.
15. Regarding the treatment of war neuroses in the Dual Monarchy, see also the contribution of Maciej Górny in this volume.
16. *Pester Lloyd*, 10 June 1922, 2.

17. *Neues Motagblatt*, 2, 3 January 1921: 5; *Reichspost*, 276, 7 October 1921: 4.
18. *Reichspost* 276, 8 October 1921, 4.

References

Baumann, Ursula. 2001. *Vom Recht auf den eigenen Tod: Die Geschichte des Suizids vom 18. bis zum 20. Jahrhundert*. Weimar.
Besnard, Philippe. 2000. "La destinée du Suicide: Réception, diffusion et posterité." In *Le Suicide un siècle après Durkheim*, edited by Massimo Borlandi and Mohamed Cherkaoui, 185–218. Paris.
———. 2002. "Suicide and Anomie." In *Durkheim Today*, edited by W. S. F. Pickering, 81–86. New York.
Delannoy, René M. 1927. "Selbstmorde und Selbstmordversuche in Wien im Jahre 1926." In *Statistische Mitteilungen der Stadt Wien*, Jg. 1927 (3).
Durkheim, Émile. 1983. *Der Selbstmord*. Translated by Sebastian and Hanne Herkommer. Berlin.
Eissler, Kurt R. 2007. *Freud und Wagner-Jauregg vor der Kommission zur Erhebung militärischer Pflichtverletzungen*. Wien.
Freud, Sigmund. 2009. *Beyond the Pleasure Principle*. Authorized translation from the second German edition of 1922 by C. J. M. Hubbeck. Mansfield Center, CT.
Gerwarth, Robert, and John Horne. 2012. *War in Peace: Paramilitary Violence in Europe after the Great War*. Oxford.
Goda, Norman J. W. 2012. "Review of Christian Goeschel 'Suicide in Nazi Germany.'" *Journal of Contemporary History* 45(4): 883–85.
Goeschel, Christian. 2009. *Suicide in Nazi Germany*. New York.
Gruhle, Hans. 1940. *Selbstmord*. Leipzig.
Hofer, Hans-Georg. 2004. *Nervenschwäche und Krieg: Modernitätskritik und Krisenbewältigung in der österreichischen Psychiatrie, 1880-1920*. Wien/Köln/Weimar.
Leidinger, Hannes. 2012. *Die BeDeutung der SelbstAuslöschung: Aspekte der Suizidproblematik in Österreich von der Mitte des 19. Jahrhunderts bis zur Zweiten Republik*. Innsbruck/Wien/Bozen.
Leidinger, Hannes, and Verena Moritz. 2013. "Nervenschlacht: 'Hysterie,' 'Trauma' und 'Neurosen' am Beispiel der Ostfront 1914–1918." In *Jenseits des Schützengrabens: Der Erste Weltkrieg im Osten; Erfahrung -Wahrnehmung—Kontext*, edited by Bernhard Bachinger and Wolfram Dornik, 157–77. Innsbruck/Wien/Bozen.
Lerner, Paul. 2003. *Hysterical Men. War, Psychiatry, and the Politics of Trauma in Germany, 1890-1930*. Ithaca/London.
Lukes, Steven. 1973. *Emile Durkheim: His Life and Work; A Historical and Critical Study*. London.
MacDonald, Michael, and Terence R. Murphy. 1990. *Sleepless Souls: Suicide in Early Modern England*. Oxford.
Masaryk, Thomas Garrigue. 1881. *Der Selbstmord als sociale Massenerscheinung der modernen Civilisation*. Wien.
Mengg, Heinrich. 1929. "Gespräche mit einer Mutter über Selbstmord." *Zeitschrift für psychoanalytische Pädagogik* III.
Morrissey, Susan K. 2011. *Suicide and the Body Politic in Imperial Russia*. Cambridge.
Murray, Alexander. 1998. *Suicide in the Middle Ages*. Vol. 1: *The Violent against Themselves*. Oxford.

Pickering, W. S. F. 2002. "Durkheim: The Man Himself and his Heritage." In *Durkheim Today*, edited by W. S. F. Pickering, 9–17. New York.
Quinodoz, Jean-Michel. 2005. *Reading Freud*. London.
Wedler, Hans. 2000. "Entwicklung der Suizidprävention in Europa." In *Suizidforschung und Suizidprävention am Ende des 20. Jahrhunderts*, edited by Manfred Wolfersdorf and Christoph Franke, 197–222. Regenburg.
Weichbrodt, Raphael. 1937. *Der Selbstmord*. Basel.

CHAPTER 7

The "Healthy Nerves" of the Nation
War Neuroses in Austria-Hungary and its Successor States

Maciej Górny

Though foreseen by many, the Great War took almost everyone by surprise. The generals ignored the experience of the Russo-Japanese War of 1904–1905 and the Balkan Wars. They underestimated the power of new and modernized weapons—artillery and machine guns. Despite some quite precise estimates of the potential for human casualties in the conflict (suffice it to mention Jan Gottlieb Bloch's multivolume study and the less ambitious work by Jan Baudouin de Courtenay [Courtenay 1913; Bloch 2005]), the numbers of dead and wounded exceeded the capacity of the combatants' field hospitals. Equally surprising were the thousands of prisoners of war who had to be fed and accommodated. This last issue grew in importance as soon as it became clear that hope for a peace before Christmas 1914 would not materialize. War clearly differed from its prewar image.

Human reactions to the experience of war were no less of a surprise. August Krasicki, a Polish aristocrat in Austro-Hungarian uniform, noted in summer 1915,

> A crazy woman from Starawieś near Bychawa was brought here. She lost her senses in fear and among heavy shooting. The woman constantly cries, lamenting after her children, money, home and—surprisingly—she does it in verse just like in *The Wedding* by Wyspiański. The rhythm is precisely the same. This woman died suddenly in Rzeszów. Probably she was given an overdose of morphine by a doctor because she tossed on her bed and had to be tied up. (Krasicki 1988: 265)

The nervous breakdown of a woman, even if accompanied by such an unusual performance, was not completely at odds with contemporary ideas about the human psyche. Hysteria was popularly attributed to women in general. "Nervous exhaustion" was less popular as a diagnosis of the source of a man's psychosis. Men in uniform were expected to radiate strength of body and mind and possess a certain immunity to extreme external stimulation. This was another instance where the war forced specialists to change their opinion. Obviously, soldiers predominated among those suffering from variously defined war-related psychoses. In the Austro-Hungarian army, this problem became apparent in the first months of the war, which were marked by constant offensives and retreats.

In summer 1914, a soldier of the 20th Infantry Regiment, Stanisław Kawczak, took part in a chaotic retreat from the Congress Kingdom of Poland:

> A couple of dozen men, crowded on an island, fight each other. A Slovak takes off his clothes and laughing diabolically, points at me, crying: "Pod' sem kamrát [Come here, comrade]!" In front of me I see a captain from the 100th Regiment shoot himself in the head. (Kawczak 1991: 40)

Approximately a month later, an Austrian medical officer described the behavior of some entrenched soldiers: "[The] mentally ill cannot stand this infernal shooting. . . . They either sit on the bottom of the trenches or run up to avenge dead comrades and try to go over the top. At night they are all sent to the rear" (Składkowski 1990: 30, 31). Both quoted authors stress the fact that officers were among those affected.

A certain nervousness among the Habsburg Empire's high ranks was also observed by Józef Piłsudski. In his opinion, fear was the proper diagnosis:

> There are many things in war that happen to soothe the nerves of lower and higher rank commanders. You overload your subalterns with work, you set fire to windmills, you hang innocent people—everything under the pretext of avoiding danger, but actually to calm the shattered nerves of this or that gentleman. À la guerre comme à la guerre! (Piłsudski 1988: 44f.)

Though many of Piłsudski's psychological observations proved quite correct with time, in this case he seems to have underestimated the scale of the phenomenon, which was typical not only of the Dual Monarchy but of all other belligerents as well (Duroselle 1994; Borodziej and Górny 2014: 115–25).

However, repressions against civilians, typically entirely groundless, were not the most spectacular evidence of a psychological crisis. The first months of the war were marked by a massacre of the high ranks of the Austro-Hungarian army. According to Manfried Rauchensteiner, by the end of 1914, approximately forty officers above the rank of colonel had died, a striking number in comparison to only thirty who fell in the subsequent four years of fighting (Rauchensteiner 2010: 67–76). Even more striking were the circumstances of their death. Not by accident, these circumstances were kept secret by the military authorities. Nonetheless, rumors of a wave of suicides among the generals were soon heard across the whole country. Generals Friedrich Wodniansky von Wildenfeld, Ernst von Froreich, and Franz Peukert were among the first victims (Rauchensteiner 2010: 74).

Those casualties were accompanied by an unusually high number of officers who were dismissed from service on grounds of "neurasthenia," or nervous breakdown. Although official communiqués named various accidents and illnesses (like falling from a horse, stomach problems, rheumatism, or sudden deafness) as causes, no extraordinarily sharp intellect was necessary to discern the real reason for the couple of dozen dismissals among higher officers in the first months of the war (Rauchensteiner 2010: 74). Francis Joseph's attempt to stop this storm among his personnel failed (Rauchesnteiner 2010: 76). The problem could no longer be ignored.

Quite naturally the experts—the psychiatrists—were expected to find a solution. Their activities have been subject to historical research of growing intensity since the 1990s (Dührssen 1993; Rousseau 1997; Lerner 1998; Lerner 2000 Hofer 2004; Hofer 2011; Hermes 2012; Leidinger and Moritz 2013; Ruszała 2016), although they have never occupied as prominent a place within World War I studies as shell shock and psychiatric cure on the Western Front. Much less can be said about the continuities of wartime practices in East Central Europe after 1918. This chapter attempts to deliver a preliminary outline of this particular aspect of military psychiatry.

Within the Habsburg army, they constituted a small fraction of the body of medical doctors gathered in the Militär-Sanitäts-Komitee, a specialized unit of the War Ministry in Vienna, which was led by *Generalstabsarzt* Zdzisław Ritter von Juchnowicz-Hordyński. Under the directorship of Bruno Drastich, the psychiatry department of the Militär-Sanitäts-Komitee included a number of renowned Vienna-based specialists: Alexander Pilcz, Emil Redlich, Julius Wagner-Jauregg, Erwin Stransky, Alfred Fuchs, Artur Schüller, and Otto Marburg (Ruszała 2016: 270–72). Many of them were quite confident about their contributions to the war effort. Along with proponents of the sciences of man, psychiatrists can rightly be said to have profited from the conflict. It gave them new career possibilities and a lot of research material (Wolf 2008: 167). However, there were some barriers to successful psychiatric practice in the Habsburg army, both theoretical and practical. The year 1917 marked both a climax and a serious crisis in Austro-Hungarian war psychiatry, a crisis that subsequently affected the successor states of the Habsburg Empire.

This chapter analyzes the psychiatrists' responses to war neuroses in the Habsburg army during World War I and the postwar social and political conflicts that followed in Austria-Hungary's successor states. Although in many respects they copied the trends and methods of their German colleagues, psychiatrists of Austria-Hungary developed a particular attitude toward their patients. Unable to communicate with non-German-speaking subjects of the monarchy (and thus deprived of the ability to influence them by means of suggestion or hypnosis), specialists such as Julius Wagner-Jauregg responded to the challenge with particularly harsh treatment based on discipline, coercion, and electroshock therapy.

Though the Austrian specialists occupied prominent places at the center of the monarchy's medical milieu, their opinions met with rather lukewarm acceptance among Polish and Czech military doctors in the Habsburg service and were ignored altogether after 1918. While they were close to their Austrian and Hungarian colleagues in their medical practice, military psychiatrists in the successor states were very different in their understanding of the ethnic hierarchies of the Empire. Rather than following Viennese psychiatry, specialists in Poland and Czechoslovakia contributed to the positive self-assessment of their newly dominant nationalities. "Healthy nerves" that had once been attributed by the Viennese doctors to the German Austrians within the Habsburg army were now understood to characterize their Slavic ex-brothers in arms.

The Short Career of Electroshock Therapy

Before 1914, Hermann Oppenheim placed the burden of responsibility for psychic disturbance on physical impairments of the nervous system. His concept was still widely endorsed at the time of the German Reich's entry into the war. Indeed, during the first months of the conflict, German psychiatrists identified psychological disorders as the immediate effect of physical or psychological shock endured when witnessing bullet wounds or dead comrades. While Oppenheim's diagnoses shaped state policies in Germany, they were eventually abandoned.

Two factors contributed to that decision. First, patriotic fervor impelled doctors to look to the war as an opportunity to heal the nation's psyche. The "weak nerves" and "emasculation" that had increasingly been remarked upon in the previous decades were expected to give way to true warrior masculinity. Second, Oppenheim's concepts had particular financial and military consequences: traumatized soldiers were released from duty and received remuneration comparable to that offered for physical injuries in peacetime. Both facts played into the hands of the critics and detractors of the neuropsychiatrist from Berlin. The official change in paradigm took place in September 1916, during a conference of psychiatrists and neurologists in Munich. Most of those in attendance agreed that soldiers suffering from psychological disorders owed their misery to a lack of will to fight rather than to injuries.

This position was also adopted (by and large) by Austro-Hungarian psychiatrists, regardless of their attitudes toward psychoanalysis. In Hungary, a clash similar to that which took place in Germany saw Artur Sarbó defeated by a coalition of opponents of psychoanalysis and advocates of the therapeutic effect of frontline service, such as Ernő Jendrassik and Jenő Kollarits. Even Sigmund Freud postulated the birth of a new, combative "war ego" that would incite fear in the old *Friedens-Ich*, or "peace ego." One of the speakers at the 1918 Budapest psychiatric congress claimed that, in a state of war, healthy individuals are typically—and normally—ready to sacrifice their lives for the sake of a community. Deviations from this attitude required a corrective, by way of psychoanalysis or traditional methods of psychological therapy (Wolf 2008: 135f.).

During the Munich conference, participants were particularly impressed by the presentation of the neurologist Max Nonne, who had served in the western theater. He related his experiences with hypnosis, claiming that he had successfully eliminated the symptoms of frontline hysteria. Nonne, a disciple of Charcot (Lerner 1998: 79–101), used hypnotic suggestion to convince patients that they suffered no symptoms. Once he succeeded, the patients were deemed to have achieved a full psychological recovery. According to Nonne, this form of therapy only worked if both the doctor and the patient believed it to be the only option, and that it would be effective. Nonne downplayed the role of one "therapeutic" element that often seemed even more necessary for the success of the healing process—the element of coercion.

The alternative to Nonne's therapy of suggestion and hypnosis was hardly enticing. Since war was perceived as conducive to psychological health (rather than destructive to the nervous system), therapy centered on the separation of the afflicted from their families (and civilian communities in general) and the maintenance of military discipline (Lerner 2000: 13–28). The prominent Austrian psychiatrist Julius Wagner-Jauregg and his students (Erwin Stransky et al.) created a therapeutic model that cited Nonne's ideas but mostly relied on repression. The declared reason for this bias in Austria-Hungary was the multiethnicity of the army. No hypnotic suggestion was possible—Wagner-Jauregg claimed—between a German-speaking doctor and a non-German-speaking patient (Wagner v. Jauregg 1917: 18). Yet, taking a wider perspective, he did not hesitate to consider his approach at least closely akin to suggestion. In his memoirs published in the 1950s, Wagner-Jauregg took some pains to show his course of treatment in a favorable light:

> There was not a single one among the patients of our hospital who couldn't be healed in a matter of days. The means we were using can be deemed suggestive in a broad sense of that word. In some situations, and in some cases, they were also, probably, deterring: isolation, monotonous though sufficient diet, distasteful medicine or faradization. (Wagner-Jauregg 1950: 69)

Wagner-Jauregg claimed to have tested all these "deterring" measures on himself, notably to make sure the electric current applied in "faradization" (electroshock therapy) was not too strong. He suggested the same self-sacrifice to his colleagues, albeit, as he later confessed, rather without success. In his postwar memoirs he emphasized that almost none of his patients had been sent back to the trenches. They were all, as he claimed, situated in the rear, still useful for the war effort but without immediate contact with the battlefield (Wagner-Jauregg 1950: 70f.). Contradictory of those claims, Wagner-Jauregg and many of his fellow doctors soon acquired dubious fame as hunters of malingerers. The "cure" they offered has been subjected to historical study in the last ten years. Let us recall some of the relevant elements of the treatment.

Suggestion, as meant by Wagner-Jauregg, could not be easily performed in a multiethnic environment, yet there was a way to communicate despite nearly insurmountable linguistic hurdles. He put emphasis on positive and negative visual strategies. The positive consisted of showing examples of successful treatments to new patients, suggesting that they could expect a short hospitalization and prompt relief. The negative visual stimulus was closely connected to the positive. Patients were shown all the main elements of the treatment in detail. Wagner-Jauregg remembered an officer who, having been shown another soldier undergoing faradization, asked not to be subjected to the same cure. After two days of superficial treatment, this officer, who had not been able to walk for two years, declared himself fully capable of returning to the ranks (Wagner v. Jauregg 1917: 16).

Naturally, reducing the role of Austro-Hungarian psychiatrists to this kind of sadistic treatment alone would be unjust. Along with the methods preferred by Wagner-Jauregg, many others were attempted, and thousands of patients happily avoided faradization. Psychoanalysts had quite differing views of war neuroses. In general, selection of the most efficient cure was a matter of lively discussion. Some doctors believed that bromides and rest sufficed.[1] On the other hand, with casualties growing rapidly, there was a dire need for a swift and efficient cure. None of the available methods could possibly surpass faradization, which offered seemingly immediate relief and, in addition, emanated from the flowering of modern technology (there were some attempts to go further in this direction by using the Roentgen apparatus).

The climax of the popularity of electroshock in Austria-Hungary coincided with the Brusilov Offensive in summer 1916. It was Viktor Gonda, director of the clinic at the military hospital at Rózsahegyi (after 1918 known as Ružomberok, in Slovakia) who, in summer 1916, declared the sensational results of his lightning-paced therapy based on electric shocks of varying intensity. His reward was a promotion, laudatory pieces in the daily press, and the adoption of his method throughout Hungary. In May 1917, Gonda's treatment was thoroughly explained to readers of the *Prager Tageblatt* (Prague daily) by Alexander Roda Roda, a star of Austro-Hungarian journalism:

> I saw Doctor Gonda at work some time ago. He let faradic current run through the body of a patient until he noticed tetanic contraction of his muscles. The current's voltage and the duration of the treatment differed with every case. Until now, Doctor Gonda has treated 822 patients this way; that is, 822 were immediately cured without any retraction or accident, even by heart disease. . . . Now, I will restrain my excitement and fantasy and simply try to tell what I saw at Doctor Gonda's hospital. To begin with, Doctor Viktor Gonda, *k.u.k Assistenzarzt*, currently with the rank of a lieutenant, 27 years old. . . . Doctor Gonda is tall, slim, pale and silent—a prototype of the modern scientist. Two aid-workers carry an infantryman, Demeter Papp, on a litter. Paralyzed for fifteen months. . . .
> "Stand up!"
> He cannot. The aid-workers help him to rise from the litter and to stay straight.
> "Go!"
> He takes two crutches and creeps shakily a few steps before he falls completely exhausted. Doctors examine the patient. . . . Diagnosis: traumatic neurosis. The patient lies down on a bed. Doctor Gonda sits by him and mildly whispers: "Don't give up, lad! Take it as a hero and as a Hungarian! It will hurt a little. Just bite in the towel and don't cry!"
> The nurse installs an electrode, Doctor Gonda uses the other. Two seconds. Demeter Papp moans loudly while his legs stretch up.
> "Now take a rest, my son." And after a short pause: "sit down . . . !" Again, pause and Gonda says: "Attention!"
> Demeter Papp stands up shakenly, visibly moved.
> "On the march!"
> Papp marches—without any help—several steps to the next chair. There he is allowed to rest for a moment. And then he jogs, yes, he jogs, three times round the room. He makes a stop by Doctor Gonda and tries to kiss his hand. Laughing gently, Gonda refuses. "Number 819," he murmurs. (Roda Roda 1917: 2–3)[2]

Electroshock was widely implemented in Cisleithania, the lands of the Austrian crown, as well. In some cases—contrary to the claims made by Doctor Gonda (Gonda 1916a: 445)—to deadly effect for the patients.[3] Though similar treatment was even more common in the German Reich (there it was known as the "Kaufmann treatment" [Hermes 2012; Eckart 2014: 148–50]),[4] Austria-Hungary was particularly fertile soil for faradization. This was at least partly due to the organizational structure of psychiatric hospitals. Contrary to most other belligerents, Austria-Hungary tended to centralize this branch of medical care after 1917. Vienna and Graz were the biggest centers for psychiatric treatment (Hofer 2004: 309). Only a little more than a year after the publication of Gonda's story, however, treatment with electroshock gradually began to be abandoned, first in Germany and subsequently in Austria-Hungary.

The evolution of the soldiers' treatment can be seen as illustrative of the changes in the way their suffering was interpreted. In the first phase, relief of "neurasthenic" officers was the main objective of the cure. At this stage, patients were still distributed among many local hospitals, with some units provisionally turned into psychiatric clinics. As the situation worsened on all fronts, the standard of medical care deteriorated, and the attitude toward patients changed. At the same time, therapy for mental illness was centralized, and in July 1917 the procedure for transport of mentally ill soldiers was finally settled upon by the Ministry of War (Ruszała 2016: 276–78). Gonda's therapy was based on an assumption—widely shared by German and Austrian psychiatrists—that it was essential to break the will of the patient in order to force him out of his illness. To Wagner-Jauregg, there was practically no difference between a malingerer and a neurotic. The symptoms were similar, but the neurotic cheated not only on everybody around him but also on himself (Wagner v. Jauregg 1917: 14).

To be fair to the Austro-Hungarian military medical service, one should remember that being an inpatient could be the best possible option for a soldier. First of all, transport of aggressive or overactive soldiers to the rear was difficult and could be dangerous. As some memoirs indicate, they were sometimes left behind to an unknown fate (Składkowski 1990: 362f.). Second of all, patients who did not respond to their treatment and were released from hospital joined the starving masses, more than eight thousand of whom died of hunger in the Austrian part of the empire alone (a similar calculation for the German Reich exceeds seventy thousand victims [Faulstich 1998: 61; Eckart 2014: 136]). Finally, only now are appearing the first case studies devoted to smaller hospitals (Maria Hermes on Bremen [2012]), which show that the psychiatrists' radicalism expressed itself more vividly in their writings than in their everyday work.

There were at least two reasons for abandoning electroshock therapy. First, after the reintroduction of the Parliament in Vienna, and the softening of censorship, a huge scandal was a real threat. The fact that some of the patients did not survive their treatment could no longer be covered up by stories about the efficiency of faradization (Kloocke, Schmiedebach, and Priebe 2005: 47f.). The number of complaints against psychiatrists grew. In spring 1917, newspapers published articles about suicidal patients desperate to avoid electroshock. Social democratic deputies picked up the story and made it political (Leidinger and Moritz 2013: 157–77). Another reason was practical: faradization proved inefficient. The reported number of those actually cured had been massively massaged. In fact, many resisted their treatment, and most of those who were supposedly healed returned to their symptoms shortly after their cure.

The Ethnic Interpretation of War Neurosis

The demise of electroshock therapy was a relief not only for patients. Sigmund Freud and his disciples had every reason to expect psychoanalysis to take the lead over such therapies. Late in September 1918, the Fifth International Psychoanalytic Congress in Budapest was held under the general theme "On the Psychoanalysis of War Neuroses." It was on this particular occasion that Freud delivered his first (and last) lecture based on a preexisting text that he prepared especially for the purpose. His main objective, and the reason for his diligence, was to suggest the establishment of a network of psychoanalytic therapy units for military patients (Dührssen 1993: 200–204). Due to his somehow unlucky timing, this idea had no chance of being fulfilled. As a matter of fact, it never came under discussion in government circles.

Despite being hated symbols of state oppression, none of the leading psychiatrists of the day faced important charges or even any inconvenience after 1918. Some of them, including Wagner-Jauregg, were nominated to the Kommission zur Erhebung militärischer Pflichtverletzungen (Commission for Eliminating Military Violations of Duty), which had been set up in December 1918. In 1920, former military patients charged Wagner-Jauregg with particular brutality, and he resigned from the commission. The trial against him and his collaborators ended in their exculpation (Eissler 1979: 55). Freud's role in the trial was that of an independent expert. While his written opinion basically supported Wagner-Jauregg, he took advantage of the opportunity to criticize him as one of the enemies of psychoanalysis.

Though the trial had no practical consequences, hostility between the two psychiatrists grew even more. Their conflict contributed to the image of psychoanalysis as a "humanistic" form of psychiatry. As a consequence, only one of Wagner-Jauregg's assistants, the Pole Michał Kozłowski, was dismissed on grounds of sadistic behavior (Rousseau 1997: 13–27). But even in his case, no relevant punishment was meted out. In 1918, Kozłowski became a Polish citizen and a successful doctor in Cracow. The only reminder of his wartime cooperation with Wagner-Jauregg was Kozłowski's translation of Wagner-Jauregg's brochure devoted to hypnosis, telepathy, and suggestion, published in Cracow in 1920 (Wagner-Jauregg 1920). Wagner-Jauregg characterized the dissolution of the Austro-Hungarian monarchy as the main reason for Kozłowski's postwar impunity:

> Had all those connivers whom I happened to treat somewhat indelicately in our clinic during the war thought of accusing me, the resulting case would be a sight to see. But most found themselves in the successor states, happily disconnected from Vienna; the remaining few questionable neurotics felt slightly ashamed and

did not want their heroic achievements to become the subject of public interest. (Wagner-Jauregg 1950: 71)

In fact, most of the "connivers" hailed from the linguistic peripheries of the monarchy. Czechs and Ukrainians (Ruthenians) predominated among the victims of Wagner-Jauregg's cure. Hans-Georg Hofer points to the Viennese doctors' anti-Slavic resentment as the catalyst for their radicalism (Hofer 2004: 340). In fact, there is something to that. During the war, Wagner-Jauregg described various kinds of malingerers who unmistakably and without exception belonged to the Slavic nationalities, predominantly Czechs:

> Another soldier ... pretended to be a deaf mute, successfully passing through two hospitals. In the third, he became so impertinent that he was seen talking to his friends on the street, after which he confessed to have been cheating. He imitated other patients' symptoms claiming that his neurosis was the effect of an explosion. In this case simulating ... was meant to cover desertion. (Wagner v. Jauregg 1917: 10)

Certainly, the conviction that practically no Austrian Germans or Hungarians malingered or deserted the army was a stereotype, equally as "true" as the stories told about Bohemian regiments deserting en masse to the enemy.[5] Nonetheless, these stories were believed not only among the common folk but also among the intellectual elites, psychiatrists included. For some of them, the empire's multiethnicity was clearly its weakest spot. This idea was formulated scientifically by Erwin Stransky, a student of Wagner-Jauregg. According to his interpretation, the Slavs were intellectually inferior to Germans and subconsciously hated their benefactors (Górny 2014: 239–41). Some other psychiatrists searched for correlations between nationality and psychic neurosis.

The tendency to see the nondominant nationalities of the Habsburg monarchy as especially prone to mental disorders was not restricted to medical publications. The feuilleton by Alexander Roda Roda that introduced Viktor Gonda to the wider German-speaking audience also subscribed to this narrative. The brave Demeter Papp, a proud member of Hungary's "ruling race," was an exception to the rule. Most other patients of Gonda's belonged to non-Magyar ethnic groups. Roda Roda mentioned a Bosnian (who probably "actually was a little bit crazy") and a Romanian (i.e., a representative of a nationality that, according to Roda Roda, tended to be extremely heavily affected by neuroses [1917]). The unofficial creation of ethnic hierarchies on the shaky ground of psychiatric diagnoses had a tacit agenda, namely that of rebuilding the threatened self-esteem of Austria-Hungary. The healthy nerves of the Germans and Austro-Germans were a common element in the majority of these theories (Hofer 2004: 333). And healthy nerves, German-speaking psychiatrists never failed to mention, were badly needed to win the Great War.

Unpublished memoirs by Stransky give some interesting insight into the worldview of the Habsburg psychiatrists. Stransky was born into a Jewish family (as were many other Austro-Hungarian psychiatrists) in the ethnically mixed area of Moravian Silesia. Anti-Czech attitudes are clearly discernible in Stransky's comments, as well as in the opinions of others he quotes. To Stransky, the abyss between civilized Germandom and the barbaric Slavs was insurmountable, as illustrated by his memories of the Galician campaign. Crossing the border, he was shocked, "as if I was saying 'adieu' to Europe."[6] Lemberg (present-day Lviv) was an obscure mixture of Vienna and Asia. In these circumstances, the sight of the distant Carpathians was a relief, because they resembled Stransky's native region. In contrast to Moravia, Galicia was a wild country, inhabited by equally wild people. In Stransky's estimation, many of them remained on the level of children:

> [The] representatives of the Slavic lower classes are like women: good and faithful as long as they feel you are a "Pan" ("Lord") with a whip in one hand that should be decisively and energetically used in case of need, and with a sugar cube in the other hand. . . . [A] boring teacher who has neither the one nor the other will inevitably be laughed at.[7]

Stransky claimed to have drawn his conclusions from this observation. He describes himself slapping Jewish soldiers in the face in order to teach them proper German pronunciation.[8] This does not necessarily mean that after his return to Vienna in 1915 he applied the same roughness to his patients. Nevertheless, he seems to fit into the category proposed by Hofer: German nationalists with patronizing and, at times, hostile attitudes toward the "East," in this case to Slavs and backward Jewish-Slavic Galicia.

There is, however, another interesting element in Stransky's memories, something we could call his auto-psychoanalysis. He stresses his early fascination with strong (especially physically strong) individuals. His stern father was the first of this kind. Next came Swiss youngsters he met on holidays. They despised him as a small and weak Jewish child and harassed him for his "Jewish behavior," as Stransky puts it. His wish was to be strong and rooted in the native soil, "like an Aryan."[9] The greatest authority in his life was, however, Wagner-Jauregg. Wagner-Jauregg embodied three features that Stransky most admired: "right origin," physical strength, and hostility toward Jewish "psychologizing" (which was characteristic of Sigmund Freud).[10] The ideal of the nonpsychologizing psychiatrist, an authority who controls his emotions and also dominates his patients, is a returning motif in Stransky's autobiography and in his professional self-perception:

> I myself had the opportunity to see the rightfulness of these psychological rules during my first fight. It was an extremely dangerous Cossack night assault on a

medical column marching to the south-east from Lemberg in the days of our withdrawal from Galicia, late August 1914. Stress and excitement when the shooting started were soon replaced by calm. My colleagues and I did not even try to hide from bullets. We discussed with restraint our possible actions in case the enemy would attack us. Later on, with shrapnel exploding over our heads ... I did not think, I only wished to be able to fall asleep; but when the danger started to threaten us, I immediately was possessed by strong nervous excitement. That was the "reaction" described by many authors in similar cases. (Stransky 1918: 62)

We should not overemphasize conclusions made on the basis of Stransky's autobiography. Surely, they do not sufficiently explain either his or his colleagues' attitude toward their soldier-patients. On the other hand, they may, perhaps, help to supplement the list of motivations for the ruthlessness of the doctors. Because Freud talked about psychiatrists acting as "machine guns behind the lines," it has become customary to associate their behavior with opportunism, which led them to value the interests of the army over their patients' lives and health. But there were other motivations as well. One, elaborated by Hofer and others, was ethnic and racial prejudice. The other, as in Stransky's case, was based on the doctors' desire to overcome their own weaknesses and to control their bodies and minds. Their privileged position and authority led them to believe they actually had succeeded in that, as Stransky's Galician memoirs show. Having overcome their fear, they expected uniformed patients to do the same. Unfortunately, few "connivers" lived up to this ideal. In the doctors' eyes, most of the war's neurotics and malingerers were weak. And weakness was something neither Wagner-Jauregg nor Stransky were ready to tolerate.

Center and Peripheries

The crude chauvinism manifested by Stransky and Wagner-Jauregg offers a highly suggestive yet misleading picture of Habsburg military psychiatry. Their position was central both in spatial terms and in terms of their professional authority in the country. Nevertheless, not every military psychiatrist in Austria-Hungary belonged to the country's titular nations. Notably, Galician and Bohemian hospitals employed dozens of specialists who, while fluent in German and part of the Austro-Hungarian medical milieu, were Polish or Czech in their language, national identity, and culture. How did they receive the emotional statements of their Viennese colleagues?

The outcome of analysis of wartime and postwar issues of the main medical and military medical journals in both Czech and Polish surprises the historian with the scarcity of local opposition to the narratives of the imperial center. The absence of openly critical polemics in the presence of wartime censorship is unsurprising, but any references at all are largely missing after 1918. Military hospitals, notably in Galicia and Bohemia, continued their work after 1918 without revolutionary personal changes. During the war, central Galician and Bohemian medical journals devoted surprisingly little attention to the luminaries of Austro-Hungarian psychiatry. In the *Časopis lékařů českých* (Czech doctors' magazine), Gonda's treatment techniques received altogether only two short and hardly enthusiastic notes.[11]

The Cracow-based *Przegląd Lekarski* (Medical review) went much further in ignoring Gonda's therapy, which was hotly discussed in German circles, instead publishing a thorough analysis of the modern treatment of "war neurotics" penned by Professor Jan Piltz of the Jagiellonian University (Piltz 1917: 395–405). Besides medical literature, Piltz's study was based on his personal experience with up to ten thousand military psychiatric patients hospitalized in Cracow after 1914. Neither Wagner-Jauregg nor Gonda (nor any other of their Austrian and Hungarian colleagues for that matter) received mention in Piltz's article, which described therapies used in Cracow. Piltz chose to refer to his former French professors, something that would hardly be seen in wartime medical journals in Vienna or Berlin. Among German-language psychiatrists, he referred primarily to Karl Bonhoeffer. While he admitted that he had used faradization himself (though, as he notes, only applying low current and never on a large scale), the Polish doctor refused to accept that there was any miraculous cure for wartime neurotics. In his view, every case required a different combination of psychotherapy (which he believed to include the usage of electroshock), and other, more traditional means of "healing the nerves." A similar line of reasoning was advanced by one of Piltz's subordinates, Eugeniusz Artwiński. In 1918 he summarized his observations from the Cracow university hospital, discussing the theoretical positions of Charcot, Oppenheim, and Struempell. He stressed the value of practical experience with psychoanalysis, understood broadly (Artwiński 1918: 278–79).

Such a plethora of opinions, and the relative open-mindedness of Polish psychiatrists even during the war, seem to confirm a situation analogous to the Bremen psychiatric hospital analyzed by Maria Hermes: that is, regional eclecticism as opposed to the radical, exclusive approach to therapy promoted by those practicing in the center. It was probably Leo Taussig, a Czech psychiatrist whose scientific career was accelerated by his research into war neuroses, who offered interpretations that were closest to those penned by Wagner-Jauregg. The Prague doctor based his university habilitation (dissertation) on his wartime experience with neurotics. Starting with some typical criticism of Oppenheim's theory, he subscribed to the thesis that war-related psychoses merely reflected preexisting mental disorders. Like Oppenheim's German critics, he considered his patients primarily as obsessive hypochondriacs. However, contrary to them, he did not deem it necessary to break the neurotic's will immediately and brutally. Instead of the bellicose language used by his German and Austrian colleagues, he preferred to offer long-term administrative measures. Thus, in his view, it was essential for the state to reduce the perverse incentive of financial compensation for mental disability and offer neurotics a cure rather than a reward for their illness (Taussig 1918: 425).

After 1918, the trend was to more or less ignore the Austro-Hungarian wartime debate about neuroses and instead explore other "national" schools and multiple methodologies. To some extent, political calculations seem to have played a role in determining which studies would be cited in the military medical press of the successor states. On the pages of the initial volumes of the Polish *Lekarz Wojskowy* (Army doctor) (established in 1920) and the Czechoslovak *Vojenské zdravotnické listy* (Military medical sheets) (established in 1925), references to German and Austrian colleagues were indeed very rare. Decisively more space was devoted to French military medicine (Gepner 1920: 14–18). Not only there did international esteem for the former Central Powers deteriorate. Germans, Austrians, Hungarians, and Bulgarians (as well as Soviets) were absent from the international congresses of military doctors held in Brussels (1921), Rome (1923), and Paris (1925) (Franz 1925: 110–16).

In some cases, the scarcity of references to German and Austro-Hungarian wartime psychiatric celebrities resulted from the different personal and scholarly experiences of medical personnel. Zygmunt Bychowski, a Polish military neurologist, was one of the first to summarize his wartime psychiatric experience in a lecture given in Warsaw in September 1919 and published in *Lekarz Wojskowy* in 1920 (1920: 13–24). In Bychowski's opinion, which he based on his personal experience in Moscow military hospitals during the Great War and in Warsaw military hospitals after 1918, any theorizing about the cause of war neuroses was futile. "The whole debate on this matter was, to my mind, premature, as it would be premature to discuss about the victims of an earthquake while the earthquake still isn't over and new victims keep coming" (Bychowski 1920: 22).

Nevertheless, Bychowski believed himself to have identified a "phylogenetic" reflex that resulted in strong physical symptoms, primarily in the case of soldiers who were in danger of being sent back to the trenches. No such symptoms could be identified among prisoners of war and, interestingly, soldiers as well after 1917, when the Russian army lost its power to discipline them. Though Bychowski's observations in many ways echoed Wagner-Jauregg's opinions (including putting terms like "traumatized" in quotation marks), he made no reference to the Austro-Hungarian wartime discussion. Similarly to other Polish and Czech authors, he shared some of the Austrian's conclusions, but he claimed to have reached them based on his own observations.

From the perspective of the history of psychiatry, the collapse of the Habsburg monarchy resulted in two quite contradictory developments. First,

Austrian attempts at centralizing the regulation of the methods of psychiatric treatment ceased to play any relevant role in the successor states. Given that even before 1918 the Austro-Hungarian medical milieu was far from unanimous and united on their theories, this is hardly surprising. The decentralization of medical practice, which was promoted even in Germany during the Great War, as shown by Maria Hermes, became the rule in the successor states and was promoted in wartime medical journals such as the *Przegląd Lekarski*. As a matter of fact, the multiplicity of therapies applied and openness toward a variety of interpretations of the cause of war neuroses came to be perceived as a merit of medical science in East-Central Europe. An impressive expression of this understanding of military psychiatry was delivered by the Polish general Janusz Gąsiorowski, who was the author of an extensive bibliography of the discipline published in 1938.

Second, shortly after the end of hostilities, war neuroses ceased to attract the attention of medical scholars to the extent they did in the wartime Austro-Hungarian and German psychiatric milieu. Joanna Urbanek, who recently analyzed the content of interwar Polish military medical journals and other publications, ranked such neuroses as the fourth most popular topic of the contemporary literature, yet even that ranking owes much to Urbanek's including all texts devoted to neurology. Interest in the subject was decisively decreasing.[12] This was partly due to wartime research by Constantin von Economo, an Austro-Hungarian military doctor who was at the time an assistant at Wagner-Jauregg's clinic in Vienna.

In 1917, von Economo described cases of encephalitis lethargica, a brain disease with symptoms largely similar to those that had been observed among war neurotics. An epidemic of the disease affected Romania, Austria, France, Germany, and the United States from 1917 to 1924. Von Economo's intuition was that the disease was caused by a virus attacking the brain, causing somnolence, among other symptoms:

> The blood vessels of the cortex were surrounded by a mantel of lymphocytes and plasma cells. Here, too, we found the peculiar nests of polymorphonuclear leukocytes, as well as much more distinct neuronophagia than in the other parts of the nervous system. The peculiar inflammatory alterations appear in spots. (Economo 1997: 581–85).

The "Economo disease" was an argument for seeking out a physical, neurological background for neurotic symptoms and thus weakened the position held by military psychiatry.

Though it was hardly a surprise at a time of pandemic influenza, typhoid, and malaria, as well as an emotional debate about the influence of sexual diseases on the military, there was a change in the discourse. On the one hand, with the dissolution of the Habsburg monarchy and emergence of the new states, studies of war neuroses lost much of their appeal. On the other hand, they acquired a nationalist stimulus. Ethnic hierarchies, such as those imagined by Wagner-Jauregg and Stransky, were not congruent anymore with the self-perception of the armies of the new nations. The theoretical foundations of the expertise of medical professionals in the successor states recalled the time before the Great War and, specifically, before the great nervous crisis of the Habsburg army.

In some respects, this return to the prewar understanding of how psychiatry can contribute to national defense involved simply ignoring the practical experience of wartime. In a characteristic study by a Czech psychiatrist, Vilém Forster, fear, which had been at the very heart of Wagner-Jauregg's, Gonda's and Stransky's diagnoses, and those of their Polish and Czech contemporaries as well, was replaced by bravery:

> Moral preparation and education for war is just as important a factor in victory as technical and organizational preparations. The confidence of the army in the meaning of their fight is of decisive importance here. Consciousness of its importance to your existence, and that of your family and nation, whose interests cannot be separated from your own, gives the soldier the impetus to sacrifice and heroism, an impetus a mercenary or someone who is forced to fight could never sense and follow. Precisely these two characteristics made the Hussites invincible fighters. They believed their cause was righteous and they knew they could not count on mercy if they lose a battle. (Forster 1926: 55–62)

Conclusion

Forster's article pointedly marks a shift of perspective. "'Healthy nerves," which for some Austro-Hungarian psychiatrists belonged primarily to the dominant nationalities of the monarchy and—above all—to the doctors themselves, became a characteristic of the new nations. Rooted in the military history of the Bohemian Middle Ages (and in other positive self-stereotypes elsewhere), national pride paved the way for a swift passage out of "nervousness" to national consolidation. Yet it would be misleading to claim that military psychiatry in East Central Europe simply turned back to where it stood in 1914. War-related medical science thrived on two neighboring yet different fields: that of the medical discourse and that of the actual cure. Sometimes, as in the case of Gonda, discourse overwhelmed practice with effects detrimental to the patients. Sometimes, as in the early postwar Polish and Czech medical publications, theorizing was manifestly subordinated to practical experience of wartime doctors. Between these two extremes there was a broad field of negotiation most of psychiatrists in this period fit in quite comfortably.

Maciej Górny is deputy director of the Tadeusz Manteuffel Institute of History Polish Academy of Sciences and research fellow at the German Historical Institute in Warsaw. His research interests are East-Central Europe in the nineteenth and twentieth centuries, history of historiography, discourses on race, and World War I. His latest publications include *Science Embattled: Eastern European Intellectuals and the Great War* (2019, Polish 2014) and *Nasza wojna*, 2 vols. (together with Włodzimierz Borodziej, 2014, German 2018, English edition forthcoming). Between 2014 and 2019 he was editor in chief of *Acta Poloniae Historica*.

Notes

1. F. Erős, "Pszichiátria és pszichoanalízis az első világháborúban," accessed 16 May 2017, http://www.balassiintezet.hu/attachments/article/562/Pszichiatria percent20es percent20pszichoanalizis percent20az percent20elso percent20vilaghaboruban perc ent20(Eros percent20Ferenc).pdf, 10.
2. I am grateful to Kamil Ruszała for pointing out this feuilleton.
3. Same text: "Rasche Heilung der Symptome der im Kriege entstandenen 'traumatischen Neurose.'" *Wiener klinische Wochenschrift* 29 (1916): 951.
4. For more information on Fritz Kaufmann and his "treatment," see the contribution of Hannes Leidinger in this volume.
5. For the most recent study of this topic, see Lein (2011).
6. Österreichische Nationalbibliothek (ÖNB), Sign. Cod.Ser.n.24109, Nachlaß Erwin Stransky, Autobiographie, 325.
7. Österreichische Nationalbibliothek (ÖNB), Sign. Cod.Ser.n.24109, Nachlaß Erwin Stransky, Autobiographie, 333.
8. Österreichische Nationalbibliothek (ÖNB), Sign. Cod.Ser.n.24109, Nachlaß Erwin Stransky, Autobiographie, 387.
9. Österreichische Nationalbibliothek (ÖNB), Sign. Cod.Ser.n.24109, Nachlaß Erwin Stransky, Autobiographie, 390–91.
10. Der Mensch Wagner-Jauregg, Sign.Cod.Ser.n.24041, Erwin Stransky collection, Österreichische Nationalbibliothek, Vienna, Austria.
11. *Časopis lékařů* 38, 1916: 1177; 13, 1917: 35.
12. The study by Joanna Urbanek on Polish military psychiatry in the interwar period has been accepted for publication in *Acta Poloniae Historica* for 2021.

Bibliography

Artwiński, Eugeniusz 1918. "W sprawie nerwic urazowych." *Przegląd Lekarski* 57(41): 278–83.
Baudouin de Courtenay, Jan 1913. *Bracia Słowianie*. Kraków.
Bloch, Jan 2005. *Przyszła wojna pod względem technicznym, ekonomicznym i polityczny*. Warszawa.
Borodziej, Włodzimierz, and Maciej Górny. 2014. *Nasza wojna: Imperia 1912–1916*. Warszawa.
Bychowski, Zygmunt 1920. "Neurologja wojenna." *Lekarz Wojskowy* 1(4): 13–24.

Duroselle, Jean-Baptiste 1994. *La Grande Guerre des Français, 1914–1918: L'incompréhensible*. Paris.
Dührssen, Annemarie 1993. "Die 'strenge tendenzlose Analyse' und die Psychoanalyse der Kriegsneurosen." *Zeitschrift für Psychosomatische Medizin und Psychoanalyse* 39(3): 200–204.
Eckart, Wolfgang U. 2014. *Medizin und Krieg. Deutschland 1914–1924*. Paderborn.
Eissler, Kurt R. 1979. *Freud und Wagner-Jauregg von der Kommission zur Erhebung militärischer Pflichtverletzungen*. Vienna.
Faulstich, Heinz 1998. *Hungersterben in der Psychiatrie 1914–1949: Mit einer Topographie der NS-Psychiatrie*. Freiburg im Breisgau.
Franz, Karel 1925. "Třetí mezinárodní sjezd vojenských lékářů a lékárníků v Paříži (od 20. do 25. dubna 1925)." *Vojenské zdravotnické listy* 1(2): 110–16.
Forster, Vilém 1926. "Emoce strachu a hněvu, jejich fysiologie a vojenský význam." *Vojenské zdravotnické listy* 2(2): 55–63.
Gąsiorowski, Janusz 1938. *Bibliografia psychologii wojskowej*. Warszawa.
Gepner, Tadeusz 1920. "Z praktyki wojskowo-lekarskiej. Neurologia w armji francuskiej." *Lekarz Wojskowy* 1(6): 14–18.
Gonda, Viktór 1916a. "A háború okozta 'traumás neurosis' tüneteinek gyors gyógyitása." *Orvosi Hétilap*, 13 August.
———. 1916b. "Rasche Heilung der Symptome der im Kriege entstandenen 'traumatischen Neurose.'" *Wiener klinische Wochenschrift* 29.
Górny, Maciej 2014. *Wielka Wojna profesorów: Nauki o człowieku (1912–1923)*. Warszawa.
Hermes, Maria 2012. *Krankheit: Krieg; Psychiatrische Deutungen des Ersten Weltkrieges*. Essen.
Hofer, Hans-Georg 2004. *Nervenschwäche und Krieg: Modernitätskritik und Krisenbewältigung in der österreichischen Psychiatrie (1880–1920)*. Vienna.
———. 2011. "Beyond Freud and Wagner-Jauregg: War, Psychiatry and the Habsburg Army." In *War, Trauma and Medicine in Germany and Central Europe (1914–1939)*, edited by H.-G. Hofer, C.-R. Prüll, and W. U. Eckart, 49–71. Freiburg.
Kawczak, Stanisław 1991. *Milknące echa. Wspomnienia z wojny 1914–1920*. Warszawa.
Kloocke, Ruth, Heinz-Peter Schmiedebach, and Stefan Priebe. 2005. "Psychological Injury in the Two World Wars: Changing Concepts and Terms in German Psychiatry." *History of Psychiatry* 16(1): 43–60.
Krasicki, August 1988. *Dziennik z kampanii rosyjskiej 1914–1916*. Warszawa.
Lein, Richard 2011. *Pflichterfüllung oder Hochverrat? Die tschechischen Soldaten Österreich-Ungarns im Ersten Weltkrieg*. Münster.
Leidinger, Hannes, and Verena Moritz. 2013. "Nervenschlacht: 'Hysterie,' 'Trauma' und 'Neurosen' am Beispiel der Ostfront 1914–1918." In *Jenseits des Schützengrabens: Der Erste Weltkrieg im Osten; Erfahrung—Wahrnehmung—Kontext*, edited by Bernhard Bachinger and Wolfram Dornik, 157–77. Innsbruck.
Lerner, Paul 1998. "Hysterical Cures: Hypnosis, Gender and Performance in World War I and Weimar Germany." *History Workshop Journal* 45(1): 79–102.
———. 2000. "Psychiatry and Casualties of War in Germany, 1914–18." *Journal of Contemporary History* 35(1): 13–28.
Piłsudski, Józef 1988. *Moje pierwsze boje*. Łódź.
Piltz, Jan 1917. "Przyczynek do nauki i t.zw. nerwicach wojennych i ich leczeniu na podstawie własnych spostrzeżeń." *Przegląd Lekarski* 56(48): 395–408.
Rauchensteiner, Manfried 2010. "Der Tod des Generals Wodniansky." In *Österreichisch-polnische militärische Beziehungen im 20. Jahrhundert: Symposium 6. November 2009. Acta*, edited by C. Reichl-Ham and I. Nöbauer, 67–76. Vienna.

Roda Roda, A. 1917. "Stehe auf und Wandle." *Prager Tageblatt*, 17 May.
Rousseau, Frédéric 1997. "L'électrothérapie des névroses de guerre durant la première guerre mondiale." In *Guerres mondiales et conflits contemporains* 185: 13–27.
Ruszała, Kamil 2016. "Choroby duszy i ciała w armii austro-węgierskiej: Przyczynek do badań nad służbami medycznymi podczas I wojny światowej." In *Doświadczenia żołnierskie Wielkiej Wojny: Studia i szkice z dziejów frontu wschodniego I wojny światowej*, edited by M. Baczkowski and K. Ruszała, 267–90. Kraków.
Składkowski, Sławoj F. 1990. *Moja służba w brygadzie: Pamiętnik polowy*. Warszawa.
Taussig, Leo 1918. "Z našich zkušeností o válečných psychoneurosách." *Časopis lékařů českých* 58 (19): 422–26.
von Economo, Constantin. 1997. "Encephalitis Lethargica," *Wiener Klinische Wochenschrift* 30 (1917). In *Neurological Classics*, ed., R. H. Wilkins and I. A. Brody. Park Ridge.
Wagner-Jauregg, Julius 1920. *O suggestji, hypnozie i telepatji: Wykład na posiedzeniu Towarzystwa Lekarskiego we Wiedniu 13 czerwca 1919*. Translated by M. Kozłowski. Kraków.
———. 1950. *Lebenserinnerungen*. Edited by L. Schönbauer and M. Jantzsch. Vienna.
Wagner v. Jauregg, Julius 1917. *Erfahrungen über Kriegsneurosen*. Vienna.
Wolf, Maria A. 2008. *Eugenische Vernunft: Eingriffe in die reproduktive Kultur durch die Medizin 1900–2000*. Vienna.

CHAPTER

8

Forging a "Winning Spirit"
The North American YMCA and the Czechoslovak Army, 1918–1921

Ondřej Matějka

At the turn of the year 1918, the inhabitants of the newly created Czechoslovakia found themselves in a psychologically intricate situation. Until very recently subjects of the defeated Austro-Hungarian emperor, they overnight became citizens of a republic that belonged to the winning side of World War I. Masaryk's and Beneš's successes on the diplomatic front facilitated the emergence of a "culture of victory"[1] in the Czechoslovak public space, which positively identified with the postwar order. However, the building of citizens' loyalty toward the institutions of the new state represented a lengthy, gradual process. It was, in fact, a process that profoundly challenged the prevailing patterns of relationships with the state and its institutions among Czech-speaking citizens, who had interiorized an ambivalent coexistence with the Austro-Hungarian monarchy during the prewar decades.

The Czechoslovak army of the time offers a telling example of this phenomenon. When, in the early 1920s, representatives of the U.S. Army assessed the military preparedness of the Central Europeans, they rapidly understood that ordinary Czech soldiers still generally perceived it as their "patriotic duty to do as little as possible, cheat and lie, steal from the government, play sick" (Taft 1922: 469). In the domain of military defense, a radical mental transformation was thus essential for the survival of the fragile republic, surrounded as it was by frustrated states infused with revisionist "cultures of defeat." The establishment of an operational army, which could secure the Czechoslovak state in the midst of violent and revolutionary Central Europe was understandably a complicated challenge. The Czechoslovak army was formed of a heterogeneous (and potentially explosive) mixture of tired Czech and Slovak ex-soldiers of the former imperial army, recruits from the minority German and Hungarian linguistic groups,[2] and members of the "Czechoslovak Legions," who returned after several years far away from home with great expectations and ambitions as to their position in the new republic.[3]

This chapter aims to retrace one aspect of the process of constructing a "winning spirit" among those different components of the Czechoslovak army. This winning attitude was to constitute the basis for positive identification with the army by recruits and to strengthen their willingness to defend their new state against internal and external challengers rather than turn their violent impulses against it. The main field of observation for this process will be the activities of the North American Young Men's Christian Association (YMCA) in the Czechoslovak army between 1918 and 1921, when the YMCA played the role of principal provider of welfare services for Czechoslovak soldiers.[4]

I will first rapidly introduce the YMCA and summarize the genesis and modalities of the association's involvement in army work, beginning in the mid-nineteenth century. Second, I will describe the role of the YMCA in the process of establishing a stable and strong Czechoslovak army, worthy of a "victorious state" in the immediate aftermath of World War I. Finally, in the third part, I will offer hypotheses for understanding the rationale(s) behind the extensive investment of North American financial and human resources into the establishment of the YMCA in Czechoslovakia, which had the aim of contributing to the enthusiastic identification by Czechoslovak citizens (especially soldiers) with their new state in the geopolitical context of the "first cold war" (Carley 2014).

Young Men, the YMCA, and War

The YMCA movement appeared in the middle of the nineteenth century in Great Britain in reaction to dramatic social changes connected with rapid urbanization and the industrial revolution. The founding fathers of the YMCA, principally George Williams, were fed spiritually by the Second Great Awakening.[5] They decided to create an association that would take care of "morally endangered" young men, who were pouring into British cities to staff newly created factories (Shedd 1955; Latourette 1957). The YMCA's mission was to keep them away from the "dreadful delights" (Hanna 2015) that were readily accessible in urban areas, such as cheap alcohol, gambling, prostitution, and other "vices." In the YMCA's centers, young men could find, in addition to regular Bible classes and prayer meetings, libraries filled with "wholesome" literature, nonalcoholic refreshments, and a rich offering of sport activities. From the very beginning, the YMCA was a predominantly Protestant (though expressly nondenominational) movement.

The YMCA became a global phenomenon after 1851, when the first YMCA outside Britain opened in Montreal, Canada. In the following years, YMCAs quickly spread across North America and continental Europe. Already by 1855, almost one hundred delegates from nine countries met in Paris to demonstrate the association's international standing[6] and elaborate a common expression of its basic ideological principles (the so called "Paris Basis")—to which the World Alliance of YMCAs has ever since adhered.[7]

It is important to underline that the exceptional success of the YMCA in the second half of the nineteenth century, especially in the United States, was closely linked to modern warfare. The YMCA attended to large masses of often desperate young men in military camps. Its "service without partisanship" opened the gates of young men's hearts and minds for the first time during the American civil war. Over five thousand volunteers offered "wholesome Christian activities" on the battlefield, in hospitals, and in the soldiers' camps, where many of them were away from home for the first time in their lives (Lancaster 1987: 1–11). This success encouraged the leaders of the North American YMCA to expand its operations overseas. Its activities were supervised by the World Committee, which was created in 1866 and renamed the International Committee in 1879.

With the support of some of the richest U.S. families (such as the Rockefellers), and thanks to the enthusiastic involvement of some of the ablest representatives of the new generation of North American missionaries, the YMCA became an essential element of the North American "matrix of moral reform," with global ambitions (Tyrrell 2010: 74–97). Among those missionaries was John R. Mott, who, at the dawn of the twentieth century, proclaimed the objective of "evangeliz[ing] the world in a generation" (Hopkins 1979). The American YMCA was an essential component of a network of organizations aspiring to create a more Christian and more moral world, a goal that went hand in hand with the emergence of U.S. imperialism and colonialism. Ian Tyrrell precisely analyzed how the North American reformers fashioned their own version of a nonterritorial "empire," which was grounded in the networks of the moral reform organizations that were pursuing innovative policies and seeking a hegemonic position within the new arena of voluntary NGOs (Tyrrell 2010: 227–49).

World War I, which marked the emergence of the United States as a global power led by Woodrow Wilson, of course represented a substantial opportunity for this "empire" and more specifically for the YMCA.[8] Wilson's friend John R. Mott was perfectly in tune with the president's vision[9] of a "new world order" based on the basic tenets of the American progressive movement, which provided the ideological backdrop for Wilson's administration. Wilson drew his trust in the goodness and perfectibility of man from the Christian optimism of the nineteenth century that was reflected in the YMCA. At the same time, social Darwinism provided him with his faith in the superiority of Anglo-Saxon civilization (Rossini 2008: 64–65).[10]

Unsurprisingly, Mott volunteered the full services of the YMCA without hesitation to Wilson's administration in 1914. He rapidly understood that the world war represented an "unparalleled opportunity" for widening the global influence of the YMCA (Steuer 2009).[11] The first step in this cooperation was the YMCA's relief program for prisoners of war (POWs) which consisted of sending the YMCA's secretaries to POW camps in all belligerent countries in order to "alleviate the suffering of the millions of these forgotten men" (Steuer 2009: chap. 19). Such an operation was possible mainly thanks to the prewar infrastructure of the YMCA in countries on both sides of the war. Even though the YMCA's POW program was minimal from a quantitative perspective (at the peak of its operations in February 1917, the American YMCA had only sixty-eight secretaries serving over six million prisoners), YMCA secretaries were often the only Americans located deep inside enemy territory. Their work certainly bolstered the global prestige of the YMCA. But even more immediately, it significantly enhanced the YMCA's symbolical capital in the leading circles of Wilson's administration.[12]

The POW operation was only the first step in the YMCA's war activities. After the United States declared war on Germany, the North American International Committee decided to throw its full support behind the Allied war effort. The Wilson administration gladly accepted the YMCA's offer to provide welfare services for its soldiers. This dramatically changed the YMCA's standing not only in the United States but also abroad. The number of YMCA employees working with American forces in Europe attained its peak in early 1919. Twenty-six thousand paid staff of men and women served with the YMCA. Another thirty-five thousand volunteers attended to the spiritual and social needs of the U.S. armed force of 4.8 million troops. The maximum was reached in spring 1918, when there was approximately one YMCA secretary for every two hundred U.S. soldiers in France. In total, the YMCA performed 90 percent of all welfare work in the American Expeditionary Force in Europe; four thousand rapidly constructed wooden "huts" or large tents were opened for recreation and educational and religious services. YMCA activities were also closely connected with the growing production of consumer goods, which were offered to soldiers for free or at very low prices in order to "alleviate their suffering." For instance, forty-four factories were established in Europe for the production of cookies and candy for the troops.[13]

In the progressively ever more globalized logic of the YMCA action, North American YMCA workers did not limit their attention exclusively to American soldiers and to the Western Front. They always emphasized their international ambitions. YMCA archives contain extensive and passionate accounts of the workers' activities with soldiers of various nationalities in various geographic settings. For instance, their "romance" with the Czechoslovak Legions in Russia was presented as an example of a success story of the North American YMCA's international engagement.[14] The first contact in the Russian context was established thanks to prewar connections between Tomáš Garrigue Masaryk and U.S. Protestants (Miller 2010: 65–66). Subsequently, "American uncles" (the Czechoslovak legionnaires' nickname for YMCA secretaries) acquired great popularity among the legionnaires in Russia. As we can read in the diaries of one of those "uncles," Kenneth Dexter Miller,[15] his work among the Czech legionnaires resulted in their "great admiration for America" and "big faith" in the goodness of President Wilson.[16] Testimony from those receiving services confirms these perceptions. Czech soldiers sincerely appreciated the YMCA's welfare services and understood them as a symbol of the idea that "the American nation empathizes with everyone who fights for the freedom of humanity."[17]

"How to Become a Winner?" Constructing a Loyal and Efficient Army for the New State

Several months later, in direct continuation of this experience with the Czechoslovaks at the Eastern Front, Miller's YMCA colleagues started to accompany transports of Czech and Slovak soldiers on their journey from Siberia to Europe. On their arrival in Czechoslovakia, the tired legionnaires then found yet other "American uncles" and their local assistants, who took care of them in the days after their arrival and helped them in the first phase of their reintegration.[18] Their presence in the new republic resulted from an invitation to the YMCA issued by Czech Americanophile elites who hoped that the association would assist them in the creation of a new state dedicated to a democratic political culture.

It was Olga Masaryková herself whom her father, elected the first president of Czechoslovakia in November 1918,[19] sent to Geneva to persuade John Mott to support a project of active intervention by the North American YMCA in Central Europe, in order to "guide the latent potentialities"[20] of the newly born Czechoslovak nation. Olga Masaryková quite explicitly couched her request in terms of defeat and victory, and colored it with Czech nationalist historical imagery. Olga and her father expected the North American YMCA to lead a nation that had been "crushed" under the weight of the counterreformation and "Austrian oppression," which had "lived for generations in negation of the existing political order," toward a substantial change in mentality—to a true culture of victory. In the Masaryks' view, this meant genuine identification with "an independent, democratic state life,"[21] which would follow the example of the United States' political system (Masaryk 1925: 270).

To bring that about, the army was an excellent entrance point for the enterprise, because tens of thousands of young men could be addressed directly, influenced and *in fine* taught "how to become a winner." Becoming a winner meant, as one of the early propaganda brochures published by the YMCA stated, identification with modern democracy à la the United States.[22] At the same time the army was the key institution needed for the survival of the new state, which was located right in the middle of the "tempestuous sea" of Central Europe.[23] A double mission grew out of the Masaryks' ambitious objectives. On the one hand, there was the delicate and ambivalent need to keep the sometimes threatening mass of young males in relative calm during the months of intense postwar revolutionary social turmoil linked to economic difficulties and a wave of political unrest in Central Europe (Vondrášek 1993: 36–39, 66–67). On the other hand, leading elites of the new state needed to rapidly persuade the young army recruits that the Czechoslovak republic was worthy of their fighting spirit and of putting their lives at risk only a few weeks or months after the end an exhausting world conflict. The program constituted a great challenge, considering that many young Czechs had interiorized a very skeptical attitude toward state institutions in general and the army in particular.

Understandably, such intensive work with tens of thousands of young men required very experienced management. In Masaryk's view, and that of his closest advisors, the North American YMCA offered the support best suited to the delicate enterprise, thanks to its outstanding war record on the Allied side. The YMCA was expected to assist the army command in limiting the violent impulses of young soldiers as they were demobilized, with the objective of getting them ready to return to civilian life. At particular contexts when the troops, to the contrary, needed to be mobilized, the YMCA could help prepare and motivate the young recruits, along with their tired comrades who, for the most part, had experienced the war on the losing side of Austria-Hungary. In fact, the troops had to be ready for combat with neighboring states that claimed parts of the territory of the new Czechoslovak state for themselves—in particular, Hungary. Therefore, state authorities decided to support YMCA personnel and projects extensively, and by the autumn months of 1919 the majority of important Czechoslovak military units had access to a YMCA "hut."[24] At the peak of its activities in 1920, the YMCA staffed and managed fifty-four fully operating "standard centers" with canteens, game rooms and reading rooms, twenty-five branch army centers, and sixty-two mobile centers with basic equipment.[25]

What tools and strategies did the YMCA secretaries use to transform the defeatist attitudes of the Czechoslovak troops into a "winning spirit?" How did they contribute to forging loyalty toward the new state? What kind of activities did they offer to the soldiers of the Czechoslovak army in their "huts"? When observing monthly and annual reports, which both American and local personnel prepared for the YMCA's New York and Geneva headquarters, we can see that the YMCA strategists developed an elaborate road map for working with young men in a violent context. That plan was based on a hierarchy of human needs similar to Maslow's famous model, but predated it by several decades.[26] Maslow structured human needs in a pyramid whose base consisted of elementary "physiological" necessities (breathing, food, water, etc.) as well as physical safety. The upper levels of the pyramid contained more socially oriented needs and values (love, friendship) before reaching a peak in "self-actualization" (respect for norms, morality, spirituality, and high ideals).

Replicating the base of the pyramidic structure of this psychological model, every YMCA report from 1919–1920 started almost obsessively with an extensive enumeration of statistical data on cups of cocoa, tons of sugar, number of buns distributed to soldiers in various regions and units of the army. Hence we know quite precisely that, for instance, in 1920 the YMCA served 5,434,902 hot drinks to members of the Czechoslovak army, together with 5,210,170 white rolls.[27] It is striking (and symptomatic of YMCA thought) that a kind of religious language was often used to describe how food and drinks were "ministered" to soldiers.[28] This kind of imagery corresponds to the reality on the ground as perceived by the YMCA's beneficiaries. Army reports from the early 1920s repeatedly emphasized that the YMCA's focus on soldiers' basic needs played an important role in the difficult months while the territory of the new state was being stabilized. "Only those, who during the winter of 1919 and 1920 knew the Army intimately can understand what a cup of hot cocoa and a hut with its light and warmth . . . meant to those weary men."[29]

It is interesting to observe various (and sometimes contradictory) uses of favorite YMCA tools such as the famous cup of cocoa, which at different moments and in different contexts, could play a mobilizing or a demobilizing role. This early symbol of American consumer culture was the first object that awaited legionnaires returning to Czechoslovakia after the exhausting journey from Siberia. At the railway station in České Budějovice, the YMCA was entrusted with the delicate task of welcoming those soldiers (who often were frustrated and bellicose) "back home." The main objective of the cup of cocoa in that particular context, as YMCA secretaries explicitly stated, was to relax the soldiers and begin the process of demobilizing them.[30] We can, however, encounter a different purpose for the same cup of cocoa during the military operations in southern and eastern Slovakia, where, quite to the contrary, it was meant to mobilize, motivate, and reward men who had to fight the Hungarian army during the early postwar months.[31]

"Wholesome entertainment" appears just one step above the cup of cocoa in the YMCA kit of tools to satisfy soldiers' most pressing needs. Libraries and reading rooms, lectures and courses, concerts and social evenings were organized in the huts on the "sound and healthy grounds of Christianity." Such distractions were to prevent soldiers from looking for their "former foolish entertainments and time-killers"—namely the cabaret or brothel.[32] With the help of the technical advances that were enabling the rise of American mass culture, huts succeeded in attracting masses of young recruits,[33] to the great satisfaction of the Czechoslovak military authorities.[34] In the sphere of entertainment, the YMCA enjoyed an advantageous position thanks to equipment coming from the U.S. Army. Mobile movie projectors (called "kinos" by the Czech soldiers) proved to be exceptionally popular and efficient in spreading the message of Western and North American cultural supremacy. In several reports we can read how YMCA secretaries almost conceived of themselves as apostles "bringing culture to isolated and remote places of Slovakia, far away from railroads and culture—where Kino has never been seen before."[35]

The YMCA's success in its army work was attributable to its flexibility and readiness to use as well local tools that enhanced the efficiency of its activities. In Czechoslovakia for instance, YMCA secretaries rapidly noticed the traditional popularity of choral singing and started to offer opportunities for soldiers to practice this activity inside the YMCA huts, under the supervision of experienced musicians whom YMCA personnel found among officers and the local population.[36] According to the majority of accessible reports, the YMCA's offering of entertainment met with a genuinely enthusiastic response among its target group. Czech representatives of the Ministry of National Defense expressed their gratitude in December 1920:

> You have made difficult military service more agreeable to the soldier. You have cared for his moral improvement.... Thousands and thousands of soldiers were well and inexpensively entertained by you. You have secured the everlasting thankfulness of our young army, which you have helped with your unselfish humanitarian intentions in the worst times after the war.[37]

The YMCA huts provided for yet another level of the soldiers' needs, serving the higher level of the Maslow pyramid connected to relationships. Nourished, refreshed, warmed up, and relaxed thanks to YMCA entertainment, soldiers were offered sheets of paper and pens so they could write letters to their families and friends. In 1920, more than 5.8 million letters were written on paper provided free by the YMCA.[38] The rationale behind this effort was to "keep alive in [soldiers'] memories the best impulses associated with the home they had left behind them."[39] This emphasis on facilitating young men's connection with their homes had the explicit objective of reinforcing stability in the violent context of military service during the wild early postwar months and years, so that young soldiers could return smoothly to civilian life once their service ended. Significantly, tables with sheets of paper, envelopes, and pens were the second things offered by YMCA secretaries (after the cup of cocoa) to returning legionnaires, who were thus invited to take the first steps toward reintegration into nonmilitary life.[40]

In the social sphere, YMCA huts offered more than just an opportunity to sustain written contact with faraway families. The huts served as meeting places where soldiers could form new bonds with their peers in a structured and controlled context, through a set of well-tested activities. "Comradeship between soldiers was strengthened over games."[41] This was traditionally one of the strongest and most developed points of the YMCA program. Team sports, some of them invented or reinvented and popularized by the YMCA in the nineteenth century for the masses of young males pouring into the industrializing urban centers of Anglo-Saxon countries (Taft 1922: 321ff.), were instrumentalized in the wartime and postwar contexts. In different (sometimes almost contradictory) situations, YMCA sport activities in army training camps and in the huts proved to be very useful in managing the violent impulses of soldiers in allied armies during the war and in the Czechoslovak army in the early 1920s. First of all, they increased the "agility" of the men. In the military setting, favorite YMCA sports and games such as basketball and volleyball were promoted as efficient means of creating and maintaining "the habit of instant response to a touch or a signal," improving soldiers' ability to leap a trench or a strand of barbed wire "without breaking stride" (Taft 1922: 321ff.).

According to YMCA secretaries as well as numerous army officers, the capabilities developed in games had inestimable value during military operations of all kinds.[42] In their reports, better physical conditioning and shorter reaction time was immediately connected with stimulation of the "fighting spirit" (Taft 1922: 321). Furthermore, games and sports practiced in competition with other units fostered the determination to win. In the psychological perspective shared by the military leadership and YMCA secretaries, that spirit allowed the men to "exceed the powers they believe themselves to possess" (Taft 1922: 321). Last but not least, collective games promoted teamwork by explicitly showing the players the advantages of cooperation. As a consequence, "individualism yielded to that *esprit de corps* which enables men to maintain presence of mind in the face of heavy odds, because they feel themselves to be a part of an invincible force" (Taft 1922: 321).

The qualities acquired through the practice of collective games were useful in the context of mobilization for combat operations during the war, as well as during the postwar conflicts in Central Europe in 1919–1920. However, the bonding aspect and respect for rules and fair play were the main motives for YMCA sports activities as the political situation in Czechoslovakia progressively stabilized in 1920–1921. At that time, the YMCA skillfully reframed its sports offerings as the way "to make youth into citizens," by stressing "unselfish cooperation in the team, the bridging of differences of race, class and nation . . .

regard for adversary." Above all, identification with fair play through the game was meant to help "human life to emerge from the jungle" of violence connected with the recent armed conflicts.[43]

In the reports by YMCA staff about sports in the Czechoslovakia of the early 1920s, we are struck by one persistent motivation that adds a special flavor to the YMCA's general discourse on the role of collective sports in the wider postwar Europe. Josef A. Pipal, who formulated it most explicitly, was a Czech-American who directed the YMCA sports program in Czechoslovakia (first in the army but later in YMCA civilian work as well). He repeatedly underlined the educational "democratic function" of team sports in the new state as it pursued stability in postwar Central Europe.[44] During his mission in Czechoslovakia, Pipal continuously emphasized the particular importance of constructing "a real democratic army," composed not only of "brave soldiers but also of men of high principles."[45] In a 1920 analysis destined for the North American headquarters of the YMCA, Pipal argued that "years of Austrian rule have crushed out all play instinct and greatly dulled and deadened the spirit of fair play."[46] Even though he appreciated[47] the local Sokol movement devoted to gymnastics,[48] Pipal observed that the Sokols had evolved into an organization with too "heavy [an] apparatus" and "too rigid a discipline" in reaction to Austrian oppression. He conceded that stressing mechanical physical training and military discipline made sense in an era when people "were simply supposed to obey." The construction of a democracy, however, called for something else, according to Pipal. In addition to the external discipline of drills and gymnastic training, young citizens of the newborn republic needed "recreational games, play life and competitive sport with its self-discipline."[49]

The importance of collective sports in the creation of self-disciplined and self-regulated citizens of a Czechoslovak democracy permeated by a winning spirit is evident from YMCA discourse throughout the interwar period. In the early 1920s we can nevertheless observe even more directly persuasive action by the YMCA in the Czechoslovak army, which had the objective of promoting and spreading a narrative about the inevitability of Czechoslovakia's path toward peaceful democracy. Ever since the establishment of the YMCA huts in the Czechoslovak army, YMCA secretaries integrated lectures and courses on "civic education" into their daily program. These included presentations on the new constitution of the Czechoslovak republic, programs on the theory of democracy, and popularizing lectures about Masaryk and his political thought.

Reaching for the higher strata of Maslow's pyramid, the YMCA secretaries did their best to disseminate this story of "political progress" and its interiorization by young soldiers. Angry comments found in the pages of the press, representing political currents marginalized in the beginning phases of the existence of Czechoslovakia, illustrate the aggressiveness and efficiency of YMCA programs both inside the army and out. In the early 1920s, regional

Catholic journals such as *Štít* and *Nová Severní Morava* furiously lamented the "foreign elements such as the YMCA" pouring into "our towns and villages," further "subverting" the already shaken traditional Catholic social order.[50] In the Czechoslovak parliament, members of German and Slovak nationalist parties repeatedly criticized the YMCA's actions, castigating the "prodigal attribution of state financial resources" to this "foreign Protestant association."[51] Last but not least, the left wing of social democracy accused the YMCA of being "merely a tool of capitalism."[52]

YMCA representatives actively intervened to counter these critical voices as soon as they were able to identify the main cleavages dividing the population of the new state and the army as well. To tamp down religious conflicts, the YMCA in Czechoslovakia did not stop reaffirming its interdenominational openness and systematically downplayed its Protestant origins throughout the interwar period.[53] This attitude was most strongly emphasized in the very beginnings of the YMCA's work in the Czechoslovak army. The official agreement between the YMCA and the Ministry of National Defense expressly prohibited any kind of proselytizing activity by YMCA secretaries inside the army. More importantly, however, YMCA strategists in Czechoslovakia rapidly understood that in the violently anticlerical context of the early days of the republic, strict confessional neutrality, bordering at times on a kind of abstinence from religion, was the best choice for the moment.[54] It is important to note that the "C" in the YMCA acronym truly reappeared in its work only in the late 1920s, with the rise of the "Academic YMCA" led by distinguished Protestant intellectuals and theologians such as Josef L. Hromádka and Jaroslav Šimsa.[55]

In the contentious field of religion, the YMCA elites who were managing the organization's work with the Czechoslovak army opted for a temporary strategic withdrawal. They chose different tactics in the other explosive area, the ethnic divisions that were a deep cleavage in the army and in Czechoslovak society in general. YMCA leaders in Prague and in Geneva rapidly understood the enormity of the challenge that the complicated ethnic composition of Czechoslovakia presented to its existence as a unitary state. They therefore decided to promote all sorts of activities aimed at encouraging friendly contacts between young recruits coming from different linguistic communities. We can find reports from 1919 and 1920 of Czechoslovak soldiers whose mother tongues were Czech, Slovak, Polish, German, and Hungarian singing together, playing sports together, and learning one another's languages.[56] Nevertheless, a concentrated and systematic effort to promote "international-mindedness" among youth became the YMCA leadership's center of interest only after the transition from army work to the civilian sphere in 1921. This work would become the main symbol of YMCA activities in Czechoslovakia and was aimed at preventing interethnic violence and supporting the stability of the new state.[57]

"Whoever Is Master of Bohemia Is Master of Europe"

The complicated religious and ethnic conditions in Czechoslovakia inspired a great deal of caution and vigilance among YMCA leaders in Geneva and New York when they planned their activities in that area. They discussed modifications of the usual YMCA procedures to address the problem. It is interesting to observe that while they were ready to tone down the explicitly Protestant tenor of the association, they never compromised its Anglo-Saxon character. From the very beginning of their activities in Central Europe, YMCA leaders constantly repeated that their association intended to facilitate the penetration of the "ideal Americanism" or "the magic . . . of the American constructive spirit."[58] They associated that spirit with "progressive liberalism," which they presented as an essential precondition to progress along the path to the "winning side" of history.[59] A closer look at this dimension of the YMCA program helps us understand some of the principal reasons for the large extent of the North American YMCA's investment in the welfare of Czechoslovak army and in its work in the civilian sphere after 1921.

On the surface, in their official presentations, the U.S. representatives of the YMCA emphasized again and again their disinterested motives for the organization's impressive engagement in the heart of Europe, which, they stated, grew out of a noble wish "to bring the spirit of peace to a distracted world."[60] They further reassured their supporters in Czechoslovakia and the United States that "our greatest gain will unquestionably come in the course of our giving" (Taft 1922: 480). However, an attentive reading of internal reports and correspondence by the key actors on the American side, which contain numerous combative and rather violent images that carry the taint of realpolitik thinking, allows us to uncover a more complex set of motivations. We can then recognize a great deal of geopolitical self-interest[61] in the face of the new cleavages and conflict zones in Eurasia. One impressive study of the YMCA's service to wartime and postwar Europe, written in 1922, concludes with the following comments on the rationale behind the continuing YMCA investment in that region: "They [the new states in Central Europe] have had our help in their times of need; they will not soon forget us. . . . What little we have sacrificed of our surplus may be but a tithe of what they may be able to give us in return" (Taft 1922: 480).[62] This argument helped to persuade rich U.S. philanthropists to support the YMCA's activities in Europe and specifically in Czechoslovakia. Why did those Americans find it so important to invest in the construction of a stable, democratic political system in the Czechoslovakia of the immediate postwar period? What was their underlying geopolitical reasoning?

Let us emphasize that very early on, in some of the first writings published by the North American YMCA about Czechoslovakia, we find relatively extensive reflections on the geostrategic position of the country. This discourse seems to have had a persuasive effect on North American leaders and the sponsors of the YMCA. In the 1921 issue of a YMCA review "The Czechoslovak American" (published in English) the editors reminded the Anglophone public of the old adage, attributed to Bismarck, that "the man who is master of Bohemia is master of Europe."[63] Such thoughts were expressed in different words, yet with the same meaning, again and again in the early phases of the YMCA's work in Czechoslovakia. In 1919, Irving D. Kimball, who was responsible for the YMCA's work with the Czechoslovak army, wrote to his superiors in New York that "this republic is in a critical position geographically, racially, and politically."[64] His perspective was restated by his colleagues throughout the 1920s, stressing "the tremendous importance in middle Europe of the new Republic of Czechoslovakia" and furthermore arguing that "this Republic is particularly well suited to serve as the center of the dissemination of Association ideals throughout Europe."[65]

In internal YMCA debates, Czechoslovakia soon began to play an even more important role, giving meaning to the American investment in its welfare and in a larger sense to the entirety of the United States' engagement in Europe. Since the early 1920s, the country gained the status of one of the North American YMCA's principal success stories. When the financial support of its donors began to fall off with the general isolationist turn in the postwar United States, the North American YMCA needed such stories. It therefore actively contributed to the discourse that stressed Czechoslovakia's exceptionality in the difficult enterprise of constructing a stable democracy in Central Europe. Reports emphasized the important role of the YMCA in this project, providing evidence for satisfying outcomes attributable to the investment of U.S. financial and human resources.

We can thus find some truly poetic passages in internal reports destined for the North American YMCA leadership and sponsors. They presented "the story of the relation of the American YMCA to the new nation in the heart of the Old Europe as one of the romances of the Red Triangle [the YMCA logo]."[66] This reputation was the Czechoslovaks' added value, and it soon bore fruit. By the early 1920s, according to YMCA reporters, the organization had had "a wonderful effect upon the spirit and activities of the young people in many centers all over Czechoslovakia."[67] From their perspective, it was thanks to the organization's activities (among those of others[68]) that the new republic could start to fulfill its "great mission" in Central Europe. As John R. Mott himself observed when he evaluated the first years of YMCA activities in the region, Czechoslovakia, supported by the YMCA, "has taken a stand for liberty and freedom. It has become as a lighthouse sending streams of light to the peoples around in darkness." He further prophesized that "other nations will look to it for guidance and help."[69] Two years later, when applying for further funding of YMCA activities in Europe, Mott's coworkers re-emphasized that even though Czechoslovakia was "built out of fragments of a decadent Empire and suffered all the hardships of one of the chief participants in the world war,"[70] with the YMCA's support it alone had "risen like an island amid the surging sea around it."[71]

Such narratives found keen listeners among North American internationalist elites who used them for their own political purposes. In 1925, Herbert Hoover himself cited the YMCA's action in Czechoslovakia, specifically its project for a "Student Home" in Prague for students from various linguistic communities (Matějka 2016), as an example of the effectiveness of American help for Europe. He explained the impact of the continued U.S. presence in Europe for his Washington audience:

> When you replace old lines of division with strands of friendship as [the North American YMCA] is doing at home and abroad, you are removing the very roots and seeds of strife. To bring Czechs, Hungarians, Slovaks, Germans, and Jews in a city to recognize a common interest and work together for it, better guarantees the rights of a minority than treaties or legislation.[72]

In Hoover's geopolitical thinking, his enthusiasm for the North American YMCA's beneficial and successful activities in Central Europe grew out of his experience with the direction of the American Relief Administration, which he considered to be the fundamental element in the "race against both death and communism."[73] He is well known for having conceived and applied the idea of using "food diplomacy to combat the spread of Russian Bolshevik Revolution" (Tyrrell 2010: 207). In fact, Hoover was one of the highly influential U.S. politicians (with Wilson at their head) who after 1917 most acutely held the vision and most actively constructed the reality of global U.S.-Soviet antagonism. Some historians today interpret those antagonisms, which arose from the world conflict, as the "first Cold War" (Carley 2014). According to these researchers, it was precisely in 1917 that the dichotomy between Russia and America began on a global level. This dichotomy went on to characterize the history of the twentieth century until very recently (Rossini 2008: 53). The deep and abiding anticommunism of leading Western political elites was an essential component of this phenomenon.

The role of the Czechoslovak YMCA in the immediate postwar period offers numerous interesting illustrations of this "first cold war" thinking and practice. In fact, already in 1919, Irving Kimball connected the YMCA's engagement with the Czechoslovak army to the imperative of "building up a wall against the spread of bolshevism."[74] This was to be only the first, fundamental step in a larger project of YMCA "indigenous and independent" associations, which were intended to form "a great belt from the Baltic to the Black and Mediterranean Seas" with a "strong and steadying center" in Prague.[75] The anti-Soviet significance of this "belt" can clearly be deduced from numerous warnings in YMCA reports about the "threats from the East," the "red danger," and the "Bolshevik menace."[76]

YMCA activities in the autumn and winter of 1920–1921, which were critical months of social conflict in Czechoslovakia, prove that the engagement of the association in anticommunist struggle did not remain only on the level of discourse. When the specter of a socialist revolution in Central Europe was imminent, the YMCA huts received not only more cocoa and sugar to "calm down" radicalized young soldiers but also orders to produce more propaganda preaching the advantages of the currently existing social order to recruits.[77] The predominance of the nonviolent reformist wing inside the Czechoslovak Social Democratic Party was thus greeted with great fanfare in New York. The Social Democrats' November 1920 convention was reported to have had "epoch-making effects, not only on the history of Czechoslovakia, but on socialistic movements throughout the world." It became clear that "there shall be no revolution [in Czechoslovakia]," that "the emancipation of the working classes must be attained through education and cooperation," and, most importantly for the U.S. audience, that Czechoslovak social democracy "will not abandon democratic independence to place itself at the mercy of Moscow communism."[78]

Conclusion

The temporary marginalization of the revolutionary wing of Czech social democracy was considered an important threshold in the construction of a stable democratic political system, which the North American YMCA defined as one of its main objectives in its work with the Czechoslovak army during the early postwar months and years. This chapter retraced the progressive growth of the YMCA's role in this process, with an emphasis on the analysis of the tools the association used in Czechoslovakia in the critical period between 1919 and 1921. In that period, the YMCA was expected not only to take care of the welfare of young recruits but also to orient them appropriately in the contemporary sociopolitical situation. The North American YMCA's leadership in Prague always focused first on the satisfaction of soldiers' physical, material and social needs, supplying them with relaxing and demobilizing activities aimed at preparing them for return to civilian life.

However, the endangered Czechoslovak republic was located in the midst of an unsettled Central Europe. In this context, the YMCA intervened with a remobilizing agenda as well. In the sphere of propaganda and civic education it actively disseminated the idea of a democratic republic founded on

Masaryk's ideals. It promoted that idea to young Czechoslovak soldiers as a value worth defending against external and internal challengers, and a bulwark against Bolshevism. The YMCA further invested its energy and resources into preventing intra-state violence by encouraging all sorts of activities that introduced tolerant attitudes to men who came from different linguistic and ethnic milieus.

The combination of the geostrategic importance of Czechoslovakia, which was located in the center of Europe, and the good results attained by the YMCA in its army activities were abundantly publicized back in the United States. This explains the ease with which the North American YMCA agreed in 1921 to transpose its work from the military sphere to civil society, to transfer its possessions to local hands and to continue its active support of the Czechoslovak YMCA. The YMCA could thus become one of the key players in the field of youth work in Czechoslovakia in the 1920s and 1930s, with a dozen regional centers and a stable membership. Its attractive summer camps, the rich offer of varied club activities, its intense work among students, and its close connections to political elites around Masaryk and Beneš earned it significant influence among a generation of Czech and Slovak young men that came of age during the two interwar decades.[79]

Finally, the North American YMCA succeeded in creating an enduring local tradition in Czechoslovakia. The YMCA maintained a stable material base in well-equipped buildings that, despite devastating losses among the Czechoslovak YMCA's elites during World War II (Šimsová 2005) and a forty-year interruption of the YMCA's institutional existence during the Communist dictatorship (1951–1990), allowed it to regain its visibility in the Czech public sphere in the twenty-first century.[80]

Acknowledgments

I am thankful for the support of the PROGRES Q18 research funding scheme ("Social Sciences: from Multidisciplinarity to Interdisciplinarity," Charles University, Prague).

Ondřej Matějka teaches contemporary European history and methodology of social sciences at the Institute of Area Studies at Charles University (Prague, Czech Republic). He also regularly collaborates with the Department of History at the University of Geneva (Switzerland). His main research interests include transnational history of youth movements, history of psychotherapy, and social history of religion in contemporary Czech lands.

Notes

1. For an explanation of the concepts of "culture of victory" and "culture of defeat," see Eichenberg and Newman (2013: 1–19).
2. The complicated story of the integration of members of different linguistic groups into the newly formed Czechoslovak army was analyzed by Zückert (2006).
3. For an overview of the process of establishment of the Czechoslovak army, see Straka and Kykal (2013).
4. Even though this chapter is mostly based on untapped archival sources, it enlarges and completes the already existing historiographical works covering certain aspects of YMCA activities in Central and Eastern Europe, i.e. Steuer (2009), Tlustý and Štumbauer (2013), Tlustý (2017), Smith (2018).
5. This was one of the most extensive Protestant religious revivals in the Anglo-Saxon world, led by Baptist and Methodist preachers, which started in the United States in the late eighteenth century and peaked in the first half of the nineteenth century. See Conforti (1991: 99–118).
6. Nevertheless, for several decades, the YMCA's center of interest remained mainly in the Western part of Europe: the first YMCA emissaries reached the Bohemian lands only in the late 1880s.
7. The Paris Basis, which remains posted on the YMCA webpage (http://www.ymca.int/who-we-are/mission/paris-basis-1855), states that the fundamental objective of the association is "to unite those young men who, regarding Jesus Christ as their God and Savior according to the Holy Scriptures, desire to be His disciples in their doctrine and in their life, and to associate their efforts for the extension of His Kingdom amongst young men."
8. World War I was "the greatest single event of YMCA history" according to Lancaster (1987: 47).
9. The relationship between Mott and Wilson is thoroughly analyzed in Rothra (2014).
10. Both Wilson and Mott believed that America was a unique nation and the vanguard of humanity. Whatever happened in the United States prefigured and influenced what would follow in the rest of the world (including the implementation of the liberal-democratic form of mass politics).
11. Accessible online: http://www.gutenberg-e.org/steuer/index.html.
12. Steuer goes so far as to affirm that "the American YMCA and the United States government each became increasingly dependent on the resources of the other to meet their respective policy objectives during the course of the war." Steuer (2009: chap. 19).
13. Ralph Blanchard, "The History of the YMCA in World War One," *WorldWarI.com*, http://www.worldwar1.com/dbc/ymca.htm.
14. Archives of World Alliance of the YMCAs (AWA), Geneva, fund Czechoslovakia, box 2: Extension work, letter, report of D. A. Davis (undated, early 1920s).
15. In 1912, soon after finishing his studies of Protestant theology, Kenneth Dexter Miller (1887–1968) was sent to Bohemia to learn the Czech language and to become acquainted with Czech culture in order to be ready to serve as a Presbyterian minister to Czech-speaking immigrants in North America. During his stay in Bohemia he met and befriended Tomáš G. Masaryk and his family. Miller remained connected to the country all his life. Between 1917 and 1919, he served as a YMCA secretary with the Czechoslovak Legions in Siberia. In the interwar period, he spent several long stays in Czechoslovakia. After 1948, he worked with Czech political refugees in the United States. His private papers are accessible at the Immigration History Research Center

at the University of Minnesota, and I am very grateful to Daniel Nečas for having attracted my attention to those files.
16. Immigration History Research Center Archives (IHRC), Minneapolis—University of Minnesota, fund Kenneth Miller Dexter (71), box 3, Diary entry 26 July 1918.
17. IHRC Minneapolis, fund Kenneth Miller Dexter (71), box 1, Letter from 5 November 1917.
18. AWA Geneva, fund Czechoslovakia, box 1 (Czechoslovakia by subjects), Report from August 1920.
19. AWA Geneva, fund Czechoslovakia, box 2, "After ten years an American looks at the YMCA in Czechoslovakia."
20. AWA Geneva, fund Czechoslovakia, box 2, Letters from Olga Masaryková (1919).
21. AWA Geneva, fund Czechoslovakia, Survey of the YMCA in Czechoslovakia (1930), Part II, 8.
22. AWA Geneva, fund Czechoslovakia, box 1, Report from June 1920.
23. AWA Geneva, fund Czechoslovakia, box 1, Report from December 1920.
24. An order of the Ministry of Defense from 26 May 1919 assured the association "adequate quarters with furnishings, light and heat, transportation of personnel and materials on a military basis, the right to purchase supplies from the Quartermaster and the assignment of details necessary for operating the huts." Quoted in Kautz Family YMCA Archives (KFA YMCA), University of Minnesota Libraries, fund: Records of YMCA International Work in Czechoslovakia, box 1, Czechoslovakia 1924. See also KFA YMCA Minneapolis, fund Czechoslovakia, box 2, Letter from D. A. Davis (November 1919): "The Czecho-Slovakia Government is giving us more facilities than any other Government with which we have worked in any country."
25. AWA Geneva, fund Czechoslovakia, box 1, Report from December 1920.
26. Abraham Maslow formulated this psychological theory in his famous article "A Theory of Human Motivation" (Maslow 1943).
27. AWA Geneva, fund Czechoslovakia, box 1, Report from December 1920.
28. AWA Geneva, fund Czechoslovakia, box 1, Report from August 1920.
29. KFA YMCA Minneapolis, fund Czechoslovakia, box 1, Report 1924.
30. AWA Geneva, fund Czechoslovakia, box 1, Report from August 1920 (České Budějovice).
31. KFA YMCA Minneapolis, fund Czechoslovakia, box 1, Brief survey 1921.
32. AWA Geneva, fund Czechoslovakia, box 1, Report from December 1920.
33. For an analysis of a similar process in Italy, see Rossini (2008 94ff.).
34. Several messages of this type from highly placed representatives of the Czechoslovak army can be found in the Archives of the Czech YMCA (AC YMCA), Prague, file "Historie Foto YMCA 1920–1950."
35. AWA Geneva, fund Czechoslovakia, box 1, Report from November 1920.
36. AWA Geneva, fund Czechoslovakia, box 1, Report from December 1920.
37. AWA Geneva, fund Czechoslovakia, box 1, Report from December 1920.
38. KFA YMCA Minneapolis, fund Czechoslovakia, box 1, Report 1924.
39. AWA Geneva, fund Czechoslovakia, box 1, Report from November 1920.
40. AWA Geneva, fund Czechoslovakia, box 1, Report from August 1920 (České Budějovice).
41. AWA Geneva, fund Czechoslovakia, box 1, Report from November 1920.
42. The most extensive reflections about this in the Czechoslovak context can be found in AWA Geneva, fund Czechoslovakia, box 1, Czechoslovakia 1921: A study on the recreation and athletic situation in Czechoslovakia (J. A. Pipal).

43. The most concise expression of the YMCA's thought on the unifying role of sports and collective games is to be found in Basil Mathews, *Spirit of the Game* (London, 1926).
44. AWA Geneva, fund Czechoslovakia, box 1, Czechoslovakia 1921. These ideas are further developed in Josef Amos Pipal, *O americké výchově těla* (Praha, 1920).
45. There are several extensive files on the problems of the creation of a "democratic army" and the role of the YMCA in this process in *Historical Military Archives (Vojenský historický archiv) HMA* Prague, box MNO 1922, Presidium Politická kancelář 5281 6320, 28. Interesting complementary information can also be found in Vondrášek (1993: 41-62).
46. AWA Geneva, fund Czechoslovakia, box 1, Czechoslovakia 1921.
47. However, military archives show that certain influential representatives of the Czech Sokol association observed YMCA activities with suspicion (e.g. Jindřich Vaníček, who directed the educational department of the Ministry of Defense) *HMA* Prague, fund General Inspection, file GI 1920 25 1/5.
48. This association, originally devoted to gymnastics, was founded in 1862. It became one of the strongest proponents of Czech nationalism in the last decades of the nineteenth century (Nolte 2002).
49. AWA Geneva, fund Czechoslovakia, box 1, Czechoslovakia 1921.
50. *Štít. Politický týdeník Československé strany lidové* 15(11), 1921: 4; *Nová Severní Morava* 2(42), 1920: 1.
51. HMA Prague, box MNO 1922, Presidium Politická kancelář 5281 6320, 28.
52. AWA Geneva, fund Czechoslovakia, box 1, Report from August 1920.
53. AWA Geneva, fund Czechoslovakia, box 2, Correspondence 1920-1921 (Olga Masaryková).
54. HMA Prague, box MNO 1922, Presidium Politická kancelář 5281 6320, 28.
55. I analyze this aspect in more detail in my article "Returning 'Genuine Faith' to Modernity: The Academic YMCA in Interwar Czechoslovakia," which will appear in the collective volume edited by Harald Fischer-Tiné and Stefan Hübner (to be published with Hawaii University Press in 2020).
56. See various reports from 1920 in *AWA* Geneva, fund Czechoslovakia, box 1.
57. For a detailed analysis of "education towards international mindedness" promoted by the YMCA in interwar Czechoslovakia, see Matějka (2016: 153–79).
58. AWA Geneva, fund Czechoslovakia, box 5, Czechoslovakia by subjects, "America and Czechoslovak republic."
59. KFA YMCA Minneapolis, fund Czechoslovakia, box 1, report by William Caldwell.
60. AC YMCA Prague, file "YMCA—osobnosti," 1922.
61. For an in-depth analysis of the notion of self-interest in American philanthropy, see Zunz 2012.
62. In a similar way, Ian Tyrrell quotes Calvin Coolidge: "Our country was the good Samaritan that did not pass them by" (in Tyrrell 2010: 207).
63. AWA Geneva, fund Czechoslovakia, box 5, Czechoslovakia by subjects, *The Czechoslovak American*, January 1921.
64. AWA Geneva, fund Czechoslovakia, box 2, "Summary-Requirements of YMCA work in Czecho-slovak republic," 4 April 1919.
65. KFA YMCA Minneapolis, fund Czechoslovakia, box 1, report 1924.
66. AWA Geneva, fund Czechoslovakia, box 2, report of D. A. Davis (undated, early 1920s). The "Red Triangle" is the logo of the YMCA, which stands for the unification of the spirit, mind and body.
67. KFA YMCA Minneapolis, fund Czechoslovakia, box 1, report by William Caldwell.

68. Even the most passionate YMCA secretaries did not claim all the good for themselves. They developed ideas about the "providential" qualities of the Czechoslovak people, benefiting from the influence of Masaryk and Beneš, etc. (i.e. KFA YMCA Minneapolis, fund Czechoslovakia, box 2, Letter by D.A. Davis 1919).
69. AWA Geneva, fund Czechoslovakia, box 5, Czechoslovakia by subjects, *The Czechoslovak American*, January 1921.
70. KFA YMCA Minneapolis, fund Czechoslovakia, box 2, survey 1924.
71. AC YMCA Prague, file "YMCA—osobnosti," 1922.
72. AWA Geneva, fund Czechoslovakia, box 3, National work; Hoover in Washington 1925.
73. Hoover's thoughts (in this particular case linked to postwar Austria) are quoted in Rothbard (1979: 97).
74. AWA Geneva, fund Czechoslovakia, box 2, "Summary-Requirements of YMCA work in Czecho-slovak republic," April 1919.
75. AWA Geneva, fund Czechoslovakia, box 2, "The Association in Czechoslovakia in 1925."
76. Mainly in AWA Geneva, fund Czechoslovakia, box 1, reports from 1920.
77. Mainly in AWA Geneva, fund Czechoslovakia, box 1, reports from 1920.
78. AWA Geneva, fund Czechoslovakia, box 1, December report 1920. For the move of the elites of the Academic YMCA to the left see Matějka (2016: 174–79) and Matějka (2019).
79. An overview of this development can be found in Matějka (2016), but also in an older study situated in a Marxist perspective: Šiklová (1966).
80. The diversity and richness of today's activities of the Czech YMCA can be observed at www.ymca.cz.

References

Carley, Michael Jabara. 2014. *Silent Conflict: A Hidden History of Early Soviet-Western Relations*. Plymouth.
Conforti, Joseph. 1991. "The Invention of the Great Awakening 1795–1842." *Early American Literature* 26(2): 99–118.
Eichenberg, Julia, and John Paul Newman. 2013. "Introduction: The Great War and Veterans' Internationalism." In *The Great War and Veterans' Internationalism*, edited by Julia Eichenberg and John Paul Newman, 1–19. Basingstoke.
Hanna, Emma. 2015. "Young Men's Christian Association (YMCA)." In *1914–1918 Online: International Encyclopedia of the First World War*, edited by Ute Daniel, Peter Gatrell, Oliver Janz, Heather Jones, Jennifer Keene, Alan Kramer, and Bill Nasson. Berlin.
Hopkins, Charles Howard. 1979. *John R. Mott, 1865–1955: A Biography*. Grand Rapids, MI.
Hynek, Jaroslav, ed. 2011. *Ymca v proměnách času*. Praha.
Lancaster, Richard C. 1987. *Serving the U.S. Armed Forces 1861–1986*. Schaumburg.
Latourette, Kenneth Scott. 1957. *World Service: A History of the Foreign Work and World Service of the Young Men's Christian Associations of the United States and Canada*. New York.
MacAloon, John J., ed. 2008. *Muscular Christianity in Colonial and Post-Colonial Worlds*. London.
Masaryk, Tomáš G. 1925. *Světová revoluce za války a ve válce 1914–1918*. Praha.
Maslow, Abraham. 1943. "A Theory of Human Motivation." *Psychological Review* 50(4): 370–96.

Matějka, Ondřej. 2016. "Erziehung zur Weltbürgerlichkeit: Der Einfluss des Ymca auf die tschechoslowakische Jugend der Zwischenkriegszeit." In *Jugend in der Tschechoslowakei: Konzepte und Lebenswelten (1918–1989)*, edited by Christiane Brenner et al., 153–76. Göttingen.

———. 2019. "Un mur contre le bolchevisme? La Young Men's Christian Association (YMCA) dans la Tchécoslovaquie de l'entre-deux-guerres." *Le mouvement social* 267: 25–46.

Mathews, Basil. 1926. *Spirit of the Game*. London.

Miller, Kenneth Dexter. 2010. *Uncle from America*. Minneapolis.

Nolte, Claire E. 2002. *The Sokol in the Czech Lands to 1914: Training for the Nation*. New York.

Pipal, Josef Amos. 1920. *O americké výchově těla*. Praha.

Putney, Clifford. 2001. *Muscular Christianity: Manhood and Sports in Protestant America, 1880–1920*. Cambridge.

Rossini, Daniela. 2008. *Woodrow Wilson and the American Myth in Italy: Culture, Diplomacy, and War Propaganda*. Cambridge.

Rothbard, Murray N. 1979. "Hoover's 1919 Food Diplomacy in Retrospect." In *Herbert Hoover: The Great War and its Aftermath 1914-1923*, edited by Lawrence E. Gelfand. Iowa City.

Rothra, John L. 2014. "Progressivism's Impact on Evangelism: The Confluence of Ideas between Woodrow Wilson and John R. Mott, and Barack Obama and Jim Wallis." PhD diss., Southwestern Baptist Theological Seminary.

Shedd, Clarence Prouty. 1955. *History of the World's Alliance of Young Men's Christian Associations*. London.

Šiklová, Jiřina. 1966. "Československá YMCA: Příspěvek k ideologickým bojům o mládež a studenstvo v období první republiky." PhD diss., Prague.

Šimsová, Milena. 2005. *V šat bílý odění: Zápasy a oběti Akademické Ymky 1938–1945: vzpomínky, svědectví a záznamy vyprávění*. Benešov.

Smith, Erica C. 2018. "The YMCA and the Science of International Civil Statecraft in Post–World War I Czechoslovakia." In *The YMCA at War: Collaboration and Conflict during the World Wars*, edited by Jeffrey C. Copeland and Yan Xu, 101–22. Lanham, MD.

Steuer, Kenneth. 2009. *Pursuit of an "Unparalleled Opportunity": The American YMCA and Prisoner-Of-War Diplomacy among the Central Power Nations during World War I, 1914–1923*. New York.

Straka, Karel, and Tomáš Kykal. 2013. *Československá armáda v letech budování a stabilizace 1918–1932*. Praha.

Taft, William H., et al. 1922. *Service with Fighting Men: An Account of the Work of the American YMCA in the World War*. New York.

Tlustý, Tomáš. 2017. *Budování národních organizací YMCA v Československu a Polsku, Rozvoj tělesné kultury v letech 1918–1939*. Praha.

Tlustý, Tomáš, and Jan Štumbauer. 2013. *Tělesná výchova a sport v organizacích Ymca a Ywca v meziválečném Československu*. České Budějovice.

Tyrrell, Ian R. 2010. *Reforming the World: The Creation of America's Moral Empire*. Princeton, NJ.

Vondrášek, Václav. 1993. *Výchovná práce v československé armádě po roce 1918*. Praha.

Zunz, Oliver. 2012. *Philanthropy in America: A History*. Princeton.

Zückert, Martin. 2006. *Zwischen Nationsidee und staatlicher Realität: Die tschechoslowakische Armee und ihre Nationalitätenpolitik 1918–1938*. Munich.

CHAPTER 9

When the Defeated Become Victorious
Averting Violence with Football in Post-1918 Romania

Cătălin Parfene

After Greater Romania was formed in 1918, incorporating the former Habsburg provinces of Transylvania, Banat, and Bukovina, and the former Russian province of Bessarabia, the percentage of ethnic minorities living in Romania rose dramatically. According to official demographic data, ethnic minorities comprised 8 percent of the population of the Old (pre-1918) Romanian Kingdom, but that rose to 30 percent in Greater Romania after 1918. In some big cities the percentage was even higher. The minorities were predominantly "defeated" Hungarians and Germans. Romanian government efforts at integration were directed toward these new provinces and populations. Integration posed a challenge for Greater Romania because revisionist ideas persisted in opposition to the territorial rearrangements that followed World War I. In consequence of those post-1918 territorial and political changes, interethnic violence rose in the new provinces of Romania. Uprisings in Khotyn (1919), Bender (1919), and, later, Tatarbunary (1924) were among the most violent, with thousands of deaths (Clark 1927; Okhotnikov and Batchinsky 1927; Scurtu 2003; Rotari 2004).

To avoid violence and to integrate the "defeated" Hungarians and Germans, one solution found by the Romanian ruling dynasty was football, or more precisely, the Romanian national football team, a potent symbol of Romanian national identity that nevertheless had a rather paradoxical preponderance of non-Romanian ethnicities among its teammates. The Romanian royal dynasty was directly involved in the establishment of the Romanian national football team in 1922, as well as in efforts to integrate the new provinces and their peoples into their kingdom, mainly through the personal engagement of Prince Carol, the future King Carol II.

In the broader international context, sport emerged as a nonviolent competition connected to political pacification after the war. Sport came to serve as a symbolic example of the possibility of nonviolent competition between states in the twentieth century. After 1918, domestic national regeneration through sport was a common goal, and the results of international competitions mirrored, or were hoped to mirror, the nation's status. National football teams were identified with the nation itself and had to obey ideological "rules" of nation-building (Lowe, Kahn, and Strenk 1978; Hobsbawm 1992a; Riordan and Krüger 1999; Marschik 2001; Rossol 2010; Tomlinson and Young 2011).

Established in early 1922 under the direct guidance of Prince Carol, the Romanian national football team throughout the interwar period was almost exclusively composed of representatives of ethnic minorities, primarily Hungarians and Germans but also Jews, Czechs, and Poles. All those players came from Transylvanian and Banatian clubs. However, this strategy for taming the divisions in post-1918 Romanian society, by recruiting ethnic Hungarians and Germans for the Romanian national football team, did not have the hoped-for unifying effect. In the interwar political milieu of Romania, characterized by Romanian nationalism and the centralization of political power, there were sharp debates about the need to "Romanianize" the Romanian national team (Jelavich 1983; Volovici 1991; Breuilly 1993; Livezeanu 1995; Ornea 1995; Boia 2001).

In the following pages I will analyze the peculiarity of the Romanian national football team as a symbol of the Romanian nation. As I will explain in my presentation of the theoretical framework, the national team was composed mainly of Hungarians and Germans from its very beginnings in the 1920s and throughout the interwar period. I will emphasize two crucial dimensions: the first is the relationship between football and nationalism, while the second reflects the relationship between ethnic minorities and the project of Romanian nation-building, the key notions of which were Romanianization and centralization of power. I will also emphasize the influence of the Romanian Dynasty and the future King Carol II on the establishment of the national football team in the post–World War I context of ethnic violence and the construction of the Romanian nation.

The theoretical framework in which my analysis is embedded deals with two crucial dimensions: the relationship between sports, and football in particular, with nationalism in the first half of the twentieth century, and the relationship between Romanian nation-building and the country's ethnic minorities after the Greater Union in 1918.

Sport, Football, and Nationalism

> "A nation is one, exactly as a sports team is one."
> Robert Brasillach (1941)

Popular pastimes in eighteenth-century England evolved into what today we call "sports" through the establishment of rules whose aim was to avoid serious injury to participants. These nonviolent competitions emerged as an aid to the political pacification of the English upper classes after the civil wars, according to Norbert Elias (Elias and Dunning 1993: 18–40). A relationship between sport and politics was present from the birth of the former and persisted through the following centuries. In the twentieth century, international sports came to "serve as symbolic representations of a non-violent, non-military form of competition between states," and "the growing significance of achievements in sport [was seen] as a status symbol of nations" (Elias and Dunning 1993: 263–307). In Eric Hobsbawm's words,

> National identification in this era [the apogee of nationalism, 1918–1950] acquired new means of expressing itself in modern, urbanized, high-technology societies. . . . Between the wars sport as a mass spectacle was transformed into . . . contests between persons and teams symbolizing state-nations. (1992a: 142–43)

States began to introduce physical education after wars, together with the idea of sport as a salvation of the nation and a cure for its ills. Nationalist ideas were associated with mass physical exercises in the nineteenth century. The German Turner and the Slavic Sokol movements were the most representative examples in that regard (Hobsbawm 1992b: 163–307; Tomlinson and Young 2011: 489). At the beginning of the twentieth century, contemporary commentators saw sport as having "an invigorating effect on the nation as a whole . . . thereby serv[ing] the national interest" (Hoberman 1978: 224–40). The renowned founder of the modern Olympic Games, Pierre de Coubertin, saw sport as a social therapeutic and an instrument to address the psychic crisis of modern civilization (Hoberman 1978: 229–30). The country that most energized Coubertin's idea in the interwar period was, not surprisingly, Fascist Italy—"although the use of sport as a symbol of vigour and for the sake of national representation had been already discussed prior to the Great War in Britain, Germany, France, and some other countries" (Krüger 1999: 67–89).

As one recent essay states, the focus on sport as a creator of a sense of community and national identification characterized "democracies and dictatorships alike in the 1920s and 1930s" (Rossol 2010: 9). Thus, not only was sport an expression of national identity, it even had a role in constructing a national identity.

Football's high (if not highest) position in an imaginary sports hierarchy is not the subject of this chapter. However, its evolution explains football's relationship with nationalism and politics and adds other dimensions to the general framework of sport and nationhood presented above. By the end of the nineteenth century in Britain, football had evolved from an amateur, middle-class pastime to a professional, working-class sport. Other countries followed the British pattern, which helped football not only to become an international urban social phenomenon but also to gain massive popularity in comparison to other sports. According to Matthias Marschik,

> By the early 1920s, football had become a popular form of mass culture. Not only had football firmly ensconced itself in the politics of the day, it had gone beyond the realm of sport and politics and become a mass phenomenon of its own.... As an integral part of popular culture, football in the 1930s was largely politically and economically driven.... [A]lliances were often made that were entirely politically motivated, such as the exclusion of the Central European clubs and national teams from Allied competition. (2001: 11, 18)

The close relationship between football and the nation was not at all fortuitous. As Richard Giulianotti has argued, football shaped and cemented national identities just as did education and the mass media, in a period "when most nations in Europe and Latin America were negotiating their borders and formulating cultural identities" (Giulianotti 2007: 23).

Starting from the late nineteenth century and continuing throughout the interwar period, the mass media intensively covered international football matches played by national teams, where attendance by politicians became common. Newspapers appeared that were dedicated only to sport or even to football alone. Most general-circulation newspapers and cultural magazines had at least one page dealing with sports topics. At international football matches, much attention was given to symbolic gestures embodying the spirit of the modern nation-state, like a player wrapping himself in the national flag or onlookers singing the national anthem. At the same time, the cultivation of rigid nationalism in the interwar period, characterized by militarization and rising nationalist feelings, led to segregation and exclusion for some, as political views were transposed onto the football field. The impact of nationalism was most visible in totalitarian regimes like Nazi Germany, where "Jews and Marxists were systematically excluded from the game from 1933 onwards" (Giulianotti and Robertson 2009: 20).

"The imagined community of millions seems more real as a team of eleven named people," as Hobsbawm put it (1992a: 43). This brings us to the second crucial dimension to be studied in this chapter, namely the relationship between the Romania's nation-building project and its ethnic minorities after the Greater Union in 1918.

Romanian Nation-Building and "Foreign" Minorities

> "[T]he undesirable 'aliens,' *străini*, as the Roumanians call the non-Roumanian minorities, must be forced to emigrate."
> Zsombor de Szász (1927)

After Greater Romania was formed in 1918, its new minority populations, especially Hungarians, Germans, and Jews, "were more urban, more schooled, and more modern than the Romanians" (Hobsbawm 1992a: 7–8). They were added to the Old Kingdom's existing Jewish community, which already had a bourgeoisie that was very active in the economic and cultural life of the country. Following the post-1918 territorial and political changes, the already mentioned uprisings in Khotyn, Bender, and Tatarbunary took place in the new provinces of Romania, Bukovina, and Bessarabia, and were serious examples of the ethnic violence that rose in the country. The revolts were quickly suppressed by the Romanian army. Casualties among the rebels were huge: three thousand deaths during the Tatarbunary uprising (Rotari 2004: 238), and up to fifteen thousand deaths during the Khotyn insurrection, according to Ukrainian historiography.[1]

The Romanian government directed its efforts to the integration of its new provinces, especially Transylvania. Transylvania was home to formerly ruling, well-organized Hungarian and German elites that still controlled the land and businesses. It was also home to a very politically mature class of the Romanian population, which embraced the idea of unification with the Romanian state quite late and only after extracting certain guarantees. Both categories of people represented a challenge for the Old Kingdom. Demographics and the higher level of economic and cultural development led on the one hand to an effort to catch up to those standards by the Old Kingdom, and on the other, to nationalizing (Romanianization) and centralizing measures that were enacted by the government in order to oppose regionalist tendencies. This was a logical consequence of the "ethnic nationalism endemic in Eastern Europe in the interwar period" (Livezeanu 1995: xiii), when "most of the new states built on the ruins of the old empires were quite as multinational as the old 'prisons of nations' they replaced." Romania was an example of that (Hobsbawm 1992a: 133). Transylvania was indeed a big challenge for Bucharest, although the Old Kingdom had already successfully Romanianized the former Ottoman province of Dobrudja after 1878 (Iordachi 2002: 167–97).

In short, Romanianization meant the replacement of "foreign" elites with ethnic Romanians, where "foreigner" was understood as a representative of the minorities in a region. Historians like Barbara Jelavich and Irina Livezeanu argue for the use of the words "foreign" and "foreigner" in this sense, as they were applied by the national leaderships in Romania and elsewhere in the Balkans to their minority citizens (Jelavich 1983: 135–36; Livezeanu 1995: 10–11). National identity was by no means equivalent to citizenship, as historian Lucian Boia explained:

> The member of a minority has tended to be seen first as foreign, before being considered a member of the Romanian nation and a Romanian citizen. This confrontation was particularly acute in the inter-war period, when Romania, having doubled its territory, suddenly found itself with an almost endless collection of minorities. (Boia 2001: 193)

Even mainstream state measures of Romanianization were considered too soft by the representatives of radical nationalism. These groups included the "1922 generation" of extreme right-wing students (who violently demonstrated for a *numerus clausus* in the universities), the fascist Iron Guard of Corneliu Zelea Codreanu, and a wide range of young intellectuals in the 1930s who more or less followed the nationalist thinkers Nae Ionescu and Nichifor Crainic. Many nationalists would later become renowned authorities in literature, philosophy, or history of religions (e.g., Mircea Eliade, Emil Cioran, Constantin Noica, Mircea Vulcănescu, and others).

According to Lucian Boia, "the most elaborate formula of the discourse on Romanian-ness was offered by the nationalist right of the 1930s" (Boia 1997: 168). In their view, the nation had to be composed chiefly, if not only, of ethnic Romanians (and better yet, Orthodox Christian Romanians—Nae Ionescu would have excluded the Greek-Catholic Romanians in Transylvania). The first targets of segregation were the Jews in the Old Kingdom and the Hungarians in Transylvania. The Jews in Transylvania were already Magyarized (Gyémánt 2004: 103; Livezeanu 1995: 136, 153) to such an extent that the Transylvania-born future prime minister Octavian Goga spoke of a kind of Magyar danger he called the "Hungarian Semitic" (Volovici 1991: 43). Such psychoses developed from certain existing revisionist ideas, because the internal "other" "often offers more features of alterity and much more stimulates all sorts of anxieties than the external *other*" (Boia 1997: 200). "Goga illustrated... the metamorphosis of traditional nationalism into a form of *Romanianism*, an ideology of struggle against foreigners" (Volovici 1991: 42).

As old ethnic rivalries were exacerbated, new "scientific" ideas such as eugenics were employed to underline the need for exclusion of minorities from the process of nation-building and for their Romanianization. The evolution of the eugenics movement in the 1920s and 1930s is relevant in this respect. The fact that most eugenicists came from Transylvania led them to emphasize "differences between Romanians and Hungarians [described] in biological hereditary terms, even when discussing moral or intellectual characteristics" (Volovici 1991: 69).[2] As a result, almost 200,000 Transylvanian Magyars, one-fifth of the Hungarian population in Transylvania, departed for Hungary and resettled there after 1918 (Livezeanu 1995: 137). About 225,000 individuals, one-third of the total Jewish population, were stripped of their citizenship in 1938 by a decree of Octavian Goga's government (Ornea 1995: 392).

After 1922, in a milieu characterized by Romanianization, centralization, and the rise of the extreme right, under the auspices of the ruling dynasty the Romanian national football team emerged as an important symbol of the Romanian nation and state, despite the fact that it was composed mainly of Hungarians and Germans from Transylvania and Banat.

The Romanian National Football Team as a Heritage of the Defeated Austro-Hungarian Empire

Adalbert Ritter, Alois Szilágy, Elemér Hirsch, Dezsö Jakobi, Nicolae Hönigsberg, Francisc Zimmermann, Aurel Guga, Carol Frech, Paul Schiller, Ferenc Rónay, and János Auer. One look at the roster of the first ever Romanian national football team[3] begs a question in the mind of anyone familiar with the anthroponyms of Central and Eastern Europe: "Was this the *Romanian* national team?" The question is a legitimate one, because only one of the abovementioned eleven players, who played in Romania's debut match in international football on 8 June 1922 (Yugoslavia—Romania 1-2) had a Romanian name and was an ethnic Romanian. That was the team captain, Aurel Guga. Noticing the clubs that supplied the eleven national-level players—Chinezul Timişoara (three players), CA Oradea (two players), and MTK Târgu Mureş, CA Cluj, Haggibor Cluj, CA Timişoara, Universitatea Cluj, and AMEFA Arad (one player each)[4]—another question naturally arises: "Was this perhaps a Transylvanian representative side?"

A look at the second international match played by Romania (3 September 1922, a 1-1 tie with Poland) might help us answer those two questions. However, the picture only becomes more complicated. The new names that appear (Alexandru Szatmári, József Bartha, Sándor Kozovits, Emil Rigolo Koch, Stanislas Micinski, Adalbert Ströck, and Zoltán Drescher) and the clubs from which they came (Stăruinţa Oradea, Unirea Timişoara, and Polonia Chernivtsi)[5] beg yet another question, if we forget about the demise of the Austro-Hungarian Empire four years earlier: "Was this perhaps an Austro-Hungarian team?"

The Establishment of the Team in 1922 within the Austro-Hungarian Football Framework

> "[In the Austro-Hungarian Empire,] one went in for sport, but not in the madly Anglo-Saxon fashion."
> Robert Musil (1930)

Why did the Romanian national team begin in 1922 as a team all but entirely composed of minority players, mainly from Transylvania? To find the answer to this question, a regional approach is required, looking beyond the national paradigm. In Central and Eastern Europe after 1918, new states appeared, and existing states reestablished themselves on the ruins of the Austro-Hungarian Empire. As recent research has shown (Tomlinson and Young 2011: 487–507), an approach that emphasizes "the importance of regional and cross-national flows and influence" and "capture[s] the complexity of the area's trans-national and multi-ethnic communities and structures" (Tomlinson and Young 2011: 501) is necessary, in parallel with an approach focused on the nation-state, for a better understanding of sports history in post-1918 Central and Eastern Europe.

After Romania's Great Union in 1918, the former Austro-Hungarian provinces of Transylvania (including Banat) and Bukovina and the former Russian province of Bessarabia became part of the Romanian state. From then on, Romania had to deal with several different, already established models for the organization of sports in order to integrate them into one national sports culture. This was a common task for the states in Central and Eastern Europe. Poland is a good comparison with Romania in this regard, given its need to develop sport from the Habsburg, German, and Russian models (Hilbrenner and Lenz 2011: 595–610). In Romania, there were huge differences that needed to be overcome. The most striking one, which most helps us explain the establishment of the Romanian national football team, was between Transylvania's model for the development of football and that of the Old Kingdom, which, as I will explain below, drew on the Austro-Hungarian and the British paradigms, respectively.

As I mentioned before, I will refer to Transylvania in the largest sense of the term, including not only the so-called historical Transylvania but also the regions of Banat (its Romanian part), Crișana, and Maramureș. Transylvanian football developed within the Austro-Hungarian framework in the late nineteenth century. In 1902, when "the first international football match outside the British Isles confronted Austria and Hungary," such "'international' contests [initially] served to underline the unity of nations or empires in the way inter-regional contests did" (Hobsbawm 1992b: 301). In the same year, 1902, the first football club in Transylvania appeared under the name Temesvári FC (FC Timișoara, later CA Timișoara) (Ionescu and Tudoran 1984: 13). That club was soon followed by dozens of other football clubs in the region. Thus, by the beginning of the twentieth century, clubs from Temesvár (Timișoara), Kolozsvár (Cluj), Arad and Nagyvárad (Oradea) were competing in the Hungarian championship, dominated by teams from Budapest. Some of them, Kolozsvári KASK (CA Cluj), Aradi AC (CA Arad), Kolozsvári TC (TC Cluj), Nagyváradi AC (CA Oradea), and Temesvári Kinizsi (Chinezul Timișoara),[6] won the title of regional champion.

After 1918, the Transylvanian club teams continued "their traditional contacts with their former competitors from the Austro-Hungarian monarchy," preferring "encounters with Hungarian, Yugoslavian or Austrian teams rather than the quite modest ones from other Romanian provinces" (Popa 2007: 191–203). Teams frequently visited Hungary or were visited by Hungarian teams and competed in tournaments. They were coached by Hungarian and Austrian trainers almost every season. Moreover, there were players who represented both the Romanian and the Hungarian national teams in the 1920s and 1930s, like Zoltán Szaniszló, Pál Teleky (Pavel Teleki), Károly (Iuliu Alexandru) Fuhrmann, Mihai Tänzer (Mihály Táncos), István Avar (Ștefan Auer), Gyula (Iuliu) Barátky, Rudolf Wetzer, and Adalbert Ströck (Albert Török).[7] An urban phenomenon *par excellence* in Transylvania, football was played mainly by Hungarians, Germans, and Jews. The latter were already Magyarized in Transylvania (Livezeanu 1995: 136, 153; Gyémánt 2004: 103). Romanians were a small minority in the population of the multicultural Transylvanian cities. When the members of the "foreign" communities became Romanian citizens in 1918, the national team chose its international players from the abovementioned Transylvanian teams.

A look at the different path in the development of football in the Old Kingdom will explain the preeminence of the Transylvanian players in Greater Romania. Football suddenly appeared in the Old Kingdom at the beginning of the twentieth century. It was an "invention" brought in by foreigners working in Romania in industrial and financial businesses (Economu 1935: 17; Manușaride and Ghemigean 1986: 127). This was the classic British pattern, by which football was spread almost everywhere else in Europe and South America. When the first Romanian championship took place in the 1909–1910 season, only three clubs competed. The championship team, Colentina Bucharest, was composed of English and Scottish players and had no Romanians. United Ploiești had only English, Scottish, American, and Dutch players, with no Romanians. Olympia Bucharest was more of a multicultural team and was the only one where a few Romanians played alongside Englishmen (Ionescu and Tudoran 1984: 15).

The foreigners continued to be at the core of every team in the Old Kingdom. From 1918 onward, the foreign character of the Old Kingdom football clubs increased as professional players and coaches without Romanian citizenship were brought in, especially from Austria and Hungary. Moreover, as Romania's future national coach, Virgil Economu, wrote in the 1930s,

> Some cities in the Old Kingdom, beginning with Bucharest, reached a satisfactory technical level of soccer, due to the close contact they had with Transylvania.... [Romanian football] is struggling between the influences of Hungarian soccer and the adaptation to our Latin temperament. (Economu 1935: 72, 132)

Thus, the Austro-Hungarian paradigm progressively gained ground in the Old Kingdom part of Romania, and the British influence waned. In the interwar period,

> Calcio Danubiano, the specific football system played by the national teams and clubs from Hungary, Czechoslovakia and Austria ... [was among] the most admired football cultures in Europe, challenging even the traditionally leading position of English soccer. (Marschik 2001: 7)

The 1921 national championship of Greater Romania included teams from Romania's new provinces. However, because a preliminary regional competition was kept in place until the early 1930s, the Old Kingdom clubs had no chance to win the title or play in the finals, which became the quasi-exclusive playing field for Transylvanian clubs like Chinezul Timișoara, (champion every year from 1922 to 1927), Victoria Cluj, CA Oradea, and Colțea Brașov (Ionescu and Tudoran 1984: 482). The winners were "the distinguished teams which imitated the Hungarians and especially the Austrians" (Economu 1935: 17). The Old Kingdom basically lacked a football culture, even into the 1920s:

> [In Bucharest] the rules of the game were only approximately known. Many believed that three corner kicks meant a goal scored etc. There were no players' registrations. ... The players and the referee changed their clothes near the pitch, and behind every goal there was a pile of clothes. (Economu 1935: 25)

During the 1920s, Old Kingdom clubs managed only twice to play in the finals. Juventus Bucharest lost to Chinezul Timișoara in 1926, while Venus Bucharest won the title in 1929 (Ionescu and Tudor 1984: 22). Both of those teams had Hungarian and Austrian players and coaches throughout the interwar period, such as György Hlaway, László Csillay, and Gyula Feldmann (future coach of Internazionale Milano) at Juventus, and Ferenc Platko (who coached FC Barcelona), József Pozsár, Béla Jánosy (former coach of Újpest Budapest), and Károly Weszter at Venus. The Old Kingdom clubs sometimes provided the national team with naturalized foreigners like the Greek Konstandinos "Kostas" Humis (Venus Bucharest), the Swiss Charles Kohler (Unirea Tricolor Bucharest), and the Serb Svetozar "Kika" Popović (Juventus Bucharest) (Ionescu and Tudoran 1984: 608–11).

Thus it can be seen that even after Greater Romania was formed in 1918, "the old [Austro-Hungarian] networks still persisted" and "there was also a lively exchange of players, trainers and other experts" (Hilbrenner and Lenz 2011: 601), as there was everywhere else in the states built on the ruins of the Austro-Hungarian Empire. "Sporting relations between Vienna, Budapest and Prague were hardly affected by the demise of the monarchy" (Marschik 2001: 9).

The Role of the Romanian Dynasty in the Integration of "Defeated" Hungarians and Germans

> "HRH Prince Carol is almost always present at all these sports manifestations, and he is often seen among the [football] players."
>
> Daily *Rampa*, 14 June 1922

Austro-Hungarian multiculturalism was indeed the framework in which the Romanian national football team emerged with its minority representatives from the former Austro-Hungarian provinces. "By the early 1920s, football had become a popular form of mass culture ... [that] firmly ensconced itself in the politics of the day" (Marschik 2001: 18). "Between the wars ... international sport became, as George Orwell soon recognized, an expression of national struggle, and sportsmen representing their nation or state, primary expressions of their imagined communities" (Hobsbawm 1992b: 143). The establishment of the Romanian national football team was strongly connected with the Romanian Dynasty of Hohenzollern-Sigmaringen.

The first international match in Romania's history took place on the same day (8 June 1922) as the royal wedding in Belgrade between Alexander I, the king of Serbs, Croats, and Slovenes and future king of Yugoslavia, and the Romanian princess Maria, daughter of Ferdinand I, then king of Romania.[8] As the contemporary press remarked, "During the last years, due to the fact that the heir to the throne, HRH Prince Carol, is the head of the physical education movement, the development of almost all forms of sports greatly flourished" (Orășianu 1922: 1). Prince Carol, the future King Carol II, expressed himself shortly after the match with Yugoslavia, in one of the most popular Romanian newspapers in the interwar period, *Universul* (The universe). He emphasized the superior development of Transylvanian, that is, Hungarian and German, football when compared to the Old Kingdom:

> The sport which became the most popular in our country is football. I was pleased with the occasion of the football match [in Belgrade]. ... Transylvania brought us a considerable contribution in sport. There are sport societies [in Transylvania] whose teams successfully fought with teams from the Occident that have world fame.... My dream is to have a stadium. We have cities in Greater Romania that have a stadium, while Bucharest does not. (Orășianu 1922: 1)

Publicly underlining the importance of Transylvania, Carol was here trying to avoid ethnic violence like that which had broken out in the east of the country. He was aware of the large numbers of ethnic Hungarians and Germans in the province, not to mention the revisionist ideas that were circulating, especially in neighboring Hungary. One of the ways in which the crown prince tried to avoid violence was his personal involvement in the choosing of players for the national football team. Carol was considered at the time to be the shadow coach of the team, and journalists were aware of his direct intervention in the selection of players (Ionescu 1998: 178–79). His concern about Transylvania was heightened by the fact that the region was the most industrialized and urbanized province in the country. It was also the most developed in terms of sport and, especially, football. The integration of the defeated populations of Hungarians and Germans into football, and thus into the Greater Romania project, was meant not only to prevent ethnic violence in the postwar order but also to bring success in terms of international sports representation of Romania. After violent revolts in Bessarabia, the Prince intervened there too, despite that province's lack of industrialization and interest in sports. As propaganda, he basically invented a local team in Kishinev, into which he gathered some of the best players of the moment while they were serving in the Romanian military.[9]

Carol's agenda of forming a national football culture that included the ethnic minorities seemed to yield positive results in the reduction of conflict and violence and encouraging of national integration. For example, a former international, Mircea David, emphasized in his memoirs the peaceful multicultural environment of two of the teams he played for in the interwar period, CA Oradea—where he was the only ethnic Romanian—and Venus Bucharest. In the interwar years, these two clubs, along with Ripensia Timișoara, became the main providers of players for the Romanian national team. This is how David commented on the multiethnic and multiregional composition of Venus Bucharest:

> Here, at Venus, players from all over the country gathered. Me, Bodola, Juhasz and Orza came from Oradea, Ploeșteanu, Sfera and Gain arrived from Cluj, Albu from Arad, Demetrovici from Timișoara, Fredy Fieraru from Chernivtsi, Iordăchescu and Lupaș from Ploiești, Humis and Beffa from Greece. There also were the Vâlcov brothers' "clan" (Petea, Colea and Volodea) and the Bucharest true-born Andrei Bărbulescu, Gorgorin and Traian Iordache. These people with different features and temperaments formed, although it is hardly believable, a single family. There were never any disputes, frictions or animosities between the players. . . . Venus was and remained for years a united family. There were no Bucharest or Oradea "clans," it was only "our team." (Mihalache 1979: 72, 79)

Of the nineteen Venus players mentioned by David, seventeen played for the Romanian national team. Another former international player, Augustin Juhász of CA Oradea, described the relationship between David, as the only ethnic Romanian on that squad, and his ethnic Hungarian colleagues, many of whom also played for the national team:

CAO was a big family for all of us. Mircea [David] did not know Hungarian. . . . An extraordinary thing happened then. Mircea began to learn Hungarian in order to make us [the ethnic Hungarians] a surprise, while we asked him to improve our Romanian language so that we could speak it correctly. . . . When people love each other, the language (*graiul*) is not an impediment. (Mihalache 1979: 161)

Prince Carol indeed closely oversaw the establishment of the Romanian national football team in the crucial year of 1922 ("HRH Prince Carol is almost always present at all these sports manifestations, and he is often seen among the [football] players," wrote the daily newspaper *Rampa* on 14 June 1922). That was the year Carol's father, Ferdinand I, was officially crowned king of Greater Romania in a sumptuous ceremony held in the Transylvanian town of Alba Iulia. In accord with his efforts to integrate the new Romanian provinces, Carol chose the Maccabi arena in Chernivtsi, Bukovina, to host Romania's second international football match on 3 September 1922. Carol himself attended the game, which ended in a 1-1 tie with Poland.[10]

In the following years, Carol continued to supervise the development of the national team by attending various test matches and club matches in Transylvania, which were organized in order for Romania to have a competitive team at the 1924 Olympic Games in Paris.[11] The prince personally intervened with the Romanian government to highlight the propaganda value of sport for the country. He was present in Paris for the Games and, very importantly, was the patron of the selection committee for the national football team (Popa 2013: 319)—this time in an officially recognized position from which he could act as the de facto coach of the team. However, Romania's participation in the Olympic Games surfaced some divisions between Transylvania and the Old Kingdom, and problems that arose from Romania's representation in international competition by minorities, as I will show below.

The close relationship between the Royal Family and the national team continued over the years. As crown prince, Carol supported the foundation in 1912 of the Federation of Societies of Sport in Romania (Popa 2013: 190) and was involved in passing a 1929 law on physical education (Popa 2013: 193). Later, as King Carol II, he started his own mass movement, *Straja Țării* (The sentinel of the motherland). *Straja Țării* developed from a governmental office, the Office for Romanian Youth Education, whose initial mission was to determine the ethnic composition of the national football team. In the 1930s, that office evolved into a youth organization, which used big sport spectacles as propaganda. It was meant to sustain Carol II's monarchy against the growing influence of the extreme-right Iron Guard (*Enciclopedia României* [The Romanian encyclopedia], vol. 1, 1938; Popa 2013: 131).

When Romania hosted and won the 1933 Balkan Cup in football, Carol II and his son Mihai were present at Romania's matches (Boantă 1993: 3). After

Romania's success, Carol II himself decorated the entire team ("O serbare epocală" [A memorable celebration], *Gazeta Sporturilor*, 14 June 1933: 1). Moreover, both Carol II and his predecessor, Ferdinand I, were the presidents of the Romanian Sports Federation. Carol, first as heir to the throne and then as king, was also the president of the Romanian Olympic Committee.[12] To sum up, the Romanian Dynasty was directly involved in the establishment of the Romanian national football team in 1922 and in the efforts to integrate Romania's new provinces and their people—mainly through the personal involvement of Prince, and later King, Carol. Nevertheless, his strategy for taming Romania's divided post-1918 society, by drafting almost exclusively ethnic Hungarians and Germans for the Romanian national football team, was not without problems.

A Symbol of a Nation Composed of Minorities, and of Its Problems

> "The national team carries its sin which is inherent to the [Hungarian] race and to the centrifugal tendencies of the majority of the players, who have their interest beyond the Romanian borders."
> Daily *Cuvântul*, 14 October 1932

> "We want A REAL NATIONAL TEAM because the Hungarian players who monopolized our national squad . . . mocked the Romanian football."
> Daily *Cuvântul*, 15 October 1932

As I have already said in my statement of the theoretical framework for this chapter, after the Great Union in 1918, the replacement of "foreign" elites with ethnic Romanians was a continuing policy of government that pitted regions and minorities, on the one hand, against centralization and Romanianization, on the other (Livezeanu 1995: 14, 18–19). During the interwar period, "integral nationalism became widely accepted as the ideological framework for politics at large" in Romania (Livezeanu 1995: 14). One of the most intriguing sports phenomena was the predominance of minorities on the national football team. Football in Romania was essentially "invented" by foreigners and then almost completely "confiscated" by ethnic minorities. It was difficult to link the Romanian national team to Romanian national identity because of the lack of ethnic Romanians on its roster and among those playing the games.

In 1924, Romania went to the Olympic Games in Paris with a squad composed of twenty-two players, of whom only one (an ethnic Greek) came from an Old Kingdom club and only four were ethnic Romanians (all of whom came from Transylvanian clubs). Despite Prince Carol's personal involvement in the development of the national team, Romania's participation at the Olympic Games in the summer of 1924 was a disaster. The team lost its first and only game 0-6 to the Netherlands and was eliminated from the competition. The Olympics were the most important international competition of the time, since both the Balkan Cup and the World Cup were yet to be established. The apocalypse followed. Team captain Aurel Guga accused the Hungarian and German players of deliberate sabotage ("De vorbă cu un fost 'as' al football-ului românesc" [Talking to a former "ace" of Romanian football]).[13] The half-German, half-Hungarian forward Adalbert Ströck accused Old Kingdom–based officials and coaches of a lack of professionalism and of "boozing," leaving the players to devise match tactics and even to procure food for themselves ("Cum am devenit stea... Cariera lui Strök [sic] Albi, povestită de el însuşi" (12) [How I became a star: Strök Albi's career narrated by himself], *Rampa*, 23 September 1928: 3).

The Romanian press began to question the wisdom of selecting mainly minority players and to advocate the Romanianization of the team, as in the following two examples from the Bucharest daily *Comedia* (The comedy):

> [At the Olympic Games in 1924,] when our national team entered the arena, the following recommendation was heard from all the corners of the stadium: *Hungarian team from the territories stolen by Romania*.... We already have plenty of unofficial enemies, then why should we send sports deputations abroad to deny even those few good things... about the Romanian country? (Severeanu 1927a:4)

and

> The fact that our nation is rapidly degenerating physically is certain.... We should reflect if we can remain in that passivity because of which we must send to the Olympic Games minority players who are making a fool of ourselves. (Slătineanu 1927b: 3)

The disaster was complete in the autumn of 1924 when one ethnic Hungarian player, Dezsö Jakobi, died as the result of an untreated injury he suffered during a friendly match played right before the Olympic Games.[14]

During the 1920s, rumors were often spread by the press that Hungarians were playing for the Romanian national team without having Romanian citizenship (Bolintineanu 1927: 3). Some foreign newspapers, like *L'Echo des Sports* from France, embarrassingly pointed out that "the Romanian national team is composed entirely of Hungarian players" ("Foot-ball-ul şi politica: Un articol din L'Echo des Sports" [Football and politics: One article from *L'Echo des Sports*], *Comedia*, 16 October 1927: 3). Minority players like Rudolf Wetzer were labeled by the press as "felons" and "foreign elements, undesirable for our safety" (Bolintineanu 1927: 3). Right before the 1928 Olympic Games in

Amsterdam, there were two opinions current with respect to the Romanian national football team, as expressed in *Comedia*. On the one hand, the newspaper deplored the fact that some of the best players of Magyar origin left Romania to play for club teams and for the Hungarian national team: "This is too bad.... Otherwise we would have had a football team to go to Amsterdam. We could have transformed Peter [Péter, the Hungarian name] into Petrescu [the Romanian name] and sent him to the Netherlands" (Moldovanu 1927: 4).

On the other hand, the same newspaper asked, "Do we have a Romanian sport?" and challenged the Romanian identity of the Transylvanian clubs, emphasizing the particularity of football in comparison with other sports. It concluded, "We do not have a real Romanian sport. Regarding football, the answer is negative; in regard to rugby, tennis, ski, fencing, shooting, the answer is positive.... The other sports are insignificant" (Severeanu 1927: 2). In the end, the predictions of the press ("the national team would not be able to form itself because of the departures of some players to Hungary"[15]) became reality, and Romania was not able to participate in the Olympic Games in Amsterdam. The multicultural pattern based on Greater Romania's Austro-Hungarian heritage began to fade, making way for a discourse of Romanianization regarding football. In accord with official state policy in other domains, such as the economy and education, and considering the rise of extreme-right movements emphasizing Romanian ethnicity, conflict over football reached a peak in the 1930s. "In our times it is not possible for a sports conception to be without a national character, because sport is identical to the people's soul and strength," *Comedia* editorialized on 21 October 1927.

Between the wars, against a background of mainstream official policies of Romanianization and centralization, and the rise of the extreme-right movements, the Romanian national football team emerged in 1922 as a symbol of the Romanian nation and state, which counterintuitively was composed mainly of representatives of minorities, especially Hungarians and Germans from Transylvania. The national team sometimes did not even have a single ethnic Romanian or Old Kingdom–based player on its roster. Conceived by the royal family as part of a generous strategy for taming Romania's fractious post-1918 society, with its new provinces and "foreign" populations, the integration of the "defeated" Hungarians and Germans into the Romanian national football team eventually ran into problems. Coincidentally, the national team was established the same year, 1922, as the Romanian extreme-right movement called "the 1922 generation" appeared.

The campaign for Romanianization peaked in the extreme-right framework of the 1930s. It eventually took on paroxysmal and violent dimensions. A violent "crusade" against "foreigners" was carried out in the press by prominent politicians and writers like Nicolae Iorga and Camil Petrescu, not to mention the leaders of the extreme right. The Romanian government had to intervene in the mid-1930s into the national team's affairs, establishing direct state control over the team's composition in furtherance of the policy of Romanianization.

Cătălin Parfene is a PhD candidate in history at Ecole des Hautes Etudes en Sciences Sociales in Paris, France. His field of academic interest is the relationship between football, ethnic minorities, and national identity in Romania during the last century. While working as a football journalist and football content writer for the Romanian federation, he also published several academic articles and book chapters regarding the history of Romanian and international football. Genealogy, medieval history, and history of music are among his other academic interests.

Notes

1. "Hotyns'ke Povstannya, 1919" [Khotyn Rebellion, 1919]. In Ihor Pidkova, R. M. Shust, K. Bondarenko. *Dovidnyk z istoriï Ukraïny* [Directory of the history of Ukraine], 1993–1999. Kiev.
2. See also Georgescu (2010: 6, 861–80).
3. "Romanian National Team 1922–1929—Details," RSSSF.com, retrieved 5 April 2016 from http://www.rsssf.com/tablesr/roem-intres20.html.
4. "Romanian National Team 1922–1929—Details," RSSSF.com, retrieved 5 April 2016 from http://www.rsssf.com/tablesr/roem-intres20.html.
5. "Romanian National Team 1922–1929—Details," RSSSF.com, retrieved 5 April 2016 from http://www.rsssf.com/tablesr/roem-intres20.html.
6. "Hungary—List of Final Tables 1901–1910," RSSSF.com, retrieved 7 April 2016 from http://www.rsssf.com/tablesh/honghist1900.html; "Hungary—List of Final Tables 1911–1920," RSSSF.com, retrieved 7 April 2016 from http://www.rsssf.com/tablesh/honghist1910.html.
7. "Players for both Hungary and Romania," RSSSF.com, retrieved 7 April 2016 from http://www.rsssf.com/miscellaneous/roemhong-recintlp.html. However, that list is incomplete.
8. "Nunta regală dela Belgrad: Serbări în onoarea Familiei Regale Române" [The royal wedding in Belgrade: Festivities in honor of the Romanian royal family], *Universul*, 10 June 1922, 1.
9. Bogdan Popa, "Sportul în Basarabia interbelică sau povestea unei integrări eşuate" [Sport in interwar Bessarabia or the story of one failed integration], Historia.ro, retrieved 22 May 2017 from https://www.historia.ro/sectiune/general/articol/sportul-in-basarabia-interbelica-sau-povestea-unei-integrari-esuate.
10. "Serbările sportive din Cernăuţi" [Sports festivities in Chernivtsi], *Universul*, 8 September 1922: 2.
11. "Echipa reprezentativă Bucureşti bate echipa naţională cu 2-1 (2-0). Principele Carol asistă la match" [The representative team of Bucharest beats the national team with 2-1 (2-0). Prince Carol attends the match], *Universul*, 10 May 1924, 2; "Vizita A. S. R. Principelui Carol la Oradea Mare" [The visit of HRH Prince Carol to Oradea], *Universul*, 22 May 1924, 2.

12. Principele Radu al României, "Sportul românesc și Casa Regală" [Romanian sport and the royal house], Princeradublog.ro, 20 October 2008, retrieved 16 May 2016 from http://www.princeradublog.ro/jurnal/sportul-romanesc-si-casa-regala/.
13. *Sportul Național*, 8 July 1935: 3.
14. Bogdan Popa, "Un proiect eșuat: 'Românizarea' fotbalului interbelic" [A failed project: Interwar football's Romanianization], Historia.ro. Retrieved 10 May 2016 from http://www.historia.ro/exclusiv_web/general/articol/un-proiect-esuat-romaniza rea-fotbalului-interbelic.
15. "Hotyns'ke Povstannya, 1919" [Khotyn Rebellion, 1919]. In Ihor Pidkova, R. M. Shust, K. Bondarenko, *Dovidnyk z istoriï Ukraïny* [Directory of the history of Ukraine], 1993–1999. Kiev.

References

Boantă, Vladimir. 1933. "România-Grecia 1-0 (1-0)." *Calendarul*, 11 June.
Boia, Lucian. 1997. *Istorie și mit în conștiința românească* [History and myth in Romanian consciousness]. Bucharest.
Boia, Lucian. 2001. *Romania: Borderland of Europe*. Translated by James Christian Brown. London.
Bolintineanu, Petre N. 1927. "A cui e vina?" [Who is to blame?]. *Comedia*, 11 September.
Brasillach, Robert. 1941. *Notre Avant-Guerre*. Paris.
Breuilly, John. 1993. *Nationalism and the State*. 2nd ed. Manchester.
Clark, Charles Upson. 1927. *Bessarabia, Russia and Roumania on the Black Sea*. New York.
Economu, Virgil. 1935. *Football: Studiu documentar și critic* [Football: Documentary and critical study]. Bucharest.
Elias, Norbert, and Eric Dunning. 1993. *Quest for Excitement: Sport and Leisure in the Civilizing Process*. Oxford.
Enciclopedia României [The Romanian encyclopedia], vol. 1. 1938.
Georgescu, Tudor,. 2010. "Ethnic Minorities and the Eugenic Promise: The Transylvanian Saxon Experiment with National Renewal in Inter-War Romania." *European Review of History* 17(6): 861–80.
Giulianotti, Richard. 2007. *Football: A Sociology of the Global Game*. 2nd ed. Cambridge.
Giulianotti, Richard, and Roland Robertson. 2009. *Globalization and Football*. Los Angeles.
Gyémánt, Ladislau. 2004. *Evreii din Transilvania: Destin istoric* (The Jews of Transylvania: A historical destiny). Translated by Simona Făgărășanu. Cluj-Napoca.
Hilbrenner, Anke and Britta Lenz. 2011. "Looking at European Sports from an Eastern European Perspective: Football in the Multi-ethnic Polish Territories." *European Review* 19(4): 595–610.
Hoberman, John M. 1978. "Sport and Political Ideology." In *Sport and International Relations*, edited by Benjamin Lowe, David B. Kahn, and Andrew Strenk, 224–40. Champaign, IL.
Hobsbawm, Eric. 1992a. *Nations and Nationalism since 1780: Programme, Myth, Reality*. 2nd ed. Cambridge.
———. 1992b. "Mass-Producing Traditions: Europe, 1870–1914." In *The Invention of Tradition*, edited by Eric Hobsbawm and Terence Ranger, 263–308. Cambridge.
Ionescu, Andrei. 1998. "1930: Românii în Uruguay" [1930: Romanians in Uruguay]. *Secolul XX. Fotbal* 4–7.
Ionescu, Mihai, and Mircea Tudoran. 1984. *Fotbal de la A la Z: Fotbalul românesc de-a lungul anilor* [Football from A to Z. Romanian football along the years]. Bucharest.

Iordachi, Constantin. 2002. "'La Californie des Roumains': L'intégration de la Dobroudja du Nord à la Roumanie, 1878–1913." *Balkanologie* 6(1–2): 167–97.
Jelavich, Barbara. 1983. *History of the Balkans: Twentieth Century*. Vol. 2. Cambridge.
Krüger, Arnd. 1999. "Strength through Joy: The Culture of Consent under Fascism." In *The International Politics of Sport in the Twentieth Century*, edited by James Riordan and Arnd Krüger, 67–89. New York.
Livezeanu, Irina. 1995. *Cultural Politics in Greater Romania: Regionalism, Nation Building, and Ethnic Struggle, 1918–1930*. Ithaca, NY.
Lowe, Benjamin, David B. Kahn, and Andrew Strenk, eds. 1978. *Sport and International Relations*. Champaign, IL.
Manuşaride, Chiriac, and Chevorc Ghemigean. 1986. *Aproape totul despre fotbal* [Almost everything about football]. 2nd ed. Bucharest.
Marschik, Matthias. 2001. "Mitropa: Representations of 'Central Europe' in Football." *International Review for the Sociology of Sport* 36(1): 7–23.
Mihalache, George. 1979. *"Il Dio" şi "diavolii" din faţa porţii . . . Amintirile lui Mircea David, fostul portar al echipei naţionale de fotbal* ["Il Dio" and "the devils" in front of the goal: The memoirs of Mircea David, the former goalkeeper of the national football team]. Bucharest.
Mitu, Sorin. 2001. *National Identity of Romanians in Transylvania*. Translated by Sorana Corneanu. Budapest.
Moldovanu, M. 1927. "Carnetul meu" [My notebook]. *Comedia*, 27 November.
Musil, Robert. 1930. *The Man without Qualities*. London.
Okhotnikov, J., and N. Batchinsky. 1927. *L'insurrection de Khotine dans la Bessarabie et la Paix Européenne*. Paris.
Orăşianu, C. A. 1922. "A. S. R. Principele Carol vorbeşte 'Universului' în chestia educaţiei fizice" [HRH Prince Carol speaks in "Universul" on the issue of physical education]. *Universul*, 14 June.
Ornea, Zigu. 1995. *Anii treizeci. Extrema dreaptă românească* [The Romanian extreme-right: The 1930s]. Bucharest.
Pidkova, Ihor, R. M. Shust, and K. Bondarenko. 1993–1999. *Dovidnyk z istoriï Ukraïny* [Directory of the history of Ukraine]. Kiev.
Popa, Bogdan. 2013. *Educaţie fizică, sport şi societate în România interbelică* [Physical education, sport and society in interwar Romania]. Cluj-Napoca.
———. 2007. "'Our Team?' Ethnic Prejudices and Football in Interwar Romania." In *Sport zwischen Ost und West: Beiträge zur Sportgeschichte Osteuropas im 19. und 20. Jahrhundert*, edited by A. Malz, S. Rohdewald, and S. Wiederkehr, 191–203. Osnabrück.
Riordan, James, and Arnd Krüger, eds. 1999. *The International Politics of Sport in the Twentieth Century*. New York.
Rossol, Nadine. 2010. *Performing the Nation in Interwar Germany: Sport, Spectacle and Political Symbolism*. Basingstoke.
Rotari, Ludmila. 2004. *Mişcarea subversivă în Basarabia 1918–1924* [The subversive movement in Bessarabia 1918–1924]. Iaşi.
S.A.S. 1927. "În jurul echipei naţionale: Precizări pentru 'L'echo des sports'" [Concerning the national team: Explanations for *L'Echo des Sports*]. *Comedia*, 29 October.
Scurtu, Ioan. 2003. *Istoria Basarabiei de la începuturi până în 2003* [The history of Bessarabia from the beginnings until 2003]. Bucharest.
Severeanu, Saşa. 1927a. "Turneurile 'Chinezului'" [The tournaments of 'Chinezul' (Timişoara)]. *Comedia: Teatru, muzică, sport, film*, 17 October.
———. 1927b. "Adevărata problemă naţională" [The real national problem]. *Comedia*, 21 October.

Slătineanu, Sever. 1927. "Sportul universitar" [The university sport]. *Comedia*, 19 October.
Szász, Zsombor de. 1927. *The Minorities in Roumanian Transylvania*. London.
Tomlinson, Alan, and Christopher Young. 2011. "Towards a New History of European Sport." *European Review* 19(4): 487–507.
Volovici, Leon. 1991. *Nationalist Ideology and Antisemitism: The Case of Romanian Intellectuals in the 1930s*. Translated from the Romanian by Charles Kormos. New York.

Afterword

The End of the Great War and Postwar Problems

Boris Barth

The following chapter sums up some of the central conclusions of this volume and discusses some recent research perspectives. This book shows once more that World War I caused a sharp break in modern history—after the conflict ended, Europe had changed in a decisive way. This book covers a wide variety of topics associated with the end of the Great War and, in particular, with the emergence of the successor states of the Austro-Hungarian Empire. It often has been stated that categories like "victorious" and "defeated" nations are not entirely incorrect, but they are too simple for analyzing the extremely complicated postwar situation. The five Paris peace treaties did not create a new and stable world order—quite the contrary. Very often the aims of the victorious powers and the high expectations of their respective national publics were incompatible, and the compromise solutions that were found after the long debates in Paris did not satisfy influential social groups and some politicians.

With the exceptions of Great Britain, which had achieved nearly all of its war aims even before the conference started in Paris, and the newly created Czechoslovakia, all the other states in the European system of the early 1920s were revisionist powers when it came to the Paris treaties. Nationalist elites in nearly all European countries were looking for any opportunity to undermine the Paris Conference order and change it in their own favor. This was not only true for the losers in the war, but also for most of the victorious states. Many governments and nations that were clearly on the victorious side nevertheless interpreted the outcome of the Paris Peace Conference as a defeat, because they had not achieved the far-reaching aims with which they entered the war. Aggressive revisionism became one of the biggest problems after 1919.

In Italy, the epithet "crippled victory" (*vittoria mutilata*) became extremely popular, not only in radical revisionist circles. Italian public opinion reacted to the peace treaties with a storm of indignation, because liberal politicians had obviously been unable in Paris to win the territories that had been guaranteed to Italy by the secret treaty of London in 1915. Even in France, many politicians, and huge parts of the public, continued to demand setting the French-German border at the Rhine. Greece was clearly on the side of the victorious powers, but aggressive politicians and public opinion there demanded annexation of vast territories in Asia Minor. In this volume, Christopher Gilley discusses the question of whether a culture of victory or a culture of defeat developed in Ukraine. European revisionism contributed not only to the weakness of the new democratic systems but also to the near impossibility of creating a stable European order before 1923. The years between 1918 and 1923 were characterized by forces of disintegration, at least in Central and Eastern Europe.

Historians have often noted that the German request for an armistice and the downfall of the imperial governments of the Central Powers in 1918 did not mean the end of fighting (Bartov and Weitz 2013; Gerwarth et al. 2013; Gerwarth 2017). One can count more than twenty armed conflicts in Europe in the year 1919 alone. Some of them were relatively small, but others came close to being major wars, like the Russian Civil War, the Greco-Turkish war, and the many armed conflicts that accompanied the creation of the new Polish state and the State of Slovenes, Croats, and Serbs (later Yugoslavia). One other thing was typical of the postwar situation: the demobilization of minds did not really occur until well after 1918. Long after the fighting ended, the war was still going on in the hearts and minds of millions of people in Europe. The militarization of huge parts of the European population delayed the creation of civil societies. Jay Winter describes in his many publications how millions of traumatized and crippled veterans, women, widows, and orphans tried in vain to shed their memories, and Modris Eksteins shows in an impressive way how the foundations of the common European culture that existed before 1914 were shaken to the extreme (Eksteins 1989; Winter 1995; Winter, Parker, and Habeck 2000).

Several chapters in this book deal with the small wars, the civil wars, the revolutions, and the counterrevolutionary movements after the end of the Great War. Violence was omnipresent in Europe, and nation-building was sometimes a long and complicated process. Woodrow Wilson's proclamation of the right to self-determination created far-reaching ambitions, especially among the newly emerging nations of Eastern and Central Europe. However, especially in the successor states of Austria-Hungary, it was impossible to evaluate the national "will" of the various peoples. In many regions, unstable governments reacted by expelling unwanted minorities. Especially after the end of the Greco-Turkish war in 1922 and the infamous Treaty of Lausanne, millions of displaced persons aggressively demanded revisions to that treaty. The expulsion of millions of people was promoted by the Western powers as well, because leading politicians were convinced that ethnic homogeneity was conducive to minimizing international conflicts. In the 1920s, more than ten million people in Europe were on the move (Mann 2002; Naimark 2002; Schwartz 2013).

In all of those conflicts, mass expulsions and displacements were normalized, both for "ethnic" and ideological reasons. As the case of Ukraine shows, the émigrés often embraced ultranationalist politics and favored authoritarian and anti-Semitic thinking that bordered on fascism. In other regions, the ideological convictions of rank-and-file soldiers were fluid, and loyalties could change rapidly. In the civil wars and ideological conflicts after 1918, charismatic personal leadership frequently played an enormous role in forming the self-image of the troops. If a leader changed sides, his troops often followed him. Other units dissolved or simply went home if their leaders were unsuccessful or the situation on the battlefield became too dangerous.

In 1918–1919 the new borders in Central and Eastern Europe were not yet fixed. The breakdown of the empires and the demobilization of the regular armies created a space for paramilitary groups, private armies, and regional warlords. Their actions were possible because the state monopoly on violence was weakened or had even ceased to exist. Hardly any national group fully accepted the results of the Paris Peace Conference. They demanded change—if necessary, by military force. The formation of the German *Freikorps*, which fought semi-private wars, especially in the Baltics and on the Polish border, has been intensively researched for decades. Broad attention has also been paid to Gabriele D'Annunzio and his pre-fascist *Arditi* in Fiume. Much less is known about the many other paramilitary units active in Central and in Eastern Europe (Payne 2012; Plaggenborg 2012).

A typical phenomenon of asymmetric warfare is the contribution by civilians to the conduct of war. Guerillas lead a war from the shadows, and regular troops often face the problem of distinguishing between civilians and combatants. Civilians sometimes were combatants, and combatants often returned to civilian life after military clashes. The inability to draw clear lines between civilians and soldiers is one of the main reasons why partisan warfare often leads to unrestrained violence (Barth 2005).

Even by reading the sources carefully it is often difficult to distinguish ideology, hypernationalism, and simple banditry. Robbery, plunder, rape, and murder seem to have been a constant part of the paramilitary business. Although all of the regular armies in World War I committed war crimes, the established military hierarchies normally prevented brutalized soldiers from committing comparable excesses of violence. Exceptions prove the rule, however; in Belgium in 1914, during the advance of the German army, civilians were executed even though hardly any partisan activities were observed. Atrocities in the Balkans should be the subject of further detailed research, while the Armenian and Aramean genocide in the Ottoman Empire is very well documented

(Kramer and Horne 2001; Balakian 2003; Bloxham 2003; Weltecke and Barth 2019). On the Western and Italian fronts, officers normally were interested in maintaining discipline among their troops. In recent research, concepts such as "spaces of violence" and models based on those ideas have contributed to the development of new research perspectives. The existence of "spaces of violence" brings with it new tools for understanding the mechanisms of the escalation of violence.

For reasons that are not entirely clear, gender and gendered violence during and after World War I has hardly been a subject of international historical research up to now.[1] A huge and extremely interesting potential field of analysis is still wide open. It has been estimated that in the first year of the Great War alone, thousands of women were raped by regular soldiers. In the Balkans especially, the number of cases grew rapidly in the following years. To what extent were rape and sexual violence an integral part of warfare during and after World War I? It is likely that sexual violence on the Eastern Front was directly connected with anti-Semitic pogroms. As Béla Bodó correctly argues, historians normally tend to deal with rape and sexual violence in a descriptive rather than an analytical way.[2] In this volume, several authors have demonstrated their interest in developing new, analytical methodologies.

It also has been argued that massacres are a highly complex phenomenon, and that it is anything but simple to categorize and explain these forms of collective violence. Several preconditions must be fulfilled before mass killings or mass rapes become possible (Semelin 2007). Group dynamics and/or the reaction of local authorities play a role on the side of the perpetrators. Recent interdisciplinary research has shown that perpetrators do not seek sexual pleasure but to exercise their power and absolute dominance. Women's passivity often encouraged abuse. However, the interactions between victims and perpetrators are normally difficult to analyze because of a lack of source material. The same is true of the perpetrators' precise motives. The role of bystanders is extremely important; if they support the perpetrators or tolerate mass violence by remaining passive, rape is more likely to occur. In such cases, the perpetrators do not have to fear any sanction. In prisons and prison camps, on the other hand, bystanders hardly play any role or only an indirect one. Highly sexualized torture of both women and men obviously was an integral part of the civil wars that followed World War I.

In this volume, two articles focus on Hungary and the White Terror (Bodó 2006, 2010). The analysis of this specific instance of post–World War I violence is mainly based on rich Allied Powers source material, and it should encourage further research on the topic in more Central and Eastern European countries as well. Murder, torture, rape, beatings, and other atrocities were definitely not unique to Hungary. Sexual violence (like other forms of violence) very often had a particular aim—it seldom was an end in itself. On the perpetrator's side, it was aimed at reinforcing absolute male supremacy in the gender hierarchy. The bodies of women were helpless objects. Collective rape contributed to the formation or re-formation of group identities, because perpetrators normally were fully aware that they had touched upon a moral taboo together and crossed a red line. At the same time, open sexual terror could be used for deterrence or to suppress possible resistance. In the theory of sexual violence, many questions still remain open and require more intensive comparative historical research and discussion.

Historians have intensively debated the question of why a stable democracy could be established in the first Czechoslovak Republic, when all the other newly formed republics of Central and Eastern Europe failed within less than two decades (Barth 2016). We certainly do not have one single answer to that question, and a mixture of several explanations is likely. One reason among others might be that the Czechoslovak government managed to organize an army that remained loyal to democratic order. Winning the loyalty of the country's veterans was anything but easy, because in 1919 and the following years rather heterogeneous groups had to be integrated into the new armed forces: members of the German and Hungarian linguistic minorities, Czech veterans of the Great War who had fought for Austria-Hungary, and later, the battle-hardened members of the Legions, who had fought on the side of the Allies. Although the Czech soldiers in the former Austrian army had had to face defeat, at the end of 1918 they suddenly belonged to the victorious side. This fact allowed them to identify positively with the emerging postwar order.

Another reason for the successful integration of the army was the activity of the American YMCA, as one chapter in this book argues. In accordance with Wilson's vision of the new world order, the YMCA offered personal assistance and financial and material support for the reintegration of the Legions. YMCA strategists elaborated a systematic program for working with young men who had returned from a violent conflict. One of their aims was to convince the veterans that the new Czechoslovak Republic was a state that was worth fighting for. It was easy to blame everything that went wrong in the past on the Austrians, whose rule had collapsed. The YMCA also started intensive propaganda campaigns in favor of America, the leading Anglo-Saxon civilization, because American diplomacy regarded Bohemia as extremely important for geopolitical and geostrategic reasons. The new Czechoslovakia was meant to become a center of democracy in Central Europe.

The activities of the YMCA can be seen as part of an American civilizing mission in Europe. One of its aims was clearing away the mental ruins of the decadent and authoritarian Austro-Hungarian Empire and building up new civilized, democratic nation-states. Those states were expected to act as barriers against both communism and revisionist tendencies. Civilizing missions have become the subject of intensive historical discussion during the last decade (Osterhammel 2006). In some cases, the idea of "uplifting mankind" was a cynical justification for power politics, imperialist war, and colonialism. However, in other cases, the civilizing mission was an honest attempt to improve the world by the abolition of slavery, torture, and mass violence, and by the promotion of democratization. Some contemporary observers, like Joseph Roth, who is mentioned in this volume, interpreted early Bolshevism as a special kind of civilizing mission as well. Roth's view was shared by many European left-wing intellectuals, who identified the horrors of the Great War with capitalist rule.

Most of the successor states of the Austrian Hungarian Empire—with the obvious exception of Hungary—faced the problem of integrating their ethnic minorities. However, hardly any nationalist leader was willing to grant political rights to groups other than his or her own. The integration and disintegration of postwar societies are topics that scholars have intensively debated in recent years (Ther 2011; Ipek 2013). Newly constructed national identities had to incorporate rather disparate ideological elements. As a result of the growing political pressure for national integration, every aspect of daily life was politicized. Some authors have already dealt with football in East and Southeast Europe (Dahlmann, Hilbrenner, and Lenz 2006). Football was not a passion just of the lower classes. Crown Prince Carol himself personally acted as a kind of "shadow" coach of the Romanian national team, which was mainly composed of "ethnic" Hungarians and Germans from Transylvania. However, the example of football in Romania shows once more that—against all ideological expectations—sports did not succeed in promoting the identification by minorities with the nation-state but instead proved the contrary.

Only a few historians have occupied themselves with studies that show a connection between nation-building and sports in the twentieth century. Some twenty or thirty years ago, that topic would have seemed too dubious and too irrelevant to attract the attention of serious historians, who were more interested in writing political history or were looking for hard economic facts. However, this situation is now changing. Sport of all kinds has clear political side effects. It attracts the attention of hundreds of thousands of people and contributes to the creation of common local, regional, and national identities.

It might be worth mentioning some examples. In 1934 the Polish press was excited because the German football team "Schalke 04" from the highly industrialized region of the Ruhr won the national championship. Every player had a Polish name. During the following week, a furious press was occupied with the question how "German" or how "Polish" this team was. The debate was overshadowed by two facts: on the one hand, National Socialist doctrine promoted a strictly anti-Slavic racism, while on the other, Germany and Poland had signed a treaty of nonaggression in January 1934. In Central America, a war broke out in July 1969 between Honduras and El Salvador during a qualification match for the world championship. The military conflict had a complicated social background, but the football match escalated tensions. More generally, and unfortunately, violence between competing national football hooligans is a sad daily experience all over the world. Until now, however, there has been no serious theory that links nationalism, national identification, and sports, including football.

Compared to histories of nationalism and sport and of gender and violence, studies about diseases and medical treatment during and after World War I are still rare. Even the Spanish flu, which represented the greatest medical catastrophe of modern times, was never at the center of historians' attention (Crosby 2003; Beiner 2006; Vasold 2009). One of the positive aspects of this book is that it deals with so many overlooked side-effects of the conflict. Of course, suicide is not an illness, but it does belong broadly among topics connected with mental illness. It is an open question whether one can really talk about a discourse of suicide, because in most cases, suicide is an individual decision. It is interesting that according to the few quantitative studies that exist, the number of suicides in Austria dropped during the Great War. This very fact flies in the face of the enormous growth of mental disease of all other kinds, such as war neuroses, hysteria, trembling, shivering, and shell shock. The number of reliable sources that discuss suicide in Austria is relatively small, and we are still lacking any analysis that fits the national statistics into an international frame.

The relation between medical treatment, psychology, and psychiatry has already been the subject of several historical and medical studies. In all belligerent countries, the number of war neuroses, nervous breakdowns, and psychoses grew rapidly in 1914–1915. In the beginning, the phenomenon was underestimated by the medical authorities. However, after some months the growing number of psychiatric diseases and war-related psychoses could no longer be ignored. Electroshock therapy showed no convincing long-term beneficial effect. Sigmund Freud's psychoanalysis was still too new and—from the perspective of government—did not offer a realistic short-term alternative.

Some Austrian doctors preferred to lean on hierarchies of perceived national worth. Slavic people were assumed to be inferior to Germans, and psychiatrists searched for correlations between Slavic nationality and psychic neurosis. The connection between psychiatry and "ethnicity" during World War I is a new and promising area for future researchers. The creation of ethnic stereotypes was closely connected to the process of nation-building, and they influenced the "objective" findings of medical science in the successor states as well as in Austria. Ethnic and racial prejudices became part of serious intellectual and scientific dialogue.

These prejudices were closely connected with the emergence of eugenic ideas. Far-reaching eugenic concepts had already been developed before 1914 in many European countries and in the United States, but scientists and governments were unable to put them into wide practice. During the war, however, all governments had to create new institutions to supervise and control their populations. Thus, after 1918, effective technocratic means existed to initiate active eugenic policies. It is still an open question how the eugenics of the early 1920s was influenced by the debates about war neuroses. A connection is more than likely.

In 1918–1919, most European countries were democracies, but by 1938 the picture had changed completely. In Central and Eastern Europe, only Czechoslovakia remained a parliamentary democracy. In Portugal after 1932–1933 and in Spain after the civil war of 1936–1939, fascism had spread in Western Europe as well. However, even though democratic parliamentary systems had collapsed in Central and Eastern Europe, a strong fascist movement dominated only in Romania. Fascism was unable to develop in the royal dictatorships (Yugoslavia and Bulgaria) for structural reasons. A fascist dictatorship needs an urban mass movement, which did not exist or could not be mobilized in these mainly agrarian countries. Despite the devastating effects of the Great Depression, the peasantry remained too conservative. Some of the more traditional authoritarian dictators, like Piłsudski in Poland and the leaders of the three Baltic states, had no interest in mobilizing the masses. Their power was based on traditional bureaucratic and conservative elites, combined with veterans of the local post-1918 wars.

This volume of conference proceedings contributes many new views to the history of both the Great War and its aftermath. It touches upon several areas that have not yet attracted much attention from historians. From the studies presented here, it is clear that the slow, difficult, and twisted road toward liberal and republican societies was blocked in 1914, although none of the events that followed were unavoidable.

Boris Barth is a professor for modern and contemporary history at the Institute for International Studies, Charles-University Prague. Since his dissertation (1993) he had several teaching and research positions at the universities of Düsseldorf, Hagen, Prague, Jacobs University in Bremen, and Konstanz. His main research interests are history of financial imperialism and European expansion since the late eighteenth century, banking and politics, the Weimar Republic and the stab-in-the-back legend, genocide and racism, globalization in the nineteenth century, and history of democracy since the late eighteenth century.

Notes

1. Interesting material still can be found in Hirschfeld (1930).
2. See page 45 in this volume.

References

Balakian, Peter. 2003. *The Burning Tigris: The Armenian Genocide and America's Response*. New York.
Barth, Boris. 2005. "'Partisan' und 'Partisanenkrieg' in Theorie und Geschichte: Zur historischen Dimension der Entstaatlichung von Kriegen." *Militärgeschichtliche Zeitschrift* 64: 69–100.
———. 2016. *Europa nach dem Großen Krieg: Die Krise der Demokratie in der Zwischenkriegszeit*. Frankfurt am Main.
Bartov, Omer, and Eric D. Weitz, ed. 2013. *Shatterzone of Empires: Coexistence and Violence in the German, Habsburg, Russian and Ottoman Borderlands*. Bloomington, IN.
Beiner, Guy. 2006. "Out in the Cold and Back: New-Found Interest in the Great Flu." *Cultural and Social History*: 496–505.
Bloxham, Donals. 2003. "The Armenian Genocide of 1915–16: Cumulative Radicalization and the Development of a Destruction Policy." *Past and Present* 181: 141–91.
Bodó, Bélá. 2006. "'White Terror,' the Hungarian Press and the Evolution of Hungarian Antisemitism after World War I." *Yad Vashem Studies* 34: 45–86.
———. 2010. "Hungarian Aristocracy and the White Terror." *Journal of Contemporary History* 45: 703–24.
Crosby, Alfred W. 2003. *America's Forgotten Pandemic: The Influenza of 1918*. Cambridge.
Dahlmann, Dittmar, Anke Hilbrenner, and Britta Lenz, eds. 2006. *Überall ist der Ball rund: Zur Geschichte und Gegenwart des Fußballs in Ost- und Südosteuropa*. Essen.
Eksteins, Modris. 1989. *Rites of Spring: The Great War and the Birth of the Modern Age*. Boston.
Gerwarth, Robert. 2017. *The Vanquished: Why the First World War Failed to End, 1917–1923*. London.
Gerwarth, Robert, et al., eds. 2013. *Krieg im Frieden: Paramilitärische Gewalt in Europa nach dem Ersten Weltkrieg*. Göttingen.
Hirschfeld, Magnus. 1930. *Sittengeschichte des Weltkrieges*. Leipzig.
Ipek, Nedim. 2013. "The Balkans, War, and Migration." In *War and Nationalism*, edited by M. Hakan Yavuz, 621–64. Salt Lake City.
Kramer, Alan R., and John Horne. 2001. *German Atrocities: A History of Denial*. New Haven, CT.
Mann, Michael. 2002. *The Dark Side of Democracy: Ethnic Cleansing in Twentieth-Century Europe*. Boston.
Naimark, Norman. 2002. *Fires of Hatred: Ethnic Cleansing in Twentieth-Century Europe*. Cambridge, MA.
Osterhammel, Jürgen. 2006. "Europe, the 'West' and the Civilizing Mission." Annual lecture of the German Historical Institute London. London.
Payne, Stanley. 2012. *Civil War in Europe, 1905–1949*. Cambridge.
Plaggenborg, Stefan. 2012. *Ordnung und Gewalt: Kemalismus, Faschismus, Sozialismus*. München.
Schwartz, Michael. 2013. *Ethnische "Säuberungen" in der Moderne: Globale Wechselwirkungen nationalistischer und rassistischer Gewaltpolitik im 19. und 20. Jahrhundert*. München.

Semelin, Jacques. 2007. *Säubern und Vernichten: Die politische Dimension von Massakern und Völkermorden*. Hamburg.
Ther, Philipp. 2011. *Die dunkle Seite der Nationalstaaten: "Ethnische Säuberungen" im modernen Europa*. Göttingen.
Vasold, Manfred. 2009. *Die Spanische Grippe: Die Seuche und der Erste Weltkrieg*. Darmstadt.
Weltecke, Dorothea, and Boris Barth, eds. 2019. *Sayfo: Das Jahr des Schwertes*. Berlin.
Winter, Jan. 1995. *Sites of Memory, Sites of Mourning: The Great War in European Cultural History*. Cambridge.
Winter, Jan, Geoffrey Parker, and Mary R. Habeck, eds. 2000. *The Great War and the Twentieth Century*. New Haven, CT.

Index

Allies *see* Entente
Ansolt, Teut, 18
anti-Semitic violence (*see also* pogroms), 1, 30, 39, 74
anti-Semitism, 4, 29–30, 36, 38–39, 59, 60, 74, 94–95, 98, 185–86
Arad, 169–70, 174
Arbeiter-Zeitung, 102, 111–12, 115
Arbeits- und Siedlungsdienst, 19
Armenian genocide, 46
Armistice, 1, 12, 65, 67–70, 78, 93, 113, 184
Artwiński, Eugeniusz, 135
Asia, 13, 49, 90, 133, 153, 184
atrocity stories, 68–69
Austria, 72, 89, 93, 101, 107–9, 112–17, 120, 171–72, 188
Austria-Hungary, 2, 45–46, 90, 110–11, 123–30, 132, 134–37, 146–47, 151, 169–71, 183–84, 187, 189
authoritarianism, 6, 29
authotelic violence (*autotelische Gewalt*), 51

Babel, Isaac, 94
Balkan Wars, 46, 123
Balla, Erich, 12, 13
baltic countries, 10
baltic fever, 12
Baltikumer, 3, 10–12, 14–15, 17–21
Baltische Landeswehr, 15
Barcelona, 172
Baudouin de Courtenay, Jan, 123
Baumann, Ursula, 109–10, 112, 121
Beevor, Antony, 48
Belgium, 80, 86, 185
Belgrade, 173
Bender, 163, 167

Beneš, Edvard, 142, 157, 161
Berlin, 16, 19, 22, 48, 89–91, 93, 98–101, 114, 116–17, 126, 135
Berliner Börsen-Courier, 90–91, 98, 100
Bethlen, István, 113
Bloch, Jan Gottlieb, 123
Bohemia, 132, 134–35, 138, 153–54, 158, 187
Böhm, Vilmos, 70
Boia, Lucian, 164, 168
Bolsheviks, 11–12, 14–15, 28–31, 33–41, 114, 136
Bolshevism, 13–14, 38, 85, 155, 157, 188
Bonhoeffer, Karl, 135
Bozhko, Iukhym, 33
Brand, Ignaz, 115
Brașov, 172
Bremen, 130, 135, 190
Breuer, Flóra, 51, 53, 61
Breuer, Ignác, 50, 53, 61
Breuer, Mór, 50–51, 53, 61
British Diplomatic Mission to Hungary, 55–56, 76
British Labour Party, 4, 68, 70
British Labour Party and Trades Union Congress Delegation, 68
Brody, 89
Brusilov, Aleksei, 128
Brussels, 136
Bucharest, 167, 171–74, 177
Budapest, 45, 53–54, 56, 58, 66–67, 69, 71–72, 76, 81–82, 113, 119, 127, 131, 170, 172
Bulgaria, 46, 136, 190
Bychawa, 123
Bychowski, Zygmunt, 136

Canada, 61, 144

194 | Index

Carol II, Prince of Romania, 164, 169, 173, 175–76, 188
Carpathians, 133
censorship, 111–12, 130, 134
Central Powers, 28, 46, 113, 136, 184
Central Rada (Ukraine), 28
Charcot, Jean-Martin, 127, 135
Chasidism, 91
Cheka, 34, 38–39
Chernivtsi, 169, 174–75
Chernyakhovsk, 95
Christian Social Party (Austria), 117
Cioran, Emil, 168
civil war, 4, 6, 11, 14, 29–33, 35–37, 41, 45, 47, 114, 144, 165, 184–86, 190
Cluj, 169–70, 172, 174
coercion, 126–27
Cold War 1, 143, 155
collective violence, 10, 15–16, 21, 186
Collins, Randall, 49, 52, 57, 60
combatants, 11–12, 16, 18–21, 41, 123, 185
communism, 56, 74, 77, 79, 81, 155–56, 187
Congress Kingdom of Poland, 124
Constituent Assembly (Ukraine), 37
Cossacks, 30, 33, 38, 40, 94
Coubertin, Pierre de, 165
Counterrevolution, 17, 30, 39, 47, 49, 60, 65, 67–68, 70, 76–80, 184
Cracow, 131, 135
Crainic, Nichifor, 168
Croats, 173, 184
Czechoslovak Legions, 143, 146, 158
Czechoslovakia, 2, 5–6, 36, 47, 60, 108, 126, 142–43, 146, 148–58, 161, 172, 183, 187, 190

D'Annunzio, Gabriele, 185
David, Mircea, 174
death marches, 46
Delannoy, René M., 109, 110
demobilization, 3, 5, 17–18, 184–85
democracy, 37, 81, 95, 147, 151–52, 154, 156, 187, 190
democratization, 188
Denikin, Anton, 30, 44
depression, 107, 112–13, 190
Der Reiter gen Osten, 19–20
Diszel, 49–53, 56–58, 60
Döblin, Alfred, 91–93, 98, 103

Dontsov, Dmytro, 36
Douglas, Jack D., 107
Drastich, Bruno, 125
Durkheim, Émile, 52, 108–10, 113, 118

Eastern Front, 1, 69, 146, 186
"Eastern Jews" (*Ostjuden*), 91, 103
Economo, Constantin, von, 137
Economu, Virgil, 171
Eichendorff, Joseph von, 98
El Salvador, 189
electric shocks, 128
electroshock therapy, 126, 128, 130–31, 189
Eliade, Mircea, 168
Elias, Norbert, 165
Ełk, 93
England *see* Great Britain
Entente, 12, 28, 67–68, 76–77, 80–81, 87
Ercsi, 54, 74
ethnic violence, 1, 152, 163–164, 167, 173–174
ethnicity, 79, 127, 132, 163, 178, 189
eugenics, 114, 190

faradization, 127–30, 135
feminists, 48, 65, 69
femme fatale, 59
Ferdinand I., King of Romania, 173, 175–76
fin de siècle, 111–12, 117
Finland, 110
Foelkersahm, Hamilkar von, 19
football, 6, 163–66, 169–79, 188–89
Forster, Vilém, 138
France, 1, 68, 89, 137, 145, 165, 177, 179, 184
Francis Joseph I, Emperor of Austria, 125
Frankfurter Zeitung, 90, 92, 101
Freikorps, 11–12, 19, 22–24, 95–96, 98–101, 185
Freud, Sigmund, 116–117, 127, 131, 133, 189
Froreich, Ernst von, 125
Fuchs, Alfred, 125

Galicia, 36, 46, 89–90, 133–35
Garami, Ernő, 70
Gąsiorowski, Janusz, 137
gender, 65, 67–68, 72, 77–80, 186–87, 189
gendered violence, 67, 186

German Army, 10, 110, 185
German Free Corps *see* Freikorps
German-Jewish culture, 92
Germany, 1–4, 10–13, 16, 18–20, 22, 24, 46, 49, 61, 68, 85, 89–90, 94–98, 100, 102, 108, 113–14, 126–27, 129–30, 137, 145, 165–66, 188
Gerwarth, Robert, 17, 47, 100, 102
Giulianotti, Richard, 166
Goda, Norman J. W., 107–8
Goeschel, Christian, 108
Goga, Octavian, 168–69
Goltz, Rüdiger Graf von der, 14
Gonda, Viktor, 128–30, 132, 135, 138
GPU *see* Soviet Secret Police 35
Graz, 129
Great Britain, 1, 68, 74, 143–44, 165–66, 107, 165, 183
Great War *see* World War I
Greco-Turkish War, 184
Greece, 174, 184
Grodno, 89
Grote, Nikolaus von, 15
group identity, 11, 15, 19
guerilla warfare, 21
Guga, Aurel, 169, 177
Gyöngyös, 67

Habsburg Empire *see* Austria-Hungary
Hajmáskér, 57
Hajnal, Eugen, 67, 73–74, 82, 84, 87
Hamburger, Jenő, 53, 67
Hamburger, Mrs. Sándor, 53, 65, 67
Hamburger, Sándor, 53
Héjjas Detachment, 71
Héjjas, Iván, 71
Hermes, Maria, 130, 135, 137
Hirschfeld, Magnus, 73
historiography, 1–2, 167
Hitler Youth, 113
Hobsbawm, Eric, 165–66
Hofer, Hans-Georg, 132–34
Höfer, Karl, 100
Honduras, 189
Hoover, Herbert, 155, 161
Hromádka, Josef Lukl, 152
Hryhor'iev, Nykyfor, 30, 33, 35, 37–39
Hungarian Republic of Councils *see* Hungarian Soviet Republic
Hungarian Soviet Republic, 67, 69

Hungary, 2, 4, 45–49, 53, 56, 60–61, 65–73, 75–80, 82–85, 147, 168, 170–172, 174, 178, 186, 188
Huysmans, Camille, 70
hypernationalism, 185
hysteria, 115, 118, 124, 127, 189

independence, 1, 11, 28–29, 31–32, 36, 156
Independentists, 29, 32, 34–35
Influenza *see* Spanish Flu
Insterburg, 95
interactional theory of violence, 49, 51, 59, 60
Inter-Allied Commission to Upper Silesia, 96
interethnic violence *see* ethnic violence
International Socialist Bureau, 69–70
internment camps, 56–57, 70–71
interwar period, 1–6, 10, 17–18, 20–21, 24, 30, 32, 45–48, 60, 67–68, 74, 78, 81, 90–91, 98, 100–2, 107, 110–14, 116–19, 125–26, 128, 131, 134–36, 138, 142, 147–58, 161, 163–79, 183–85, 187–88, 190
Ionescu, Nae, 168
Iorga, Nicolae, 178
Istanbul, 46
Italy, 1, 165, 183–84

Jakobi, Dezsö, 169, 177
Jelavich, Barbara, 167
Jendrassik, Ernő, 127
Jewish assimilationism, 91
Jewish heritage, 90
Jewish identity, 91
Jewish immigrants, 101
Jewish life, 73, 92
Jewish towns, 94
Jews (*see also* "Eastern Jews") 35–36, 38–39, 41, 45–47, 49–52, 59–60, 65, 67, 69, 72, 77–78, 85, 89–94, 155, 164, 166–69, 171
Juchnowicz-Hordyński, Zdzisław Ritter von, 125
Judeo-Bolshevism, 38, 85
Judson, Pieter, 6
Juhász, Augustin, 174

Kameradschaft ehemaliger Baltikumer- und Freikorpskämpfer, 19

Károlyi, Mihály, 65, 67
Kattowitz, 96, 97
Kaufmann, Fritz, 115–16, 129
Kawczak, Stanisław, 124
Kecskemét, 66, 71
Kelenföld, 53–54, 57–58, 65–66, 71
Khmel'nyts'kyi, Bohdan, 33, 36
Khotyn, 163, 167
Kimball, Irving D., 154–55
Kingdom of Romania, 163
Kishinev, 174
Kollarits, Jenő, 127
Kolozsvár, 170
Königsberg, 95
Korfanty, Wojciech, 99
Koval', Roman, 31, 42
Kozłowski, Michał, 131
Krasicki, August, 123
Kraus, Karl, 115
Kun, Béla, 4, 65, 67, 80

Latvia, 11–13, 15–20, 95
Lausanne, Treaty of *see* Treaty of Lausanne
Le Rond, Henri, 100
Lemberg *see* Lviv
liberal democracy, 95
libido theory, 116
Lima, Peru, 73
Livezeanu, Irina, 167
localizing violence (*lozierende Gewalt*), 51
Łódź, 91, 102
Lviv, 46, 133–34
Lwów *see* Lviv
Lyck, 93, 95

MacDonald, Michael, 107
Makhno, Nestor, 29–31, 39–40, 42
Marburg, Otto, 125
Marcus, Joseph, 72
Maria, Princess of Romania, 173
Mariategui, J. C., 73
Marschik, Matthias, 166
Masaryk, Tomáš G., 108, 142, 146–47, 151, 157–58, 161
Masaryková, Olga, 146
masculinity, 2, 41, 126
Maslow, Abraham Harold, 148–49, 151
melancholia, 113, 117
mercenaries, 16, 21
Mihai, King of Romania, 171, 175

Milano, 172
military hospital, 128, 135–36
militia violence, 45
Miller, Kenneth Dexter, 146, 158
minorities, 6, 16, 28, 46, 102, 142, 155, 163–64, 166–68, 170–71, 173–79, 184, 187–88
modernity, 97, 108, 111
modernization, 112
Moravia, 133
Moravian Silesia, 133
Moscow, 38, 136, 156
Mott, John R., 144–46, 154–55, 158
Müller, Karl Christian, 18
Munich, 102, 126–27
Mureş, Tărgu, 169
Murphy, Terence R., 107
Musil, Robert, 169
mutilation, 46, 49, 52, 60, 67, 79, 120

Nagyrév, 48
Nagyvárad, 170
Naimark, Norman, M. 49, 185
national character, 178
national identity, 134, 163, 165, 168, 176, 179, 189
National Socialists, 114
nationalism, 4, 6, 29–31, 35–36, 45–46, 70, 75, 90, 97–98, 100–1, 164–68, 176, 185, 189
nation-building, 164, 166–68, 184, 188–89
Netherlands, 110, 177–78
Neue Berliner Zeitung, 89–91, 93, 99–100
Neumann, Béla, 54, 58–59, 66, 71, 73, 79, 84
Neumann, Imre, 73–74, 84
neurosis, 115, 117–19, 129, 131–32, 189
Noica, Constantin, 168
Nonne, Max, 127
Nord, Franz, 13
Norway, 110
Noske, Gustav, 12

offensive warfare, 18
Oppenheim, Hermann, 116, 126, 135
Oradea, 169–70, 172, 174
Organisation of Ukrainian Nationalists, 29
Orgovány, 71
orientalism, 92–93
Orwell, George, 173

Ostjuden see "Eastern Jews"
otamans *see* warlords
Ottoman Empire, 46, 185

Papp, Demeter, 129, 132
Pappenheim, Martin, 115
paramilitaries, 1–3, 6, 10–14, 20–21, 41, 90, 95–96, 98–100, 102, 185
paranoia, 59, 115
Paris, 2, 73, 89, 92, 96, 108–10, 124, 136, 144, 166, 170, 175–76, 178–79, 183–85
Paris Peace Conference (*see also* Treaty of Lausanne, Treaty of Trianon, Treaty of Versailles), 96, 183, 185
partisans *see* peasant partisans
patriarchy, 48
Peace Treaties *see* Treaty of Lausanne, Treaty of Trianon, Treaty of Versailles
peasant partisans, 28–29, 31, 34
Petliura, Symon, 29–30, 33, 39
Petrescu, Camil, 178
Peukert, Franz, 125
Pilcz, Alexander, 125
Piłsudski, Józef, 96, 124, 190
Piltz, Jan, 135
Pipal, Josef A., 151
Ploieşti 171, 174
pogroms, 11, 28, 30, 37–39, 46, 56, 186
Poland, 2, 4–5, 29, 35–36, 82, 89–103, 124, 126, 169–70, 175, 184, 188, 190
Polish-Soviet War, 47, 91, 93, 95, 98
Poósz, Jénő, 73, 75, 76, 84
Portugal, 190
Post-Traumatic Stress Disorder (PTSD), 116, 119
Prague, 129, 135, 152, 155–56, 172, 190
prison violence, 56
prisoners-of-war, 94, 123, 136, 145
Prónay Battalion, 53–54
Prónay Officers' Detachment, 65, 70
Prónay, Pal, 53, 55
Prussia, 16, 90–91, 93, 95–96, 98, 110
psychiatry, 5, 125–26, 131, 134–38, 189
psychoanalytical circle, 116
PTSD *see* Post-Traumatic Stress Disorder

radicalization, 21, 49, 58–60
Rakovsky (*or* Rakovskii), Christian, 38, 43
rape, 15, 46, 48–49, 51–55, 57–60, 66–67, 71, 80, 89, 94, 185–87

raptive violence (*raptive Gewalt*), 51
Rathenau, Walther, 18, 41
Rauchensteiner, Manfried, 124
reconstruction, 2–3, 5, 6, 119
Red Army, 14, 28, 30, 35, 67, 94
Redlich, Emil, 115, 125
Reemtsma, Jan Philipp, 14, 51
Reichardt, Sven, 2
revisionism, 183–84
revolution, 3, 6, 11, 14, 17, 29–30, 32, 34–37, 39, 41, 45, 47, 49, 60, 65, 67–70, 73, 76–80, 82, 85, 109, 113, 115, 135, 142–43, 147, 155–56, 184
Riga, 11, 19, 21
robbers, 51
Roda, Alexander, 129, 132
Rohrscheidt, Walter von, 13
Romania, 2, 6, 36, 43, 45, 54, 67, 77, 132, 137, 163–64, 166–79, 188, 190
Romanianization, 164, 167, 168, 169, 176, 177, 178, 179
Romanov Empire *see* Russia
Rome, 136
Roßbach,, Gerhard 19
Roßbacher, 19
Roth, Joseph, 4, 89–103, 188
Rózsahegyi, 128
rumors, 69, 125, 177
Russia, 1, 11, 14, 16, 28–30, 32, 34–41, 46–49, 60, 89–91, 93–98, 101, 108, 110, 115, 136, 146, 155, 163, 170, 184
Russian Civil War, 35, 184
Russian Empire *see* Russia
Russo-Japanese War, 123
Ružomberok, 128
Rzeszów, 123

Salomon, Ernst von, 13, 16, 18, 41
Sarbó, Artur, 127
Schirach, Karl von, 113
Schmidt-Pauli, Edgar von, 13
Schüller, Artur, 125
Semon, Richard, 113
Serbs, 173, 184
sexual violence (*see also* rape), 45–48, 57, 59–60, 65, 67–68, 73–74, 77–80, 186
Shchus', Fedor, 40
shell shock, 115, 118, 125, 189
silent movies, 112
Silesian Uprising, 96, 100

Šimsa, Jaroslav, 152
Skaret, Ferdinand, 115
Skoropads'kyi, Pavlo, 30
Slovakia, 2, 5–6, 36, 47, 60, 108, 126, 128, 142–43, 146, 148–58, 161, 172, 183, 187, 190
soccer *see* football
Social Darwinism, 145
social democracy, 152, 156
Social Democratic Party (Austria), 111–12, 115
Social Democratic Party (Czechoslovakia), 156
Social Democratic Party (Germany), 101
Social Democratic Party (Hungary), 57
Socialist Party (Italy), 69
soldiers, 12–14, 16, 18, 21, 34, 36, 38, 46, 48–49, 52–55, 57–58, 60, 68, 71, 73, 77, 89, 93–94, 99, 109–10, 113–14, 119–20, 124, 126, 130, 133, 136, 142–52, 156–57, 185–87
Sosnowiec, 97
Soviet Russia *see* Soviet Union
Soviet Secret Police (GPU), 35
Soviet Ukraine, 35–36, 38
Soviet Union, 1, 22, 47, 60, 89, 94, 96, 101
Soviets *see* Bolsheviks
space of violence (*Gewaltraum*), 4, 11, 17, 31–32, 34, 40
Spain, 110, 190
Spanish Flu, 189
Squadre d'Azione, 2
stabilization, 2, 21
Starawieś, 123
Statistics, 5, 45, 107, 109–11, 114, 118–19, 189
Stettin, 91
Stransky, Erwin, 116, 125, 127, 132–34, 138
Ströck, Adalbert, 169, 171, 177
Strök, Albi, 177
Struempell, Adolph, 135
Struk, Il'ko, 30, 32
Sturmabteilung, 2
suffering, 2, 46, 49, 53, 60, 68, 73, 80, 115, 118, 124, 126, 130, 145
suicide, 5, 107–19, 125, 189
suicide statistics, 107, 109–11, 114
Suwałki, 89, 93

Sweden, 110
Switzerland, 110
Szücs, Katalin, 56

Tacitus, 92
Tambov Revolt, 37
Tapolca, 49–50
Tarcali, Robert, 72
Tatarbunary, 163, 167
Taussig, Leo, 135
Temesvár *see* Timişoara
Terpylo, Danylo, 30
Timişoara, 54, 169–70, 172, 174
Tiutiunnyk, Iurii "Iurko," 35–37
torture, 4, 46–47, 49, 51–52, 54–57, 59–60, 65–66, 71–75, 78–79, 186, 188
Transylvania, 54, 163–164, 167–76, 178, 188
trauma, 116–19, 126, 129, 136, 184
Treaty of Lausanne, 184
Treaty of Trianon, 113
Treaty of Versailles, 96, 100
Trianon, Treaty of *see* Treaty of Trianon

Ukraine, 3, 28–32, 35–39, 41, 184, 185
Ukrainian Military Organization, 36
Ukrainian People's Republic, 6, 12, 28–30, 32, 33, 34, 35, 36, 67, 98, 114, 147, 185
Ukrainian Socialist Soviet Republic, 29
unemployment, 107–8
United States of America, 5, 137, 144–47, 153–54, 157–58, 190
Urbanek, Joanna, 137

Váry, Albert, 45, 55–56
Versailles, Treaty of *see* Treaty of Versailles
Vértes, Marcel, 73, 83
Vienna, 53, 56–57, 65–67, 70–71, 73–74, 82, 84, 89, 110, 113, 115–17, 119, 125, 129–31, 133, 135, 137, 172
Vilnius, 92
violence (*see also* anti-Semitic, authotelic, collective, ethnic, gendered, interactional theory of, localizing, militia, prison, raptive, sexual violence), 1–6, 10–11, 14–21, 30–35, 37–41, 45–49, 51–52, 56–61, 65–71, 73–80, 89–90, 94–96, 98, 100, 109, 151–52, 157, 163–64, 167, 173–74, 184–89

violence artists, 52, 57, 60
violent communities
 (*Gewaltgemeinschaften*), 11, 14–15, 17, 20–21
volunteers, 12–14, 99, 144–45
Vorwärts, 101
Vulcănescu, Mircea, 168

Wagner-Jauregg, Julius, 125–28, 130–38
war neurosis *see* neurosis, 119, 131
warlords, 3, 28–33, 35–42, 185
Weichbrodt, Raphael, 110
Weimar Republic, 11, 17, 20–21, 95, 100, 102, 190
Western Front, 125, 145
Wetzer, Rudolf, 171, 177
White Terror (Hungary), 4, 45, 49, 58, 61, 66, 69, 73–77, 83, 186
Whites, 28, 30, 32, 34, 41
Wildenfeld, Friedrich Wodniansky von, 125
Williams, George, 143
Wilson, Woodrow, 95, 101–2, 144–46, 155, 158, 184, 187
Wittlin, József, 91

women's emancipation, 4, 80
women's suffrage, 48
World Depression, 107
World Health Organization, 107
World War I, 1–6, 8, 10–12, 16–21, 23–24, 29–30, 34, 41, 46–47, 49, 56, 63, 67–69, 78, 80, 86–87, 89–90, 95, 98, 100–1, 104, 107, 109–10, 112, 116, 118–19, 123, 125, 132, 136–38, 142–44, 157, 161, 163–65, 183–91
World War II, 1, 29, 49, 98, 109–10, 112, 116, 157
Wyspiański, Stanisław, 123

YMCA, 5–6, 142–58, 160–61, 187
Young Men's Christian Association *see* YMCA
Yugoslavia, 2, 47, 169, 171, 173, 184, 190

Zalaegerszeg, 56
Zaporozhian Cossacks *see* Cossacs
Zelea Codreanu, Corneliu, 168
Zelenyi, Otaman, 30, 33, 38
Zionism, 91–92

www.ingramcontent.com/pod-product-compliance
Lightning Source LLC
Chambersburg PA
CBHW071343080526
44587CB00017B/2945